Poems

1962–2020

'One of the purest and most accomplished lyric poets now writing'
Robert Hass

'No American poet writes better than Louise Glück, perhaps none
can lead us so deeply into our own nature' Stephen Dobyns

'Beneath the austere beauty, Glück is also a sharp and sly writer
who knows that the salt of poetry is the moment of surprise'
Jeremy Noel-Tod, *Sunday Times*

'Put together, these compact volumes have a great novel's cohesiveness
and raking moral intensity. They display a supple and prosecutorial
mind interrogating not merely her own life but also the sensual and
political nature of the world that spins around it . . . No other poet
slices with such accuracy and deadly intent . . . Glück is fearless'
Dwight Garner, *The New York Times*

'Glück is among the most moving poets of our era . . . This voice is not
going to go away' Dan Chiasson, *New Yorker*

'Glück's is a voice unlike any other, teeming with phrases and stanzas
that are sets of instructions on how to be human' Ian McMillan

'As with other great poets, Glück does not invite paraphrase. Her poems
at their best – and they are very often at their best – embody not just the
rage to order, but also the rage to identify a "truth" that no order can
approximate or touch' Robert Boyers, *Nation*

Louise Glück is the author of twelve books of poems and two essay collections. Her many awards include the Nobel Prize in Literature, the National Humanities Medal, the Pulitzer Prize, the National Book Award, the National Book Critics Circle Award, the Bollingen Prize, and the Wallace Stevens Award from the Academy of American Poets. She teaches at Yale University and Stanford University and lives in Cambridge, Massachusetts.

POEMS 1962-2020

LOUISE GLÜCK

PENGUIN BOOKS

PENGUIN CLASSICS

UK | USA | Canada | Ireland | Australia
India | New Zealand | South Africa

Penguin Classics is part of the Penguin Random House group of companies
whose addresses can be found at global.penguinrandomhouse.com

Poems 1962–2012 first published in the USA by Farrar, Straus and Giroux 2012
Published in Great Britain with additional poems under the present title in Penguin Classics 2021
Paperback edition published 2022

011

Copyright © Louise Glück, 2012, 2021

The moral right of the author has been asserted

Firstborn, The House on Marshland, Descending Figure, The Triumph of Achilles, Ararat, The Wild Iris, Meadowlands, Vita Nova and *The Seven Ages* were originally published by Ecco. *Averno, A Village Life* and *Faithful and Virtuous Night* were originally published by Farrar, Straus and Giroux

Printed and bound in Great Britain by Clays Ltd, Elcograf S.p.A.

The authorized representative in the EEA is Penguin Random House Ireland,
Morrison Chambers, 32 Nassau Street, Dublin D02 YH68

A CIP catalogue record for this book is available from the British Library

ISBN: 978-0-241-52608-8

CONTENTS

FIRSTBORN (1968)

THE HOUSE ON MARSHLAND (1975)

DESCENDING FIGURE (1980)

THE TRIUMPH OF ACHILLES (1985)

I

ARARAT (1990)

THE WILD IRIS (1992)

MEADOWLANDS (1996)

VITA NOVA (1999)

THE SEVEN AGES (2001)

AVERNO (2006)

I

A VILLAGE LIFE (2009)

FAITHFUL AND VIRTUOUS NIGHT (2014)

FIRSTBORN

(1968)

TO MY TEACHER

I   THE EGG

THE CHICAGO TRAIN

Across from me the whole ride
Hardly stirred: just Mister with his barren
Skull across the arm-rest while the kid
Got his head between his mama's legs and slept. The poison
That replaces air took over.
And they sat—as though paralysis preceding death
Had nailed them there. The track bent south.
I saw her pulsing crotch . . . the lice rooted in that baby's hair.

THE EGG

Everything went in the car.
Slept in the car, slept
Like angels in the duned graveyards,
Being gone. A week's meat
Spoiled, peas
Giggled in their pods: we
Stole. And then in Edgartown
I heard my insides
Roll into a crib . . .
Washing underwear in the Atlantic
Touched the sun's sea
As light welled
That could devour water.
After Edgartown
We went the other way.

II

Until aloft beyond
The sterilizer his enormous hands
Swarmed, carnivorous,
For prey. Beneath which,
Dripping white, stripped
Open to the wand,
I saw the lamps
Converging in his glasses.
Dramamine. You let him
Rob me. But
How long? how long?
Past cutlery I saw
My body stretching like a tear
Along the paper.

III

Always nights I feel the ocean
Biting at my life. By
Inlet, in this net
Of bays, and on. Unsafe.
And on, numb
In the bourbon ripples
Of your breath
I knot . . .
Across the beach the fish
Are coming in. Without skins,
Without fins, the bare
Households of their skulls
Still fixed, piling
With the other waste.
Husks, husks. Moons
Whistle in their mouths,
Through gasping mussels.
Pried flesh. And flies
Like planets, clamped shells
Clink blindly through
Veronicas of waves . . .
The thing
Is hatching. Look. The bones
Are bending to give way.
It's dark. It's dark.
He's brought a bowl to catch
The pieces of the baby.

THANKSGIVING

In every room, encircled by a name-
less Southern boy from Yale,
There was my younger sister singing a Fellini theme
And making phone calls
While the rest of us kept moving her discarded boots
Or sat and drank. Outside, in twenty-
nine degrees, a stray cat
Grazed in our driveway,
Seeking waste. It scratched the pail.
There were no other sounds.
Yet on and on the preparation of that vast consoling meal
Edged toward the stove. My mother
Had the skewers in her hands.
I watched her tucking skin
As though she missed her young, while bits of onion
Misted snow over the pronged death.

HESITATE TO CALL

Lived to see you throwing
Me aside. That fought
Like netted fish inside me. Saw you throbbing
In my syrups. Saw you sleep. And lived to see
That all that all flushed down
The refuse. Done?
It lives in me.
You live in me. Malignant.
Love, you ever want me, don't.

Under cerulean, amid her backyard's knobby rhubarb squats
My cousin to giggle with her baby, pat
His bald top. From a window I can catch them mull basil,
Glinty silica, sienna through the ground's brocade
Of tarragon or pause under the oblong shade
Of the garage. The nervous, emerald
Fanning of some rhizome skims my cousin's knee
As up and down she bends to the baby.
I'm knitting sweaters for her second child.
As though, down miles of dinners, had not heard her rock her bed
In rage and thought it years she lay, locked in that tantrum . . .
Oh but such stir as in her body had to come round. Amid violet,
Azalea, round around the whole arriving garden
Now with her son she passes what I paused
To catch, the early bud phases, on the springing grass.

RETURNING A LOST CHILD

Nothing moves. In its cage, the broken
Blossom of a fan sways
Limply, trickling its wire, as her thin
Arms, hung like flypaper, twist about the boy . . .
Later, blocking the doorway, tongue
Pinned to the fat wedge of his pop, he watches
As I find the other room, the father strung
On crutches, waiting to be roused . . .
Now squeezed from thanks the woman's lemonade lies
In my cup. As endlessly she picks
Her spent kleenex into dust, always
Staring at that man, hearing the click,
Click of his brain's whirling empty spindle . . .

Requiring something lovely on his arm
Took me to Stamford, Connecticut, a quasi-farm,
His family's; later picking up the mammoth
Girlfriend of Charlie, meanwhile trying to pawn me off
On some third guy also up for the weekend.
But Saturday we still were paired; spent
It sprawled across that sprawling acreage
Until the grass grew limp
With damp. Like me. Johnston-baby, I can still see
The pelted clover, burrs' prickle fur and gorged
Pastures spewing infinite tiny bells. You pimp.

THE WOUND

The air stiffens to a crust.
From bed I watch
Clots of flies, crickets
Frisk and titter. Now
The weather is such grease.
All day I smell the roasts
Like presences. You
Root into your books.
You do your stuff.
In here my bedroom walls
Are paisley, like a plot
Of embryos. I lie here,
Waiting for its kick.
My love. My tenant.
As the shrubs grow
Downy, bloom and seed.
The hedges grow downy
And seed and moonlight
Burbles through the gauze.
Sticky curtains. Faking scrabble
With the pair next door
I watched you clutch your blank.
They're both on Nembutal,
The killer pill.

And I am fixed. Gone careful,
Begging for the nod,
You hover loyally above my head. I close
My eyes. And now
The prison falls in place:
Ripe things sway in the light,
Parts of plants, leaf
Fragments . . .

You are covering the cot
With sheets. I feel
No end. No end. It stalls
In me. It's still alive.

SILVERPOINT

My sister, by the chiming kinks
Of the Atlantic Ocean, takes in light.
Beyond her, wreathed in algae, links on links
Of breakers meet and disconnect, foam through bracelets
Of seabirds. The wind sinks. She does not feel the change
At once. It will take time. My sister,
Stirring briefly to arrange
Her towel, browns like a chicken, under fire.

EARLY DECEMBER IN CROTON-ON-HUDSON

Spiked sun. The Hudson's
Whittled down by ice.
I hear the bone dice
Of blown gravel clicking. Bone-
pale, the recent snow
Fastens like fur to the river.
Standstill. We were leaving to deliver
Christmas presents when the tire blew
Last year. Above the dead valves pines pared
Down by a storm stood, limbs bared . . .
I want you.

II   THE EDGE

THE EDGE

Time and again, time and again I tie
My heart to that headboard
While my quilted cries
Harden against his hand. He's bored—
I see it. Don't I lick his bribes, set his bouquets
In water? Over Mother's lace I watch him drive into the gored
Roasts, deal slivers in his mercy . . . I can feel his thighs
Against me for the children's sakes. Reward?
Mornings, crippled with this house,
I see him toast his toast and test
His coffee, hedgingly. The waste's my breakfast.

GRANDMOTHER IN THE GARDEN

The grass below the willow
Of my daughter's wash is curled
With earthworms, and the world
Is measured into row on row
Of unspiced houses, painted to seem real.
The drugged Long Island summer sun drains
Pattern from those empty sleeves, beyond my grandson
Squealing in his pen. I have survived my life.
The yellow daylight lines the oak leaf
And the wire vines melt with the unchanged changes
Of the baby. My children have their husbands' hands.
My husband's framed, propped bald as a baby on their pianos,
My tremendous man. I close my eyes. And all the clothes
I have thrown out come back to me, the hollows
Of my daughters' slips . . . they drift; I see the sheer
Summer cottons drift, equivalent to air.

PICTURES OF THE PEOPLE IN THE WAR

Later I'll pull down the shade
And let this fluid draw life out of the paper.
Telling how. Except instead
Of showing you equipment I would first off share
My vision of the thing: the angle of that head
Submerged in fixer there, the bare
Soul in its set; you see, it's done with speed
And lighting but my point is that one never
Gets so close to anyone within experience. I took
These pictures of the people in the war
About a year ago—their hands were opening to me like
Language; tanks and dwellings meanwhile misty in the rear.

The elements have merged into solicitude.
Spasms of violets rise above the mud
And weed and soon the birds and ancients
Will be starting to arrive, bereaving points
South. But never mind. It is not painful to discuss
His death. I have been primed for this,
For separation, for so long. But still his face assaults
Me, I can hear that car careen again, the crowd coagulate on asphalt
In my sleep. And watching him, I feel my legs like snow
That let him finally let him go
As he lies draining there. And see
How even he did not get to keep that lovely body.

As my father, the late star, once told me,
Son, he told me, son, and all the while
That emerald fortune mewing on his pinky,
Satin wallowing about his shoulders
With his latest wife, fat
Misfit, so profoundly straight
She tried to own me in her Rolls
As Muriel, my mother, spread their staircase
With the surfeit of her dress
Before that party wound up in the garden.
Where—myself! myself!—O oven-
fresh and black from Mexico—they kept me
Soloing right into dawn
When the musicians quit as, far away,
The pool foamed with dim, lit chickies . . .
Past which, in that still grass
Beyond the canopies, my father's ex-
Producer drifted petals on her lifted mound
As Mama held the gauze body of some girl across
Her legs . . . I have not always lived like this,
You know. And yet my sequined, consequential past
Enables me to bear these shrieking nights
And disasters. I do not mean you. No, you, love,
Are as delightful as those coupled dancers strung
Like hand props down the back lawn
Of my former mansion,
Wherever that was, or as I was
When my mother's boys would rise and stir
Like dogs for me, make offers,
Women oozing from their stays
Go wild . . . I also was a hot property in those days.

BRIDAL PIECE

Our honeymoon
He planted us by
Water. It was March. The moon
Lurched like searchlights, like
His murmurings across my brain—
He had to have his way. As down
The beach the wet wind
Snored . . . I want
My innocence. I see
My family frozen in the doorway
Now, unchanged, unchanged. Their rice congeals
Around his car. He locked our bedroll
In the trunk for laughs, later, at the deep
End. Rockaway. He reaches for me in his sleep.

M. le professeur in prominent senility
Across the hall tidies his collected prose
And poems. Returning from a shopping spree
Not long ago, I caught him pausing to pose
Before the landing mirror in grandiose semi-profile.
It being impossible to avoid encounter on the stairs
I thought it best to smile
Openly, as though we two held equal shares
In the indiscretion. But his performance of a nod
Was labored and the infinite *politesse* of rose palm
Unfurled for salutation fraud-
ulent. At any rate, lately there's been some
Change in his schedule. He receives without zeal
Now, and, judging by his refuse, eats little but oatmeal.

Sometimes at night I think of how we did
It, me nailed in her like steel, her
Over-eager on the striped contour
Sheet (I later burned it) and it makes me glad
I told her—in the kitchen cutting homemade bread—
She always did too much—I told her Sorry baby you have had
Your share. (I found her stain had dried into my hair.)
She cried. Which still does not explain my nightmares:
How she surges like her yeast dough through the door-
way shrieking It is I, love, back in living color
After all these years.

THE LADY IN THE SINGLE

Cloistered as the snail and conch
In Edgartown where the Atlantic
Rises to deposit junk
On plush, extensive sand and the pedantic

Meet for tea, amid brouhaha
I have managed this peripheral still,
Wading just steps below
The piles of overkill:

Jellyfish. But I have seen
The slick return of one that oozed back
On a breaker. Marketable sheen.
The stuffed hotel. A shy, myopic

Sailor loved me once, near here.
The summer house we'd taken for July
Was white that year, bare
Shingle; he could barely see

To kiss, still tried to play
Croquet with the family—like a girl almost,
With loosed hair on her bouquet
Of compensating flowers. I thought I was past

The memory. And yet his ghost
Took shape in smoke above the pan roast.
Five years. In tenebris the catapulted heart drones
Like Andromeda. No one telephones.

THE CRIPPLE IN THE SUBWAY

For awhile I thought had gotten
Used to it (the leg) and hardly heard
That down-hard, down-hard
Upon wood, cement, etc. of the iron
Trappings and I'd tell myself the memories
Would also disappear, tick-
ing jump-ropes and the bike, the bike
That flew beneath my sister, froze
Light, bent back its
Stinging in a flash of red chrome brighter
Than my brace or brighter
Than the morning whirling past this pit
Flamed with rush horror and their thin
Boots flashing on and on, all that easy kidskin.

NURSE'S SONG

As though I'm fooled. That lacy body managed to forget
That I have eyes, ears; dares to spring her boyfriends on the child.
This afternoon she told me, "Dress the baby in his crochet
Dress," and smiled. Just that. Just smiled,
Going. She is never here. O innocence, your bathinet
Is clogged with gossip, she's a sinking ship,
Your mother. Wouldn't spoil her breasts.
I hear your deaf-numb papa fussing for his tea. Sleep, sleep,
My angel, nestled with your orange bear.
Scream when her lover pats your hair.

SECONDS

Craved, having so long gone
Empty, what he had, hardness
That (my boy half-grown)
Still sucked me toward that ring, that bless-
ing. Though I knew how it is sickness
In him: lounging in gin
He knots some silken threat until
He'll twist my arm, my words—my son
Stands rigid in the doorway, seeing all,
And then that fast fist rips across my only
Child, my life . . . I care, I care.
I watch the neighbors coming at me
With their views. Now huge with cake their
White face floats above its cup; they smile,
Sunken women, sucking at their tea . . .
I'd let my house go up in flame for this fire.

LETTER FROM OUR MAN IN BLOSSOMTIME

Often an easterly churns
Emerald feathered ferns
Calling to mind Aunt Rae's decrepit
Framed fan as it
Must have flickered in its heyday.
Black-eyed Susans rim blueberry. Display,
However, is all on the outside. Let me describe the utter
Simplicity of our housekeeping. The water
Stutters fits and starts in both sinks, remaining
Dependably pure ice; veining
The ceiling, a convention of leaks
Makes host of our home to any and all weather. Everything creaks:
Floor, shutters, the door. Still,
We have the stupendously adequate scenery to keep our morale
Afloat. And even Margaret's taking mouseholes in the molding
Fairly well in stride. But O my friend, I'm holding
Back epiphany. Last night,
More acutely than for any first time, her white
Forearms, bared in ruth-
less battle with the dinner, pierced me; I saw
Venus among those clamshells, raw
Botticelli: I have known no happiness so based in truth.

THE CELL

(Jeanne des Anges, Prioress of the Ursuline nuns, Loudun, France: 1635)

It's always there. My back's
Bulging through linen: God
Damaged me—made
Unfit to guide, I guide.
Yet are they silent at their work.
I walk
The garden in the afternoon, who hid
Delusions under my habits
For my self was empty . . . But HE did
It, yes.
      My Father,
Lying here, I hear
The sun creak past granite
Into air, still it is night inside.
I hide and pray. And dawn,
Alone all ways, I can feel the fingers
Stir on me again like bless-
ing and the bare
Hump mount, tranquil in darkness.

Sugar I am CALLING you. Not
Journeyed all these years for this:
You stalking chicken in the subways,
Nights hunched in alleys all to get
That pinch . . . O heartbit,
Fastened to the chair.
The supper's freezing in the dark.
While I, my prince, my prince . . .
Your fruit lights up.
I watch your hands pulling at the grapes.

LETTER FROM PROVENCE

Beside the bridge's photogen-
ic lapse into air you'll
Find more interesting material.
In July the sun
Flatters your Popes' delicate
City as always, turning granite
Gold. The slum's at standstill then,
Choking with droppings. Still
Its children are not entirely hostile;
Proffer smiles
At intervals most charmingly. I gave
Them chocolate, softened in the heat,
Which they would not
Go near. We heard they live on love.

MEMO FROM THE CAVE

O love, you airtight bird,
My mouse-brown
Alibis hang upside-down
Above the pegboard
With its dangled pots
I don't have chickens for;
My lies are crawling on the floor
Like families but their larvae will not
Leave this nest. I've let
Despair bed
Down in your stead
And wet
Our quilted cover
So the rot-
scent of its pussy-foot-
ing fingers lingers, when it's over.

The weeks go by. I shelve them,
They are all the same, like peeled soup cans . . .
Beans sour in their pot. I watch the lone onion
Floating like Ophelia, caked with grease:
You listless, fidget with the spoon.
What now? You miss my care? Your yard ripens
To a ward of roses, like a year ago when staff nuns
Wheeled me down the aisle . . .
You couldn't look. I saw
Converted love, your son,
Drooling under glass, starving . . .

We are eating well.
Today my meatman turns his trained knife
On veal, your favorite. I pay with my life.

LA FORCE

Made me what I am.
Gray, glued to her dream
Kitchen, among bones, among these
Dripping willows squatted to imbed
A bulb: I tend her plot. Her pride
And joy she said. I have no pride.
The lawn thins; overfed,
Her late roses gag on fertilizer past the tool
House. Now the cards are cut.
She cannot eat, she cannot take the stairs—
My life is sealed. The woman with the hound
Comes up but she will not be harmed.
I have the care of her.

And yet I've lived like this for years.
All since he quit me—caught the moon as round as aspirin
While, across the hall, the heartfelt murmurs
Of the queers . . . I see my punishment revolving in its den:

Around. Around. There should have been
A lesson somewhere. In Geneva, the ferocious local whore
Lay peeled for absolution with a tricot membrane
Sticking to her skin. I don't remember

How it happened that I saw. The place was filthy. She would sit
And pick her feet until they knocked. Like Customs. She'd just wait.

III   COTTONMOUTH COUNTRY

COTTONMOUTH COUNTRY

Fish bones walked the waves off Hatteras.
And there were other signs
That Death wooed us, by water, wooed us
By land: among the pines
An uncurled cottonmouth that rolled on moss
Reared in the polluted air.
Birth, not death, is the hard loss.
I know. I also left a skin there.

PHENOMENAL SURVIVALS OF DEATH IN NANTUCKET

I

Here in Nantucket does the tiny soul
Confront the water. Yet this element is not foreign soil;
I see the water as extension of my mind,
The troubled part, and waves the waves of mind
When in Nantucket they collapsed in epilepsy
On the bare shore. I see
A shawled figure when I am asleep who says, "Our lives
Are strands between the miracles of birth
And death. I am Saint Elizabeth.
In my basket are knives."
Awake I see Nantucket, the familiar earth.

II

Awake I see Nantucket but with this bell
Of voice I can toll you token of regions below visible:
On the third night came
A hurricane; my Saint Elizabeth came
Not and nothing could prevent the rent
Craft from its determined end. Waves dent-
ed with lightning launched my loosed mast
To fly downward, I following. They do not tell
You but bones turned coral still smell
Amid forsaken treasure. I have been past
What you hear in a shell.

III

Past what you hear in a shell, the roar,
Is the true bottom: infamous calm. The doctor
Having shut the door sat me down, took ropes
Out of reach, firearms, and with high hopes
Promised that Saint Elizabeth carried
Only foodstuffs or some flowers for charity, nor was I buried

Under the vacation island of Nantucket where
Beach animals dwell in relative compatibility and peace.
Flies, snails. Asleep I saw these
Beings as complacent angels of the land and air.
When dawn comes to the sea's

IV

Acres of shining white body in Nantucket
I shall not remember otherwise but wear a locket
With my lover's hair inside
And walk like a bride, and wear him inside.
From these shallows expands
The mercy of the sea.
My first house shall be built on these sands,
My second in the sea.

EASTER SEASON

There is almost no sound . . . only the redundant stir
Of shrubs as perfumed temperatures embalm
Our coast. I saw the spreading gush of people with their palms.
In Westchester, the crocus spreads like cancer.

This will be the death of me. I feel the leaves close in,
Promise threaten from all sides and above.
It is not real. The green seed-pod, flaky dove
Of the bud descend. The rest is risen.

We had codes
In our house. Like
Locks; they said
We never lock
Our door to you.
And never did.
Their bed
Stood, spotless as a tub ...
I passed it every day
For twenty years, until
I went my way. My chore
Was marking time. Gluing
Relics into books I saw
Myself at seven learning
Distance at my mother's knee.
My favorite snapshot of my
Father shows him pushing forty
And lyrical
Above his firstborn's empty face.
The usual miracle.

The pail droops on chain, rotten,
Where the well's been
Rinsed with bog, as round and round
The reed-weed rockets down Deer Island
Amid frosted spheres of acid: berry pick-
ing. All day long I watched the land break
Up into the ocean. Happened long ago,
And lost—what isn't—bits of jetty go
Their private ways, or sink, trailing water.
Little's left. Past this window where
My mother's basil drowned
In salad, I can see our orchard, balsams
Clenched around their birds. The basil flourished on
Neglect. Open my room, trees. Child's come.

Long Island Sound's
Asleep: no wind
Rustles down the inlet
In the sagging light
As, stalled at
Vanishing, two Sunday sailboats
Wait it out,
Paralysis, or peace,
Whichever, and the drained sun
Sinks through insects coalesced
To mist, mosquitoes
Rippling over the muddy ocean.

LATE SNOW

Seven years I watched the next-door
Lady stroll her empty mate. One May he turned his head to see
A chrysalis give forth its kleenex creature:

He'd forgotten what they were. But pleasant days she
Walked him up and down. And crooned to him.
He gurgled from his wheelchair, finally

Dying last Fall. I think the birds came
Back too soon this year. The slugs
Have been extinguished by a snow. Still, all the same,

She wasn't young herself. It must have hurt her legs
To push his weight that way. A late snow hugs
The robins' tree. I saw it come. The mama withers on her eggs.

TO FLORIDA

Southward floated over
The vicious little houses, down
The land. Past Carolina, where
The bloom began
Beneath their throbbing clouds, they fed us
Coldcuts, free. We had our choice.
Below, the seasons twist; years
Roll backward toward the can
Like film, and the mistake appears,
To scale, soundlessly. The signs
Light up. Across the aisle
An old man twitches in his sleep. His mind
Will firm in time. His health
Will meet him at the terminal.

Sir: Cruising for profit
Close to Portsmouth we have not
Done well. All winds
Quarrel with our course it seems and daily the crew whines
For fresh woman-
flesh or blood again. No gain
Accumulates; this time I fear with reason. There's no
Other news. A week ago
We charged a trader stocked with Africans
I knew for royal but their skin fixed terror in my men's
Eyes—against my will they mounted her and in the slow
Dawn off Georgia stole her whole
Hold's gold and slew that living cargo.

SOLSTICE

June's edge. The sun
Turns kind. Birds wallow in the sob of pure air,
Crated from the coast . . . Un-
real. Unreal. I see the cure

Dissolving on the screen. Outside, dozing
In its sty, the neighbors' offspring
Sucks its stuffed monster, given
Time. And now the end begins:

Packaged words. He purrs his need again.
The rest is empty. Stoned, stone-
blind she totters to the lock
Through webs of diapers. It is Christmas on the clock,

A year's precise,
Terrible ascent, climaxed in ice.

Words fail me. The ocean traveling stone
Returns turquoise; small animals twinkle in a haze
Of weed as this or that sequence
Of pod rattles with complete delicacy on the rotten vine.
I know what's slipping through my fingers.
In Hatteras the stones were oiled with mud.
The sunset leaked like steak blood,
Sank, and my companion weaved his fingers
Through my fingers. Wood's Hole,
Edgartown, the Vineyard in the rain,
The Vineyard not in the rain, the rain
Fuming like snow in Worcester, like gas in the coal
Country. Grass and goldenrod come to me,
Milkweed covers me over, and reed. But this riddle
Has no name: I saw a blind baby try
To fix its fists in tendrils
Of its mother's hair, and get air. The air burns,
The seaweed hisses in its cistern . . .

    Waveside, beside earth's edge,
    Before the toward-death cartwheel of the sun,
    I dreamed I was afraid and through the din
    Of birds, the din, the hurricane of parting sedge
    Came to the danger lull.
    The white weeds, white waves' white
    Scalps dissolve in the obliterating light.
    And only I, Shadrach, come back alive and well.

SATURNALIA

The year turns. The wolf takes back her tit
As war eats at the empire
Past this waxworks, the eternal city.
We have had our round. What
Lords rise are not of Rome: now northward some two-bit
Vercingetorix sharpens his will. A star
Is born.   Caesar
Snores on his perch above the Senate.

This is history. Ice clogs the ducts; my friend,
I wake to frost
On marble and a chill men take for omen
Here. The myth contracts. All cast
For comfort, shun their works to pray,
Preening for Judgment. Judgment fails. One year,
Twenty—we are lost. This month the feasts begin.
Token slaves suck those dripping fowl we offer
To insure prosperity.

THE HOUSE ON MARSHLAND

(1975)

WITH LOVE AND GRATITUDE

KAREN KENNERLY
TOM GILSON
ELLEN BRYANT VOIGT

I   ALL HALLOWS

ALL HALLOWS

Even now this landscape is assembling.
The hills darken. The oxen
sleep in their blue yoke,
the fields having been
picked clean, the sheaves
bound evenly and piled at the roadside
among cinquefoil, as the toothed moon rises:

This is the barrenness
of harvest or pestilence.
And the wife leaning out the window
with her hand extended, as in payment,
and the seeds
distinct, gold, calling
Come here
Come here, little one

And the soul creeps out of the tree.

THE POND

Night covers the pond with its wing.
Under the ringed moon I can make out
your face swimming among minnows and the small
echoing stars. In the night air
the surface of the pond is metal.

Within, your eyes are open. They contain
a memory I recognize, as though
we had been children together. Our ponies
grazed on the hill, they were gray
with white markings. Now they graze
with the dead who wait
like children under their granite breastplates,
lucid and helpless:

The hills are far away. They rise up
blacker than childhood.
What do you think of, lying so quietly
by the water? When you look that way I want
to touch you, but do not, seeing
as in another life we were of the same blood.

GRETEL IN DARKNESS

This is the world we wanted.
All who would have seen us dead
are dead. I hear the witch's cry
break in the moonlight through a sheet
of sugar: God rewards.
Her tongue shrivels into gas . . .

        Now, far from women's arms
and memory of women, in our father's hut
we sleep, are never hungry.
Why do I not forget?
My father bars the door, bars harm
from this house, and it is years.

No one remembers. Even you, my brother,
summer afternoons you look at me as though
you meant to leave,
as though it never happened.
But I killed for you. I see armed firs,
the spires of that gleaming kiln—

Nights I turn to you to hold me
but you are not there.
Am I alone? Spies
hiss in the stillness, Hansel,
we are there still and it is real, real,
that black forest and the fire in earnest.

FOR MY MOTHER

It was better when we were
together in one body.
Thirty years. Screened
through the green glass
of your eye, moonlight
filtered into my bones
as we lay
in the big bed, in the dark,
waiting for my father.
Thirty years. He closed
your eyelids with
two kisses. And then spring
came and withdrew from me
the absolute
knowledge of the unborn,
leaving the brick stoop
where you stand, shading
your eyes, but it is
night, the moon
is stationed in the beech tree,
round and white among
the small tin markers of the stars:
Thirty years. A marsh
grows up around the house.
Schools of spores circulate
behind the shades, drift through
gauze flutterings of vegetation.

ARCHIPELAGO

The tenth year we came upon immense sunlight, a relief
of islands locked into the water. These became our course.
Eleven months we drifted, toward the twelfth
wandered into docile ocean, a harbor. We prepared for peace.
Weeks passed. And then the captain saw
the mouth closing that defined our port—we are
devoured. Other voices stir. Water
sneers against our ship, our shrunk number runs
in two packs: madness and suicide. The twelfth year
the captain calls his name, it has no meaning, and the crew
shrieks in its extremity.

THE MAGI

Toward world's end, through the bare
beginnings of winter, they are traveling again.
How many winters have we seen it happen,
watched the same sign come forward as they pass
cities sprung around this route their gold
engraved on the desert, and yet
held our peace, these
being the Wise, come to see at the accustomed hour
nothing changed: roofs, the barn
blazing in darkness, all they wish to see.

THE SHAD-BLOW TREE

—for Tom

1. *The Tree*

It is all here,
luminous water, the imprinted sapling
matched, branch by branch,
to the lengthened
tree in the lens, as it was
against the green, poisoned landscape.

2. *The Latent Image*

One year he focused on a tree
until, through sunlight pure as never afterward, he saw
the season, early spring, work upon those limbs
its white flower, which the eye
retains: deep in the brain
the shad-blow coins its leaf in this context,
among monuments, continuous with such frozen forms
as have become the trained vine,
root, rock, and all things perishing.

You have only to wait, they will find you.
The geese flying low over the marsh,
glittering in black water.
They find you.

And the deer—
how beautiful they are,
as though their bodies did not impede them.
Slowly they drift into the open
through bronze panels of sunlight.

Why would they stand so still
if they were not waiting?
Almost motionless, until their cages rust,
the shrubs shiver in the wind,
squat and leafless.

You have only to let it happen:
that cry—*release, release*—like the moon
wrenched out of earth and rising
full in its circle of arrows

until they come before you
like dead things, saddled with flesh,
and you above them, wounded and dominant.

THE MURDERESS

You call me sane, insane—I tell you men
were leering to themselves; she saw.
She was my daughter. She would pare
her skirt until her thighs grew
longer, till the split tongue slid into her brain.
He had her smell. Fear
will check beauty, but she had no fear. She talked
doubletalk, she lent
her heat to Hell's: Commissioner, the sun
opens to consume the Virgin on the fifteenth day.
It was like slitting fish. And then the stain
dissolved, and God presided at her body.

FLOWERING PLUM

In spring from the black branches of the flowering plum tree
the woodthrush issues its routine
message of survival. Where does such happiness come from
as the neighbors' daughter reads into that singing,
and matches? All afternoon she sits
in the partial shade of the plum tree, as the mild wind
floods her immaculate lap with blossoms, greenish white
and white, leaving no mark, unlike
the fruit that will inscribe
unraveling dark stains in heavier winds, in summer.

NATIVITY POEM

It is the evening
of the birth of god.
Singing &
with gold instruments
the angels bear down
upon the barn, their wings
neither white
wax nor marble. So
they have been recorded:
burnished,
literal in the composed air,
they raise their harps above
the beasts likewise gathering,
the lambs & all the startled
silken chickens . . . And Joseph,
off to one side, has touched
his cheek, meaning
he is weeping—

But how small he is, withdrawn
from the hollow of his mother's life,
the raw flesh bound
in linen as the stars yield
light to delight his sense
for whom there is no ornament.

TO AUTUMN

—for Keith Althaus

Morning quivers in the thorns; above the budded snowdrops
caked with dew like little virgins, the azalea bush
ejects its first leaves, and it is spring again.
The willow waits its turn, the coast
is coated with a faint green fuzz, anticipating
mold. Only I
do not collaborate, having
flowered earlier. I am no longer young. What
of it? Summer approaches, and the long
decaying days of autumn when I shall begin
the great poems of my middle period.

STILL LIFE

Father has his arm around Tereze.
She squints. My thumb
is in my mouth: my fifth autumn.
Near the copper beech
the spaniel dozes in shadows.
Not one of us does not avert his eyes.

Across the lawn, in full sun, my mother
stands behind her camera.

FOR JANE MYERS

Sap rises from the sodden ditch
and glues two green ears to the dead
birch twig. Perilous beauty—
and already Jane is digging out
her colored tennis shoes,
one mauve, one yellow, like large crocuses.

And by the laundromat
the Bartletts in their tidy yard—

as though it were not
wearying, wearying

to hear in the bushes
the mild harping of the breeze,
the daffodils flocking and honking—

Look how the bluet falls apart, mud
pockets the seed.
Months, years, then the dull blade of the wind.
It is spring! We are going to die!

And now April raises up her plaque of flowers
and the heart
expands to admit its adversary.

GRATITUDE

Do not think I am not grateful for your small
kindness to me.
I like small kindnesses.
In fact I actually prefer them to the more
substantial kindness, that is always eyeing you,
like a large animal on a rug,
until your whole life reduces
to nothing but waking up morning after morning
cramped, and the bright sun shining on its tusks.

In the early evening, as now, a man is bending
over his writing table.
Slowly he lifts his head; a woman
appears, carrying roses.
Her face floats to the surface of the mirror,
marked with the green spokes of rose stems.

It is a form
of suffering: then always the transparent page
raised to the window until its veins emerge
as words finally filled with ink.

And I am meant to understand
what binds them together
or to the gray house held firmly in place by dusk

because I must enter their lives:
it is spring, the pear tree
filming with weak, white blossoms.

THE SCHOOL CHILDREN

The children go forward with their little satchels.
And all morning the mothers have labored
to gather the late apples, red and gold,
like words of another language.

And on the other shore
are those who wait behind great desks
to receive these offerings.

How orderly they are—the nails
on which the children hang
their overcoats of blue or yellow wool.

And the teachers shall instruct them in silence
and the mothers shall scour the orchards for a way out,
drawing to themselves the gray limbs of the fruit trees
bearing so little ammunition.

JEANNE D'ARC

It was in the fields. The trees grew still,
a light passed through the leaves speaking
of Christ's great grace: I heard.
My body hardened into armor.

                             Since the guards
gave me over to darkness I have prayed to God
and now the voices answer I must be
transformed to fire, for God's purpose,
and have bid me kneel
to bless my King, and thank
the enemy to whom I owe my life.

DEPARTURE

My father is standing on a railroad platform.
Tears pool in his eyes, as though the face
glimmering in the window were the face of someone
he was once. But the other has forgotten;
as my father watches, he turns away,
drawing the shade over his face,
goes back to his reading.

And already in its deep groove
the train is waiting with its breath of ashes.

GEMINI

There is a soul in me
It is asking
to be given its body

It is asking
to be given blue eyes
a skull matted

with black hair
that shape
already formed & detaching

So the past put forth
a house filled with
asters & white lilac

a child
in her cotton dress
the lawn, the copper beech—

such of my own lives
I have cast off—the sunlight
chipping at the curtains

& the wicker chairs
uncovered, winter after winter,
as the stars finally

thicken & descend as snow

II   THE APPLE TREES

THE UNDERTAKING

The darkness lifts, imagine, in your lifetime.
There you are—cased in clean bark you drift
through weaving rushes, fields flooded with cotton.
You are free. The river films with lilies,
shrubs appear, shoots thicken into palm. And now
all fear gives way: the light
looks after you, you feel the waves' goodwill
as arms widen over the water; Love,

the key is turned. Extend yourself—
it is the Nile, the sun is shining,
everywhere you turn is luck.

POMEGRANATE

First he gave me
his heart. It was
red fruit containing
many seeds, the skin
leathery, unlikely.
I preferred
to starve, bearing
out my training.
Then he said Behold
how the world looks, minding
your mother. I
peered under his arm:
What had she done
with color & odor?
Whereupon he said Now *there*
is a woman who loves
with a vengeance, adding
Consider she is in her element:
the trees turning to her, whole
villages going under
although in hell
the bushes are still
burning with pomegranates.
At which
he cut one open & began
to suck. When he looked up at last
it was to say My dear
you are your own
woman, finally, but examine
this grief your mother
parades over our heads
remembering
that she is one to whom
these depths were not offered.

BRENNENDE LIEBE

—1904

Dearest love: The roses are in bloom again,
cream and rose, to either side of the brick walk.
I pass among them with my white umbrella
as the sun beats down upon the oval plots like pools
in the grass, willows and the grove
of statuary. So the days go by. Fine days
I take my tea beneath the elm
half turned, as though you were beside me saying
Flowers that could take your breath away . . .
And always on the tray
a rose, and always the sun branded on the river
and the men in summer suits, in linen, and the girls,
their skirts circled in shadow . . . Last night
I dreamed that you did not return.
Today is fair. The little maid filled a silver bowl
shaped like a swan with roses for my bedside,
with the dark red they call *Brennende Liebe*,
which I find so beautiful.

ABISHAG

I.

At God's word David's kinsmen cast
through Canaan:
It was understood
the king was dying
as they said
outright
so that my father turned to me saying
How much have I ever asked of you
to which I answered
Nothing
as I remembered

So the sun rose from his shoulders:
blue air, the desert, the small
yellowing village

When I see myself
it is still as I was then,
beside the well, staring
into the hollowed gourd half filled
with water, where the dark braid
grazing the left shoulder was recorded
though the face
was featureless
of which they did not say
She has the look of one who seeks
some greater and destroying passion:

They took me as I was.
Not one among the kinsmen touched me,
not one among the slaves.
No one will touch me now.

2.

In the recurring dream my father
stands at the doorway in his black cassock
telling me to choose
among my suitors, each of whom
will speak my name once
until I lift my hand in signal.
On my father's arm I listen
for not three sounds: *Abishag*,
but two: *my love*—

I tell you if it is my own will
binding me I cannot be saved.
And yet in the dream, in the half-light
of the stone house, they looked
so much alike. Sometimes I think
the voices were themselves
identical, and that I raised my hand
chiefly in weariness. I hear my father saying
Choose, choose. But they were not alike
and to select death, O yes I can
believe that of my body.

12. 6. 71

You having turned from me
I dreamed we were
beside a pond between two mountains
It was night
The moon throbbed in its socket
Where the spruces thinned
three deer wakened & broke cover
and I heard my name
not spoken but cried out
so that I reached for you
except the sheet was ice
as they had come for me
who, one by one, were likewise
introduced to darkness
And the snow
which has not ceased since
began

LOVE POEM

There is always something to be made of pain.
Your mother knits.
She turns out scarves in every shade of red.
They were for Christmas, and they kept you warm
while she married over and over, taking you
along. How could it work,
when all those years she stored her widowed heart
as though the dead come back.
No wonder you are the way you are,
afraid of blood, your women
like one brick wall after another.

NORTHWOOD PATH

For my part
we are as we were
on the path
that afternoon:
it is
October, I can see
the sun sink
drawing out
our parallel
shadows. And you,
for example what
were you thinking, so
attentive to your
shoes? I recall
we spoke of
your car
the whole length
of the woods:
in so much withering
the pokeweed had
branched into its
purplish berry—so
desire called
love into being.
But always the choice
was on both sides
characteristic,
as you said,
in the dark you came
to need,
you would do it again

THE FIRE

Had you died when we were together
I would have wanted nothing of you.
Now I think of you as dead, it is better.

Often, in the cool early evenings of the spring
when, with the first leaves,
all that is deadly enters the world,
I build a fire for us of pine and apple wood;
repeatedly
the flames flare and diminish
as the night comes on in which
we see one another so clearly—

And in the days we are contented
as formerly
in the long grass,
in the woods' green doors and shadows.

And you never say
Leave me
since the dead do not like being alone.

There is nothing now. To learn
the lesson past disease
was easier. In God's hotel I saw
my name and number stapled to a vein
as Marcy funneled its corrective air
toward Placid. I can breathe
again. I watch the mountain under siege
by ice give way to blocks of dungeons,
ovens manned by wives. I understand.
They coil their hair, they turn their
music on as, humming to herself, the night-
nurse smoothes her uniform. This is
the proper pain. The lights are out. Love
forms in the human body.

HERE ARE MY BLACK CLOTHES

I think now it is better to love no one
than to love you. Here are my black clothes,
the tired nightgowns and robes fraying
in many places. Why should they hang useless
as though I were going naked? You liked me well enough
in black; I make you a gift of these objects.
You will want to touch them with your mouth, run
your fingers through the thin
tender underthings and I
will not need them in my new life.

UNDER TAURUS

We were on the pier, you desiring
that I see the Pleiades. I could see
everything but what you wished.

Now I will follow. There is not a single cloud; the stars
appear, even the invisible sister. Show me where to look,
as though they will stay where they are.

Instruct me in the dark.

THE SWIMMER

You sat in the tub.
No sand stirred, the dead
waited in the ocean.
Then the tapwater
flooded over you,
sapphire and emerald.

The beach
is as you found it,
littered with objects.
They have brought me here;
I rifle through them,
shell and bone, and am not satisfied.

What brought me to rest was your body.
Far away you turn your head:
through still grass the wind
moves into a human language

and the darkness comes,
the long nights
pass into stationary darkness.

Only the sea moves.
It takes on color, onyx and manganese.
If you are there it will release you
as when, among the tame waves,
I saw your worn face,
your long arms making for shore—

The waves come forward,
we are traveling together.

THE LETTERS

It is night for the last time.
For the last time your hands
gather on my body.

Tomorrow it will be autumn.
We will sit together on the balcony
watching the dry leaves drift over the village
like the letters we will burn,
one by one, in our separate houses.

Such a quiet night.
Only your voice murmuring
You're wet, you want to
and the child
sleeps as though he were not born.

In the morning it will be autumn.
We will walk together in the small garden
among stone benches and the shrubs
still sheeted in mist
like furniture left for a long time.

Look how the leaves drift in the darkness.
We have burned away
all that was written on them.

JAPONICA

The trees are flowering
on the hill.
They are bearing
large solitary blossoms,
japonica,
as when you came to me
mistakenly
carrying such flowers
having snapped them
from the thin branches.
The rain had stopped. Sunlight
motioned through the leaves.
But death
also has its flower,
it is called
contagion, it is
red or white, the color
of japonica—
You stood there,
your hands full of flowers.
How could I not take them
since they were a gift?

THE APPLE TREES

Your son presses against me
his small intelligent body.

I stand beside his crib
as in another dream
you stood among trees hung
with bitten apples
holding out your arms.
I did not move
but saw the air dividing
into panes of color—at the very last
I raised him to the window saying
See what you have made
and counted out the whittled ribs,
the heart on its blue stalk
as from among the trees
the darkness issued:

In the dark room your son sleeps.
The walls are green, the walls
are spruce and silence.
I wait to see how he will leave me.
Already on his hand the map appears
as though you carved it there,
the dead fields, women rooted to the river.

DESCENDING FIGURE

(1980)

FOR MY MOTHER AND FATHER

FOR JOHN

I   THE GARDEN

THE DROWNED CHILDREN

You see, they have no judgment.
So it is natural that they should drown,
first the ice taking them in
and then, all winter, their wool scarves
floating behind them as they sink
until at last they are quiet.
And the pond lifts them in its manifold dark arms.

But death must come to them differently,
so close to the beginning.
As though they had always been
blind and weightless. Therefore
the rest is dreamed, the lamp,
the good white cloth that covered the table,
their bodies.

And yet they hear the names they used
like lures slipping over the pond:
What are you waiting for
come home, come home, lost
in the waters, blue and permanent.

THE GARDEN

1. *The Fear of Birth*

One sound. Then the hiss and whir
of houses gliding into their places.
And the wind
leafs through the bodies of animals—

But my body that could not content itself
with health—why should it be sprung back
into the chord of sunlight?

It will be the same again.
This fear, this inwardness,
until I am forced into a field
without immunity
even to the least shrub that walks
stiffly out of the dirt, trailing
the twisted signature of its root,
even to a tulip, a red claw.

And then the losses,
one after another,
all supportable.

2. *The Garden*

The garden admires you.
For your sake it smears itself with green pigment,
the ecstatic reds of the roses,
so that you will come to it with your lovers.

And the willows—
see how it has shaped these green
tents of silence. Yet
there is still something you need,
your body so soft, so alive, among the stone animals.

Admit that it is terrible to be like them,
beyond harm.

3. *The Fear of Love*

That body lying beside me like obedient stone—
once its eyes seemed to be opening,
we could have spoken.

At that time it was winter already.
By day the sun rose in its helmet of fire
and at night also, mirrored in the moon.
Its light passed over us freely,
as though we had lain down
in order to leave no shadows,
only these two shallow dents in the snow.
And the past, as always, stretched before us,
still, complex, impenetrable.

How long did we lie there
as, arm in arm in their cloaks of feathers,
the gods walked down
from the mountain we built for them?

4. *Origins*

As though a voice were saying
You should be asleep by now—
But there was no one. Nor
had the air darkened,
though the moon was there,
already filled in with marble.

As though, in a garden crowded with flowers,
a voice had said
How dull they are, these golds,
so sonorous, so repetitious
until you closed your eyes,
lying among them, all
stammering flame:

And yet you could not sleep,
poor body, the earth
still clinging to you—

5. *The Fear of Burial*

In the empty field, in the morning,
the body waits to be claimed.
The spirit sits beside it, on a small rock—
nothing comes to give it form again.

Think of the body's loneliness.
At night pacing the sheared field,
its shadow buckled tightly around.
Such a long journey.
And already the remote, trembling lights of the village
not pausing for it as they scan the rows.
How far away they seem,
the wooden doors, the bread and milk
laid like weights on the table.

Love long dormant showing itself:
the large expected gods
caged really, the columns
sitting on the lawn, as though perfection
were not timeless but stationary—that
is the comedy, she thinks,
that they are paralyzed. Or like the matching swans,
insular, circling the pond: restraint so passionate
implies possession. They hardly speak.
On the other bank, a small boy throws bits of bread
into the water. The reflected monument
is stirred, briefly, stricken with light—
She can't touch his arm in innocence again.
They have to give that up and begin
as male and female, thrust and ache.

PIETÀ

Under the strained
fabric of her skin, his heart
stirred. She listened,
because he had no father.
So she knew
he wanted to stay
in her body, apart
from the world
with its cries, its
roughhousing,
but already the men
gather to see him
born: they crowd in
or kneel at worshipful
distance, like
figures in a painting
whom the star lights, shining
steadily in its dark context.

DESCENDING FIGURE

1. *The Wanderer*

At twilight I went into the street.
The sun hung low in the iron sky,
ringed with cold plumage.
If I could write to you
about this emptiness—
Along the curb, groups of children
were playing in the dry leaves.
Long ago, at this hour, my mother stood
at the lawn's edge, holding my little sister.
Everyone was gone; I was playing
in the dark street with my other sister,
whom death had made so lonely.
Night after night we watched the screened porch
filling with a gold, magnetic light.
Why was she never called?
Often I would let my own name glide past me
though I craved its protection.

2. *The Sick Child*
   —Rijksmuseum

A small child
is ill, has wakened.
It is winter, past midnight
in Antwerp. Above a wooden chest,
the stars shine.
And the child
relaxes in her mother's arms.
The mother does not sleep;
she stares
fixedly into the bright museum.
By spring the child will die.
Then it is wrong, wrong
to hold her—

Let her be alone,
without memory, as the others wake
terrified, scraping the dark
paint from their faces.

3. *For My Sister*

Far away my sister is moving in her crib.
The dead ones are like that,
always the last to quiet.

Because, however long they lie in the earth,
they will not learn to speak
but remain uncertainly pressing against the wooden bars,
so small the leaves hold them down.

Now, if she had a voice,
the cries of hunger would be beginning.
I should go to her;
perhaps if I sang very softly,
her skin so white,
her head covered with black feathers . . .

THANKSGIVING

They have come again to graze the orchard,
knowing they will be denied.
The leaves have fallen; on the dry ground
the wind makes piles of them, sorting
all it destroys.

What doesn't move, the snow will cover.
It will give them away; their hooves
make patterns which the snow remembers.
In the cleared field, they linger
as the summoned prey whose part
is not to forgive. They can afford to die.
They have their place in the dying order.

II   THE MIRROR

EPITHALAMIUM

There were others; their bodies
were a preparation.
I have come to see it as that.

As a stream of cries.
So much pain in the world—the formless
grief of the body, whose language
is hunger—

And in the hall, the boxed roses:
what they mean

is chaos. Then begins
the terrible charity of marriage,
husband and wife
climbing the green hill in gold light
until there is no hill,
only a flat plain stopped by the sky.

Here is my hand, he said.
But that was long ago.
Here is my hand that will not harm you.

ILLUMINATIONS

1.

My son squats in the snow in his blue snowsuit.
All around him stubble, the brown
degraded bushes. In the morning air
they seem to stiffen into words.
And, between, the white steady silence.
A wren hops on the airstrip
under the sill, drills
for sustenance, then spreads
its short wings, shadows
dropping from them.

2.

Last winter he could barely speak.
I moved his crib to face the window:
in the dark mornings
he would stand and grip the bars
until the walls appeared,
calling *light, light,*
that one syllable, in
demand or recognition.

3.

He sits at the kitchen window
with his cup of apple juice.
Each tree forms where he left it,
leafless, trapped in his breath.
How clear their edges are,
no limb obscured by motion,
as the sun rises
cold and single over the map of language.

THE MIRROR

Watching you in the mirror I wonder
what it is like to be so beautiful
and why you do not love
but cut yourself, shaving
like a blind man. I think you let me stare
so you can turn against yourself
with greater violence,
needing to show me how you scrape the flesh away
scornfully and without hesitation
until I see you correctly,
as a man bleeding, not
the reflection I desire.

PORTRAIT

A child draws the outline of a body.
She draws what she can, but it is white all through,
she cannot fill in what she knows is there.
Within the unsupported line, she knows
that life is missing; she has cut
one background from another. Like a child,
she turns to her mother.

And you draw the heart
against the emptiness she has created.

TANGO

1.

On evenings like this
twenty years ago:

We sit under the table,
the adults' hands
drum on our heads. Outside,
the street,
the contagious vernacular.

Remember
how we used to dance? Inseparable,
back and forth across the living room,
Adios Muchachos, like an insect
moving on a mirror: envy
is a dance, too; the need to hurt
binds you to your partner.

2.

You thrashed in the crib,
your small mouth circling
the ancient repetitions.
I watched you through the bars,
both of us
actively starving. In the other room
our parents merged into the one
totemic creature:

Come, she said. *Come to Mother.*
You stood. You tottered toward
the inescapable body.

3.

A dark board covers the sun.
Then the fathers come,
their long cars move slowly down the street,
parting the children. Then
the street is given over to darkness.

The rest follows: the labored
green of the yards, the little gardens
darned with green thread—

The trees also, whose shadows
were blue spokes.

But some the light chooses.
How they tremble
as the moon mounts them, brutal and sisterly:

I used to watch them,
all night absorbed in the moon's neutral silver
until they were finally blurred, disfigured . . .

4.

What was it like to be led?

I trusted no one. My name
was like a stranger's,
read from an envelope.

But nothing was taken from me
that I could have used.
For once, I admit that.

In the hall, posed
for the record's
passionate onset, ages
five and seven:

You were the gold sun on the horizon.
I was the judgment, my shadow
preceded me, not wavering

but like a mold that would be used again.
Your bare feet
became a woman's feet, always
saying two things at once.

Of two sisters
one is always the watcher,
one the dancer.

You were both quiet, looking out over the water.
It was not now; it was years ago,
before you were married.
The sky above the sea had turned
the odd pale peach color of early evening
from which the sea withdrew, bearing
its carved boats: your bodies were like that.
But her face was raised to you,
against the dull waves, simplified
by passion. Then you raised your hand
and from beyond the frame of the dream
swans came to settle on the scaled water.
The sea lay mild as a pool. At its edge,
you faced her, saying
These are yours to keep. The horizon burned,
releasing its withheld light.
And then I woke. But for days
when I tried to imagine you leaving your wife
I saw her motionless before your gift:
always the swans glide unmenacing across
the rigid blue of the Pacific Ocean, then rise
in a single wave, pure white and devouring.

NIGHT PIECE

He knows he will be hurt.
The warnings come to him in bed
because repose threatens him: in the camouflaging
light of the nightlight, he pretends to guard
the flesh in which his life is summarized.
He spreads his arms. On the wall, a corresponding figure
links him to the darkness he cannot control.
In its forms, the beasts originate
who are his enemies. He cannot sleep
apart from them.

You stand as rocks stand
to which the sea reaches
in transparent waves of longing;
they are marred, finally;
everything fixed is marred.
And the sea triumphs,
like all that is false,
all that is fluent and womanly.
From behind, a lens
opens for your body. Why
should you turn? It doesn't matter
who the witness is,
for whom you are suffering,
for whom you are standing still.

PORCELAIN BOWL

It rules out use:
in a lawn chair, the analogous
body of a woman is arranged,
and in this light
I cannot see what time has done to her.
A few leaves fall. A wind parts the long grass,
making a path going nowhere. And the hand
involuntarily lifts; it moves across her face
so utterly lost—
    The grass sways,
as though that motion were
an aspect of repose.
      Pearl white
on green. Ceramic
hand in the grass.

DEDICATION TO HUNGER

1. *From the Suburbs*

They cross the yard
and at the back door
the mother sees with pleasure
how alike they are, father and daughter—
I know something of that time.
The little girl purposefully
swinging her arms, laughing
her stark laugh:

It should be kept secret, that sound.
It means she's realized
that he never touches her.
She is a child; he could touch her
if he wanted to.

2. *Grandmother*

"Often I would stand at the window—
your grandfather
was a young man then—
waiting, in the early evening."

That is what marriage is.
I watch the tiny figure
changing to a man
as he moves toward her,
the last light rings in his hair.
I do not question
their happiness. And he rushes in
with his young man's hunger,
so proud to have taught her that:
his kiss would have been
clearly tender—

Of course, of course. Except
it might as well have been
his hand over her mouth.

3. *Eros*

To be male, always
to go to women
and be taken back
into the pierced flesh:

                I suppose
memory is stirred.
And the girl child
who wills herself
into her father's arms
likewise loved him
second. Nor is she told
what need to express.
There is a look one sees,
the mouth somehow desperate—

Because the bond
cannot be proven.

4. *The Deviation*

It begins quietly
in certain female children:
the fear of death, taking as its form
dedication to hunger,
because a woman's body
is a grave; it will accept
anything. I remember
lying in bed at night

touching the soft, digressive breasts,
touching, at fifteen,
the interfering flesh
that I would sacrifice
until the limbs were free
of blossom and subterfuge: I felt
what I feel now, aligning these words—
it is the same need to perfect,
of which death is the mere byproduct.

5. *Sacred Objects*

Today in the field I saw
the hard, active buds of the dogwood
and wanted, as we say, to capture them,
to make them eternal. That is the premise
of renunciation: the child,
having no self to speak of,
comes to life in denial—

I stood apart in that achievement,
in that power to expose
the underlying body, like a god
for whose deed
there is no parallel in the natural world.

HAPPINESS

A man and woman lie on a white bed.
It is morning. I think
Soon they will waken.
On the bedside table is a vase
of lilies; sunlight
pools in their throats.
I watch him turn to her
as though to speak her name
but silently, deep in her mouth—
At the window ledge,
once, twice,
a bird calls.
And then she stirs; her body
fills with his breath.

I open my eyes; you are watching me.
Almost over this room
the sun is gliding.
Look at your face, you say,
holding your own close to me
to make a mirror.
How calm you are. And the burning wheel
passes gently over us.

III   LAMENTATIONS

AUTUMNAL

Public sorrow, the acquired
gold of the leaf, the falling off,
the prefigured burning of the yield:
which is accomplished. At the lake's edge,
the metal pails are full vats of fire.
So waste is elevated
into beauty. And the scattered dead
unite in one consuming vision of order.
In the end, everything is bare.
Above the cold, receptive earth
the trees bend. Beyond,
the lake shines, placid, giving back
the established blue of heaven.
                    The word
is *bear*: you give and give, you empty yourself
into a child. And you survive
the automatic loss. Against inhuman landscape,
the tree remains a figure for grief; its form
is forced accommodation. At the grave,
it is the woman, isn't it, who bends,
the spear useless beside her.

AUBADE

Today above the gull's call
I heard you waking me again
to see that bird, flying
so strangely over the city,
not wanting
to stop, wanting
the blue waste of the sea—

Now it skirts the suburb,
the noon light violent against it:

I feel its hunger
as your hand inside me,

a cry
so common, unmusical—

Ours were not
different. They rose
from the unexhausted
need of the body

fixing a wish to return:
the ashen dawn, our clothes
not sorted for departure.

APHRODITE

A woman exposed as rock
has this advantage:
she controls the harbor.
Ultimately, men appear,
weary of the open.
So terminates, they feel,
a story. In the beginning,
longing. At the end, joy.
In the middle, tedium.

In time, the young wife
naturally hardens. Drifting
from her side, in imagination,
the man returns not to a drudge
but to the goddess he projects.

On a hill, the armless figure
welcomes the delinquent boat,
her thighs cemented shut, barring
the fault in the rock.

ROSY

When you walked in with your suitcase, leaving
the door open so the night showed
in a black square behind you, with its little stars
like nailheads, I wanted to tell you
you were like the dog that came to you by default,
on three legs: now that she is again no one's,
she pursues her more durable relationships
with traffic and cold nature, as though at pains
to wound herself so that she will not heal.
She is past being taken in by kindness,
preferring wet streets: what death claims
it does not abandon.
You understand, the animal means nothing to me.

THE DREAM OF MOURNING

I sleep so you will be alive,
it is that simple.
The dreams themselves are nothing.
They are the sickness you control,
nothing more.

I rush toward you in the summer twilight,
not in the real world, but in the buried one
where you are waiting,
as the wind moves over the bay, toying with it,
forcing thin ridges of panic—

And then the morning comes, demanding prey.
Remember? And the world complies.

Last night was different.
Someone fucked me awake; when I opened my eyes
it was over, all the need gone
by which I knew my life.
And for one instant I believed I was entering
the stable dark of the earth
and thought it would hold me.

THE GIFT

Lord, You may not recognize me
speaking for someone else.
I have a son. He is
so little, so ignorant.
He likes to stand
at the screen door, calling
oggie, oggie, entering
language, and sometimes
a dog will stop and come up
the walk, perhaps
accidentally. May he believe
this is not an accident?
At the screen
welcoming each beast
in love's name, Your emissary.

I look out over the sterile snow.
Under the white birch tree, a wheelbarrow.
The fence behind it mended. On the picnic table,
mounded snow, like the inverted contents of a bowl
whose dome the wind shapes. The wind,
with its impulse to build. And under my fingers,
the square white keys, each stamped
with its single character. I believed
a mind's shattering released
the objects of its scrutiny: trees, blue plums in a bowl,
a man reaching for his wife's hand
across a slatted table, and quietly covering it,
as though his will enclosed it in that gesture.
I saw them come apart, the glazed clay
begin dividing endlessly, dispersing
incoherent particles that went on
shining forever. I dreamed of watching that
the way we watched the stars on summer evenings,
my hand on your chest, the wine
holding the chill of the river. There is no such light.
And pain, the free hand, changes almost nothing.
Like the winter wind, it leaves
settled forms in the snow. Known, identifiable—
except there are no uses for them.

At first when you went away
I was frightened; then
a boy touched me on the street,
his eyes were level with mine,
clear and grieving: I
called him in; I spoke to him
in our language,
but his hands were yours,
so gently making their murderous claim—
And then it didn't matter
which one of you I called,
the wound was that deep.

LAMENTATIONS

1. *The Logos*

They were both still,
the woman mournful, the man
branching into her body.

But god was watching.
They felt his gold eye
projecting flowers on the landscape.

Who knew what he wanted?
He was god, and a monster.
So they waited. And the world
filled with his radiance,
as though he wanted to be understood.

Far away, in the void that he had shaped,
he turned to his angels.

2. *Nocturne*

A forest rose from the earth.
O pitiful, so needing
God's furious love—

Together they were beasts.
They lay in the fixed
dusk of his negligence;
from the hills, wolves came, mechanically
drawn to their human warmth,
their panic.

Then the angels saw
how He divided them:
the man, the woman, and the woman's body.

Above the churned reeds, the leaves let go
a slow moan of silver.

3. *The Covenant*

Out of fear, they built a dwelling place.
But a child grew between them
as they slept, as they tried
to feed themselves.

They set it on a pile of leaves,
the small discarded body
wrapped in the clean skin
of an animal. Against the black sky
they saw the massive argument of light.

Sometimes it woke. As it reached its hands
they understood they were the mother and father,
there was no authority above them.

4. *The Clearing*

Gradually, over many years,
the fur disappeared from their bodies
until they stood in the bright light
strange to one another.
Nothing was as before.
Their hands trembled, seeking
the familiar.

Nor could they keep their eyes
from the white flesh
on which wounds would show clearly
like words on a page.

And from the meaningless browns and greens
at last God arose, His great shadow
darkening the sleeping bodies of His children,
and leapt into heaven.

How beautiful it must have been,
the earth, that first time
seen from the air.

THE TRIUMPH OF
ACHILLES

(1985)

TO CHARLES CLAY DAHLBERG

First blossom in the wet grass—
O my body, you were given
only the one task, why
will you not repeat it?

"But if, as some say, . . . his suffering was only an appearance,
then why am I a prisoner, and why do I long to fight with the
wild beasts?" —IGNATIUS

"Joey was beginning to know good from evil. And whoever does
that is committed to live a human existence on earth."
—BRUNO BETTELHEIM

I

MOCK ORANGE

It is not the moon, I tell you.
It is these flowers
lighting the yard.

I hate them.
I hate them as I hate sex,
the man's mouth
sealing my mouth, the man's
paralyzing body—

and the cry that always escapes,
the low, humiliating
premise of union—

In my mind tonight
I hear the question and pursuing answer
fused in one sound
that mounts and mounts and then
is split into the old selves,
the tired antagonisms. Do you see?
We were made fools of.
And the scent of mock orange
drifts through the window.

How can I rest?
How can I be content
when there is still
that odor in the world?

METAMORPHOSIS

1. *Night*

The angel of death flies
low over my father's bed.
Only my mother sees. She and my father
are alone in the room.

She bends over him to touch
his hand, his forehead. She is
so used to mothering
that now she strokes his body
as she would the other children's,
first gently, then
inured to suffering.

Nothing is any different.
Even the spot on the lung
was always there.

2. *Metamorphosis*

My father has forgotten me
in the excitement of dying.
Like a child who will not eat,
he takes no notice of anything.

I sit at the edge of his bed
while the living circle us
like so many tree stumps.

Once, for the smallest
fraction of an instant, I thought
he was alive in the present again;
then he looked at me
as a blind man stares
straight into the sun, since

whatever it could do to him
is done already.

Then his flushed face
turned away from the contract.

3. *For My Father*

I'm going to live without you
as I learned once
to live without my mother.
You think I don't remember that?
I've spent my whole life trying to remember.

Now, after so much solitude,
death doesn't frighten me,
not yours, not mine either.
And those words, *the last time*,
have no power over me. I know
intense love always leads to mourning.

For once, your body doesn't frighten me.
From time to time, I run my hand over your face
lightly, like a dustcloth.
What can shock me now? I feel
no coldness that can't be explained.
Against your cheek, my hand is warm
and full of tenderness.

I was born in the month of the bull,
the month of heaviness,
or of the lowered, the destructive head,
or of purposeful blindness. So I know, beyond the shadowed
patch of grass, the stubborn one, the one who doesn't look up,
still senses the rejected world. It is
a stadium, a well of dust. And you who watch him
looking down in the face of death, what do you know
of commitment? If the bull lives
one controlled act of revenge, be satisfied
that in the sky, like you, he is always moving,
not of his own accord but through the black field
like grit caught on a wheel, like shining freight.

EXILE

He did not pretend
to be one of them. They did not require
a poet, a spokesman. He saw
the dog's heart, the working
lips of the parasite—
He himself preferred
to listen in the small apartments
as a man would check his camera at the museum,
to express his commitment through silence:
there is no other exile.
The rest is egotism; in the bloody street,
the I, the impostor—
He *was* there, obsessed with revolution,
in his own city,
daily climbing the wooden stairs
that were not a path
but necessary repetitions
and for twenty years
making no poetry
of what he saw: nor did he forfeit
great achievement. In his mind,
there could be no outcry that did not equate
his choice with their imprisonment
and he would not allow
the gift to be tainted.

WINTER MORNING

1.

Today, when I woke up, I asked myself
why did Christ die? Who knows
the meaning of such questions?

It was a winter morning, unbelievably cold.
So the thoughts went on,
from each question came
another question, like a twig from a branch,
like a branch from a black trunk.

2.

At a time like this
a young woman traveled through the desert settlements
looking neither forward nor backward,
sitting in perfect composure on the tired animal
as the child stirred, still sealed in its profound attachment—
The husband walked slightly ahead, older, out of place;
increasingly, the mule stumbled, the path becoming
difficult in darkness, though they persisted
in a world like our world, not ruled
by man but by a statue in heaven—

3.

Above the crowds representing
humankind, the lost
citizens of a remote time,

the insulted body
raised on a cross like a criminal
to die publicly
above Jerusalem, the shimmering city

while in great flocks
birds circled the body, not partial
to this form over the others

since men were all alike,
defeated by the air,

whereas in air
the body of a bird becomes a banner:

But the lesson that was needed
was another lesson.

4.

In untrustworthy springtime
he was seen moving
among us like one of us

in green Judea, covered with the veil of life,
among the olive trees, among the many shapes
blurred by spring,

stopping to eat and rest, in obvious need,
among the thousand flowers,
some planted, some distributed by wind,

like all men, seeking
recognition on earth,
so that he spoke to the disciples

in a man's voice, lifting his intact hand:
was it the wind that spoke?
Or stroked Mary's hair, until she raised her eyes

no longer wounded
by his coldness, by his needless destruction
of the flesh which was her fulfillment—

This was not the sun.
This was Christ in his cocoon of light:

so they swore. And there were other witnesses
though they were all blind,
they were all swayed by love—

5.

Winters are long here.
The road a dark gray, the maples gray, silvered with lichen,
and the sun low on the horizon,
white on blue; at sunset, vivid orange-red.

When I shut my eyes, it vanishes.
When I open my eyes, it reappears.
Outside, spring rain, a pulse, a film on the window.

And suddenly it is summer, all puzzling fruit and light.

SEATED FIGURE

It was as though you were a man in a wheelchair,
your legs cut off at the knee.
But I wanted you to walk.
I wanted us to walk like lovers,
arm in arm in the summer evening,
and believed so powerfully in that projection
that I had to speak, I had to press you to stand.
Why did you let me speak?
I took your silence as I took the anguish in your face,
as part of the effort to move—
It seemed I stood forever, holding out my hand.
And all that time, you could no more heal yourself
than I could accept what I saw.

When the stern god
approached me with his gift
my fear enchanted him
so that he ran more quickly
through the wet grass, as he insisted,
to praise me. I saw captivity
in praise; against the lyre,
I begged my father in the sea
to save me. When
the god arrived, I was nowhere,
I was in a tree forever. Reader,
pity Apollo: at the water's edge,
I turned from him, I summoned
my invisible father—as
I stiffened in the god's arms,
of his encompassing love
my father made
no other sign from the water.

HYACINTH

1.

Is that an attitude for a flower, to stand
like a club at the walk; poor slain boy,
is that a way to show
gratitude to the gods? White
with colored hearts, the tall flowers
sway around you, all the other boys,
in the cold spring, as the violets open.

2.

There were no flowers in antiquity
but boys' bodies, pale, perfectly imagined.
So the gods sank to human shape with longing.
In the field, in the willow grove,
Apollo sent the courtiers away.

3.

And from the blood of the wound
a flower sprang, lilylike, more brilliant
than the purples of Tyre.
Then the god wept: his vital grief
flooded the earth.

4.

Beauty dies: that is the source
of creation. Outside the ring of trees
the courtiers could hear
the dove's call transmit
its uniform, its inborn sorrow—
They stood listening, among the rustling willows.
Was this the god's lament?

They listened carefully. And for a short time
all sound was sad.

5.

There is no other immortality:
in the cold spring, the purple violets open.
And yet, the heart is black,
there is its violence frankly exposed.
Or is it not the heart at the center
but some other word?
And now someone is bending over them,
meaning to gather them—

6.

They could not wait
in exile forever.
Through the glittering grove
the courtiers ran
calling the name
of their companion
over the birds' noise,
over the willows' aimless sadness.
Well into the night they wept,
their clear tears
altering no earthly color.

THE TRIUMPH OF ACHILLES

In the story of Patroclus
no one survives, not even Achilles
who was nearly a god.
Patroclus resembled him; they wore
the same armor.

Always in these friendships
one serves the other, one is less than the other:
the hierarchy
is always apparent, though the legends
cannot be trusted—
their source is the survivor,
the one who has been abandoned.

What were the Greek ships on fire
compared to this loss?

In his tent, Achilles
grieved with his whole being
and the gods saw

he was a man already dead, a victim
of the part that loved,
the part that was mortal.

BASKETS

1.

It is a good thing,
in the marketplace
the old woman trying to decide
among the lettuces,
impartial, weighing the heads,
examining
the outer leaves, even
sniffing them to catch
a scent of earth
of which, on one head,
some trace remains—not
the substance but
the residue—so
she prefers it to
the other, more
estranged heads, it
being freshest: nodding
briskly at the vendor's wife,
she makes this preference known,
an old woman, yet
vigorous in judgment.

2.

The circle of the world—
in its midst, a dog
sits at the edge of the fountain.
The children playing there,
coming and going from the village,
pause to greet him, the impulsive
losing interest in play,
in the little village of sticks
adorned with blue fragments of pottery;
they squat beside the dog

who stretches in the hot dust:
arrows of sunlight
dance around him.
Now, in the field beyond,
some great event is ending.
In twos and threes, boldly
swinging their shirts,
the athletes stroll away, scattering
red and blue, blue and dazzling purple
over the plain ground,
over the trivial surface.

3.

Lord, who gave me
my solitude, I watch
the sun descending:
in the marketplace
the stalls empty, the remaining children
bicker at the fountain—
But even at night, when it can't be seen,
the flame of the sun
still heats the pavements.
That's why, on earth,
so much life's sprung up,
because the sun maintains
steady warmth at its periphery.
Does this suggest your meaning:
that the game resumes,
in the dust beneath
the infant god of the fountain;
there is nothing fixed,
there is no assurance of death—

4.

I take my basket to the brazen market,
to the gathering place.
I ask you, how much beauty
can a person bear? It is
heavier than ugliness, even the burden
of emptiness is nothing beside it.
Crates of eggs, papaya, sacks of yellow lemons—
I am not a strong woman. It isn't easy
to want so much, to walk
with such a heavy basket, either
bent reed, or willow.

LIBERATION

My mind is clouded,
I cannot hunt anymore.
I lay my gun over the tracks of the rabbit.

It was as though I became that creature
who could not decide
whether to flee or be still
and so was trapped in the pursuer's eyes—

And for the first time I knew
those eyes have to be blank
because it is impossible
to kill and question at the same time.

Then the shutter snapped,
the rabbit went free. He flew
through the empty forest

that part of me
that was the victim.
Only victims have a destiny.

And the hunter, who believed
whatever struggles
begs to be torn apart:

that part is paralyzed.

II

THE EMBRACE

She taught him the gods. Was it teaching? He went on
hating them, but in the long evenings of obsessive talk,
as he listened, they became real. Not that they changed.
They never came to seem innately human.
In the firelight, he watched her face.
But she would not be touched; she had rejected
the original need. Then in the darkness he would lead her back—
above the trees, the city rose in a kind of splendor
as all that is wild comes to the surface.

MARATHON

1. *Last Letter*

Weeping, standing still—then going out again into the garden.
In the field, white heads of dandelions making rows of saints,
now bending, now stiff with awe—
and at the edge, a hare: his eyes fixed, terrified.
Silence. Herds of bells—

Without thinking, I knelt in the grass, like someone meaning to pray.
When I tried to stand again, I couldn't move,
my legs were utterly rigid. Does grief change you like that?
Through the birches, I could see the pond.
The sun was cutting small white holes in the water.

I got up finally; I walked down to the pond.
I stood there, brushing the grass from my skirt, watching myself,
like a girl after her first lover
turning slowly at the bathroom mirror, naked, looking for a sign.
But nakedness in women is always a pose.
I was not transfigured. I would never be free.

2. *Song of the River*

Once we were happy, we had no memories.
For all the repetition, nothing happened twice.
We were always walking parallel to a river
with no sense of progression
though the trees across from us
were sometimes birch, sometimes cypress—
the sky was blue, a matrix of blue glass.

While, in the river, things were going by—
a few leaves, a child's boat painted red and white,
its sail stained by the water—

As they passed, on the surface we could see ourselves;
we seemed to drift
apart and together, as the river
linked us forever, though up ahead
were other couples, choosing souvenirs.

3. *The Encounter*

You came to the side of the bed
and sat staring at me.
Then you kissed me—I felt
hot wax on my forehead.
I wanted it to leave a mark:
that's how I knew I loved you.
Because I wanted to be burned, stamped,
to have something in the end—
I drew the gown over my head;
a red flush covered my face and shoulders.
It will run its course, the course of fire,
setting a cold coin on the forehead, between the eyes.
You lay beside me; your hand moved over my face
as though you had felt it also—
you must have known, then, how I wanted you.
We will always know that, you and I.
The proof will be my body.

4. *Song of Obstacles*

When my lover touches me, what I feel in my body
is like the first movement of a glacier over the earth,
as the ice shifts, dislodging great boulders, hills
of solemn rock: so, in the forests, the uprooted trees
become a sea of disconnected limbs—
And, where there are cities, these dissolve too,
the sighing gardens, all the young girls

eating chocolates in the courtyard, slowly
scattering the colored foil: then, where the city was,
the ore, the unearthed mysteries: so I see
that ice is more powerful than rock, than mere resistance—

Then for us, in its path, time doesn't pass,
not even an hour.

5. *Night Song*

Look up into the light of the lantern.
Don't you see? The calm of darkness
is the horror of Heaven.

We've been apart too long, too painfully separated.
How can you bear to dream,
to give up watching? I think you must be dreaming,
your face is full of mild expectancy.

I need to wake you, to remind you that there isn't a future.
That's why we're free. And now some weakness in me
has been cured forever, so I'm not compelled
to close my eyes, to go back, to rectify—

The beach is still; the sea, cleansed of its superfluous life,
opaque, rocklike. In mounds, in vegetal clusters,
seabirds sleep on the jetty. Terns, assassins—

You're tired; I can see that.
We're both tired, we have acted a great drama.
Even our hands are cold, that were like kindling.
Our clothes are scattered on the sand; strangely enough,
they never turned to ashes.

I have to tell you what I've learned, that I know now
what happens to the dreamers.
They don't feel it when they change. One day
they wake, they dress, they are old.

Tonight I'm not afraid
to feel the revolutions. How can you want sleep
when passion gives you that peace?
You're like me tonight, one of the lucky ones.
You'll get what you want. You'll get your oblivion.

6. *The Beginning*

I had come to a strange city, without belongings:
in the dream, it was your city, I was looking for you.
Then I was lost, on a dark street lined with fruit stands.

There was only one fruit: blood oranges.
The markets made displays of them, beautiful displays—
how else could they compete? And each arrangement had, at its center,
one fruit, cut open.

Then I was on a boulevard, in brilliant sunlight.
I was running; it was easy to run, since I had nothing.
In the distance, I could see your house; a woman knelt in the yard.
There were roses everywhere; in waves, they climbed the high trellis.

Then what began as love for you
became a hunger for structure: I could hear
the woman call to me in common kindness, knowing
I wouldn't ask for you anymore—

So it was settled: I could have a childhood there.
Which came to mean being always alone.

7. *First Goodbye*

You can join the others now,
body that wouldn't let my body rest,
go back to the world, to avenues, the ordered
depths of the parks, like great terminals
that never darken: a stranger's waiting for you
in a hundred rooms. Go back to them,
to increment and limitation: near the centered rose,
you watch her peel an orange
so the dyed rind falls in petals on her plate. This
is mastery, whose active
mode is dissection: the enforced light
shines on the blade. Sooner or later
you'll begin to dream of me. I don't envy you
those dreams. I can imagine how my face looks,
burning like that, afflicted with desire—lowered
face of your invention—how the mouth betrays
the isolated greed of the lover
as it magnifies and then destroys:
I don't envy you that visitation.
And the women lying there—who wouldn't pity them,
the way they turn to you, the way
they struggle to be visible. They make
a place for you in bed, a white excavation.
Then the sacrament: your bodies pieced together,
churning, churning, till the heat leaves them entirely—
Sooner or later you will call my name,
cry of loss, mistaken
cry of recognition, of arrested need
for someone who exists in memory: no voice
carries to that kingdom.

8. *Song of Invisible Boundaries*

Last night I dreamed we were in Venice;
today, we are in Venice. Now, lying here,
I think there are no boundaries to my dreams,
nothing we won't share.
So there is nothing to describe. We're interchangeable
with anyone, in joy
changed to a mute couple.

Then why did we worship clarity,
to speak, in the end, only each other's names,
to speak, as now, not even whole words,
only vowels?

Finally, this is what we craved,
this lying in the bright light without distinction—
we who would leave behind
exact records.

9. *Marathon*

I was not meant to hear
the two of them talking.
But I could feel the light of the torch
stop trembling, as though it had been
set on a table. I was not to hear
the one say to the other
how best to arouse me,
with what words, what gestures,
nor to hear the description of my body,
how it responded, what
it would not do. My back was turned.
I studied the voices, soon distinguishing
the first, which was deeper, closer,
from that of the replacement.

For all I know, this happens
every night: somebody waking me, then
the first teaching the second.
What happens afterward
occurs far from the world, at a depth
where only the dream matters
and the bond with any one soul
is meaningless; you throw it away.

SUMMER

Remember the days of our first happiness,
how strong we were, how dazed by passion,
lying all day, then all night in the narrow bed,
sleeping there, eating there too: it was summer,
it seemed everything had ripened
at once. And so hot we lay completely uncovered.
Sometimes the wind rose; a willow brushed the window.

But we were lost in a way, didn't you feel that?
The bed was like a raft; I felt us drifting
far from our natures, toward a place where we'd discover nothing.
First the sun, then the moon, in fragments,
shone through the willow.
Things anyone could see.

Then the circles closed. Slowly the nights grew cool;
the pendant leaves of the willow
yellowed and fell. And in each of us began
a deep isolation, though we never spoke of this,
of the absence of regret.
We were artists again, my husband.
We could resume the journey.

III

THE REPROACH

You have betrayed me, Eros.
You have sent me
my true love.

On a high hill you made
his clear gaze;
my heart was not
so hard as your arrow.

What is a poet
without dreams?
I lie awake; I feel
actual flesh upon me,
meaning to silence me—
Outside, in the blackness
over the olive trees,
a few stars.

I think this is a bitter insult:
that I prefer to walk
the coiled paths of the garden,
to walk beside the river
glittering with drops
of mercury. I like to lie
in the wet grass beside the river,
running away, Eros,
not openly, with other men,
but discreetly, coldly—

All my life
I have worshiped the wrong gods.
When I watch the trees
on the other side,
the arrow in my heart
is like one of them,
swaying and quivering.

THE END OF THE WORLD

1. *Terra Nova*

A place without associations—
Where, in the other country, there were mountains
so the mind was made to discover
words for containment, and so on,
here there was water, an extension of the brilliant city.
As for detail: where there had been, before,
nurturing slopes of grass on which, at evening or before rain,
the Charolais would lie, their many eyes
affixed to the traveler, here
there was clay. And yet it blossomed astoundingly:
beside the house, camellia, periwinkle, rosemary in crushing profusion—
in his heart, he was a lover again,
calling *now, now*, not restricted
to *once* or *in the old days*. He lay on his back in the wild fennel.
But in fact he was an old man.
Sixty years ago, he took his mother's hand. It was May, his birthday.
They were walking in the orchard, in the continuous present,
gathering apple blossoms. Then she wanted him to watch the sun;
they had to stand together as it sank in the possessive earth.
How short it seemed, that lifetime of waiting—
this red star blazing over the bay
was all the light of his childhood
that had followed him here.

2. *The Tribute*

In that period of strange calm
he wandered down stone steps to the wide harbor:
he was moved; the lights of the city moved him deeply
and it seemed the earth was being offered to him
as a source of awe—he had no wish to change.
He had written, he had built his temple.
So he justified a need to sacrifice.
He leaned against the railing: in the dark bay, he saw the city waver;

cells of light floated on the water, they rocked gently, held by white threads.
Behind him, on the steps, he heard a man and woman
arguing with great intensity.
In a poem, he could bring them together
like two pieces of a broken toy that could be joined again—
Then the voices ceased, replaced by sighs, rustlings, the little sounds
of which he had no knowledge
though the wind persisted
in conveying them to where he stood,
and with them all the odors of summer.

3. *The End of the World*

It is difficult to describe, coming as it still does
to each person at a different time.
Unique, terrible—and in the sky, uncanny brilliance
substituting for the humanizing sun.
So the blessed kneel, the lucky who expect nothing,
while those who loved the world
are returned by suffering
to what precedes attachment, namely
hatred of pain. Now the bitter are confirmed
in loneliness: they watch the winter sun
mockingly lower itself over the bare earth,
making nothing live—in this light
god approaches the dying.
Not the true god, of course. There is no god
who will save one man.

THE MOUNTAIN

My students look at me expectantly.
I explain to them that the life of art is a life
of endless labor. Their expressions
hardly change; they need to know
a little more about endless labor.
So I tell them the story of Sisyphus,
how he was doomed to push
a rock up a mountain, knowing nothing
would come of this effort
but that he would repeat it
indefinitely. I tell them
there is joy in this, in the artist's life,
that one eludes
judgment, and as I speak
I am secretly pushing a rock myself,
slyly pushing it up the steep
face of a mountain. Why do I lie
to these children? They aren't listening,
they aren't deceived, their fingers
tapping at the wooden desks—
So I retract
the myth; I tell them it occurs
in hell, and that the artist lies
because he is obsessed with attainment,
that he perceives the summit
as that place where he will live forever,
a place about to be
transformed by his burden: with every breath,
I am standing at the top of the mountain.
Both my hands are free. And the rock has added
height to the mountain.

It was an epoch of heroes.
So this young boy, this nobody,
making his way from one plain to another,
picks up a small stone among the cold, unspecified
rocks of the hillside. It is a pleasant day.
At his feet, normal vegetation, the few white flowers
like stars, the leaves woolly, sage-green:
at the bottom of the hill are corpses.

Who is the enemy? Who has distributed
the compact bodies of the Jews
in this unprecedented silence? Disguised in dirt,
the scattered army sees the beast, Goliath,
towering above the childish shepherd.
They shut their eyes. And all the level earth
becomes the shattered surface of a sea, so disruptive
is that fall. In the ensuing dust, David
lifts his hand: then it is his, the hushed,
completed kingdom—

Fellow Jews, to plot a hero's journey
is to trace a mountain: hero to god, god to ruler.
At the precipice, the moment we don't want to hear about—
the stone is gone; now
the hand is the weapon.

On the palace roof, King David stares across
the shining city of Jerusalem
into the face of Bathsheba and perceives
his own amplified desire. At heart, he feels nothing.
She is like a flower in a tub of water. Above his head,
the clouds move. And it comes to him he has attained
all he is capable of dreaming.

DAY WITHOUT NIGHT

The angel of god pushed the child's hand
away from the jewels, toward the burning coal.

1.

The image
of truth is fire: it mounts
the fortress of heaven.

Have you never felt
its obvious power?
Even a child
is capable of this joy.

Apparently,
a like sun
burns in hell. It *is* hell,
day without night.

2.

It was as though Pharaoh's daughter
had brought home a lion cub
and for a few weeks
passed it off as a cat.
You did not press this woman.
She said she came upon
a child in the rushes;
each time she told the story,
her handmaidens recreated
their interminable chorus of sighs.
It had to be:
A little prince. A little lion cub.

3.

And then with almost no encouragement
a sign came: for awhile
the child is like
a grandson to Pharaoh.
Then he squirms; on Pharaoh's lap
he reaches for the crown of Egypt—

4.

So Pharaoh set before the child
two trays, one of rubies, one of burning embers:

Light of my heart, the world
is set before you:
fire on either side, fire
without alternative—

5.

It was like a magic act: all you saw
was the child move; the same hand that took
such active interest in
the wealth of Egypt showed
this sudden preference for a pile of coal.
You never saw the actual angel.
And to complete the act,
the child maimed himself—
And a cry arose,
almost as though a person
were in hell,
where there is nothing to do
but see—

6.

Moses
lay in the rushes:
he could see
only in one direction,
his perspective being
narrowed by the basket.
What he saw
was great light, like
a wing hovering.
And god said to him,
"You can be the favored one,
the one who tastes fire
and cannot speak,
or you can die now
and let the others
stay in Egypt: tell them
it was better to die in Egypt,
better to litter the river
with your corpse, than face
a new world."

7.

It was as though a soul emerged,
independent of the angel,
a conscious being choosing
not to enter paradise—
at the same time, the true
sun was setting.
As it touched the water
by necessity the mirrored sun rose
to meet it from
the depths of the river:
Then the cry ended.
Or was hidden

in the stammering
of the redeemer—

8.

The context
of truth is darkness: it sweeps
the deserts of Israel.

Are you taken in
by lights, by illusions?

Here is your path to god,
who has no name, whose hand
is invisible: a trick
of moonlight on the dark water.

ELMS

All day I tried to distinguish
need from desire. Now, in the dark,
I feel only bitter sadness for us,
the builders, the planers of wood,
because I have been looking
steadily at these elms
and seen the process that creates
the writhing, stationary tree
is torment, and have understood
it will make no forms but twisted forms.

ADULT GRIEF

—for E. V.

Because you were foolish enough to love one place,
now you are homeless, an orphan
in a succession of shelters.
You did not prepare yourself sufficiently.
Before your eyes, two people were becoming old;
I could have told you two deaths were coming.
There has never been a parent
kept alive by a child's love.

Now, of course, it's too late—
you were trapped in the romance of fidelity.
You kept going back, clinging
to two people you hardly recognized
after what they'd endured.

If once you could have saved yourself,
now that time's past: you were obstinate, pathetically
blind to change. Now you have nothing:
for you, home is a cemetery.
I've seen you press your face against the granite markers—
you are the lichen, trying to grow there.
But you will not grow,
you will not let yourself
obliterate anything.

HAWK'S SHADOW

Embracing in the road
for some reason I no longer remember
and then drawing apart, seeing
that shape ahead—how close was it?
We looked up to where the hawk
hovered with its kill; I watched them
veering toward West Hill, casting
their one shadow in the dirt, the all-inclusive
shape of the predator—
Then they disappeared. And I thought:
one shadow. Like the one we made,
you holding me.

FROM THE JAPANESE

1.

A cat stirs in the material world.
And suddenly sunlight pours into the room
as though somewhere a blind had been opened.
And on the floor, the white bars of a ladder appear.

2.

Gwen is sobbing in the front yard; she is three.
The Spanish maid strokes her hair—Gwen
is bilingual; she dries her eyes,
a few petals falling from the jacaranda tree.

Now the door opens: here is Jack, the athlete, in his combat boots.
For the next hour he runs
first away from, then toward his family.

And here is Trixie, roaming the driveway,
huge in comparison
to the rigid bird. Boring bird,
that will not chirp and fight anymore.
She flicks it once or twice,
under the grapefruit, under the lemon tree.

Early summer: fog covers the mountains.
Under each tree, a doily of shade.

3.

At first, I saw you everywhere.
Now only in certain things,
at longer intervals.

4.

We were walking in the Japanese gardens
among the bare cherry trees,
a path you chose
deliberately in desolate November

as though I myself had ordered down
the petals, the black
nuggets of the fruit—

Nearby, a boy sailed his wooden boat,
home and away, home and away.
Then the thread snapped; the boat
was carried toward the waterfall.

"From this moment I will never know
ease," you said, "since you have lied to me,
nor joy." The boy
covered his face with his hands.

There is another world,
neither air nor water
but an emptiness which now
a symbol has entered.

5.

The cat
misses her master.
She climbs the brick wall,

a feat
Gwen determines
to copy: loud
objections from the Spanish maid.

Tears, shuffling. At the water's edge,
the boy finally
lowered his hands.
He had a new toy, a thread
tied to a lost thing—

Twilight: in her blue sombrero,
Gwen reconstructs the summer garden.

6.

Alone, watching the moon rise:
tonight, a full circle,
like a woman's eye passing over abundance.

This is the most it will ever be.
Above the blank street, the imperfections
solved by night—

Like our hearts: darkness
showed us their capacity.
Our full hearts—at the time, they seemed so impressive.

Cries, moans, our important suffering.
A hand at the small of the back
or on the breast—

And now across the wall
someone is clearing the table,
wrapping the dark bread and the white ceramic pot of butter.

What did we think?
What did we talk about?

Upstairs, a light goes on.
It must be
Gwen's, it burns
the span of a story—

7.

Why love what you will lose?
There is nothing else to love.

8.

Last night in bed your
hand fell heavily upon
my shoulder. I thought

you slept. Yet we are
parted. Perhaps the sheet moved,
given your hand's weight by

the dampness of
my body. Morning: I have
written to thank you.

9.

The cat sleeps on the sidewalk,
black against the white cement.

The brave are patient.
They are the priests of sunrise,
lions on the ramparts, the promontory.

LEGEND

My father's father came
to New York from Dhlua:
one misfortune followed another.
In Hungary, a scholar, a man of property.
Then failure: an immigrant
rolling cigars in a cold basement.

He was like Joseph in Egypt.
At night, he walked the city;
spray of the harbor
turned to tears on his face.

Tears of grief for Dhlua—forty houses,
a few cows grazing the rich meadows—

Though the great soul is said to be
a star, a beacon,
what it resembles better is a diamond:
in the whole world there is nothing
hard enough to change it.

Unfortunate being, have you ceased to feel
the grandeur of the world
that, like a heavy weight, shaped
the soul of my grandfather?

From the factory, like sad birds his dreams
flew to Dhlua, grasping in their beaks
as from moist earth in which a man could see
the shape of his own footprint,
scattered images, loose bits of the village;
and as he packed the leaves, so within his soul
this weight compressed scraps of Dhlua
into principles, abstractions
worthy of the challenge of bondage:

in such a world, to scorn
privilege, to love
reason and justice, always
to speak the truth—

which has been
the salvation of our people
since to speak the truth gives
the illusion of freedom.

The virtuous girl wakes in the arms of her husband,
the same arms in which, all summer, she moved
restlessly, under the pear trees:
it is pleasant to wake like this,
with the sun rising, to see the wedding dress
draped over the back of a chair,
and on the heavy bureau, a man's shirt, neatly folded;
to be restored by these
to a thousand images, to the church itself, the autumn sunlight
streaming through the colored windows, through
the figure of the Blessed Virgin, and underneath,
Amelia holding the fiery bridal flowers—
As for her mother's tears: ridiculous, and yet
mothers weep at their daughters' weddings,
everyone knows that, though
for whose youth one cannot say.
At the great feast there is always the outsider, the stranger to joy,
and the point is how different they are, she and her mother.
Never has she been further from sadness
than she is now. She feels no call to weep,
but neither does she know
the meaning of that word, youth.

HORSE

What does the horse give you
that I cannot give you?

I watch you when you are alone,
when you ride into the field behind the dairy,
your hands buried in the mare's
dark mane.

Then I know what lies behind your silence:
scorn, hatred of me, of marriage. Still,
you want me to touch you; you cry out
as brides cry, but when I look at you I see
there are no children in your body.
Then what is there?

Nothing, I think. Only haste
to die before I die.

In a dream, I watched you ride the horse
over the dry fields and then
dismount: you two walked together;
in the dark, you had no shadows.
But I felt them coming toward me
since at night they go anywhere,
they are their own masters.

Look at me. You think I don't understand?
What is the animal
if not passage out of this life?

ARARAT

(1990)

*". . . human nature was originally one and we were a whole,
and the desire and pursuit of the whole is called love."*

—PLATO

Long ago, I was wounded.
I learned
to exist, in reaction,
out of touch
with the world: I'll tell you
what I meant to be—
a device that listened.
Not inert: still.
A piece of wood. A stone.

Why should I tire myself, debating, arguing?
Those people breathing in the other beds
could hardly follow, being
uncontrollable
like any dream—
Through the blinds, I watched
the moon in the night sky, shrinking and swelling—

I was born to a vocation:
to bear witness
to the great mysteries.
Now that I've seen both
birth and death, I know
to the dark nature these
are proofs, not
mysteries—

A FANTASY

I'll tell you something: every day
people are dying. And that's just the beginning.
Every day, in funeral homes, new widows are born,
new orphans. They sit with their hands folded,
trying to decide about this new life.

Then they're in the cemetery, some of them
for the first time. They're frightened of crying,
sometimes of not crying. Someone leans over,
tells them what to do next, which might mean
saying a few words, sometimes
throwing dirt in the open grave.

And after that, everyone goes back to the house,
which is suddenly full of visitors.
The widow sits on the couch, very stately,
so people line up to approach her,
sometimes take her hand, sometimes embrace her.
She finds something to say to everybody,
thanks them, thanks them for coming.

In her heart, she wants them to go away.
She wants to be back in the cemetery,
back in the sickroom, the hospital. She knows
it isn't possible. But it's her only hope,
the wish to move backward. And just a little,
not so far as the marriage, the first kiss.

A NOVEL

No one could write a novel about this family:
too many similar characters. Besides, they're all women;
there was only one hero.

Now the hero's dead. Like echoes, the women last longer;
they're all too tough for their own good.

From this point on, nothing changes:
there's no plot without a hero.
In this house, when you say *plot* what you mean is *love story*.

The women can't get moving.
Oh, they get dressed, they eat, they keep up appearances.
But there's no action, no development of character.

They're all determined to suppress
criticism of the hero. The problem is
he's weak; his scenes specify
his function but not his nature.

Maybe that explains why his death wasn't moving.
First he's sitting at the head of the table,
where the figurehead is most needed.
Then he's dying, a few feet away, his wife holding a mirror under his mouth.

Amazing, how they keep busy, these women, the wife and two daughters.
Setting the table, clearing the dishes away.
Each heart pierced through with a sword.

LABOR DAY

It's a year exactly since my father died.
Last year was hot. At the funeral, people talked about the weather.
How hot it was for September. How unseasonable.

This year, it's cold.
There's just us now, the immediate family.
In the flower beds,
shreds of bronze, of copper.

Out front, my sister's daughter rides her bicycle
the way she did last year,
up and down the sidewalk. What she wants is
to make time pass.

While to the rest of us
a whole lifetime is nothing.
One day, you're a blond boy with a tooth missing;
the next, an old man gasping for air.
It comes to nothing, really, hardly
a moment on earth.
Not a sentence, but a breath, a caesura.

LOVER OF FLOWERS

In our family, everyone loves flowers.
That's why the graves are so odd:
no flowers, just padlocks of grass,
and in the center, plaques of granite,
the inscriptions terse, the shallow letters
sometimes filling with dirt.
To clean them out, you use your handkerchief.

With my sister, it's different,
it's an obsession. Weekends, she sits on my mother's porch,
reading catalogues. Every autumn, she plants bulbs by the brick stoop;
every spring, waits for flowers.
No one discusses cost. It's understood
my mother pays; after all,
it's her garden, every flower
planted for my father. They both see
the house as his true grave.

Not everything thrives on Long Island.
Sometimes the summer gets too hot;
sometimes a heavy rain beats down the flowers.
That's how the poppies died, after one day,
because they're very fragile.

My mother's tense, upset about my sister:
now she'll never know how beautiful they were,
pure pink, with no dark spots. That means
she's going to feel deprived again.

But for my sister, that's the condition of love.
She was my father's daughter:
the face of love, to her,
is the face turning away.

My mother's playing cards with my aunt,
Spite and Malice, the family pastime, the game
my grandmother taught all her daughters.

Midsummer: too hot to go out.
Today, my aunt's ahead; she's getting the good cards.
My mother's dragging, having trouble with her concentration.
She can't get used to her own bed this summer.
She had no trouble last summer,
getting used to the floor. She learned to sleep there
to be near my father.
He was dying; he got a special bed.

My aunt doesn't give an inch, doesn't make
allowance for my mother's weariness.
It's how they were raised: you show respect by fighting.
To let up insults the opponent.

Each player has one pile to the left, five cards in the hand.
It's good to stay inside on days like this,
to stay where it's cool.
And this is better than other games, better than solitaire.

My grandmother thought ahead; she prepared her daughters.
They have cards; they have each other.
They don't need any more companionship.

All afternoon the game goes on but the sun doesn't move.
It just keeps beating down, turning the grass yellow.
That's how it must seem to my mother.
And then, suddenly, something is over.

My aunt's been at it longer; maybe that's why she's playing better.
Her cards evaporate: that's what you want, that's the object: in the end,
the one who has nothing wins.

CONFESSION

To say I'm without fear—
it wouldn't be true.
I'm afraid of sickness, humiliation.
Like anyone, I have my dreams.
But I've learned to hide them,
to protect myself
from fulfillment: all happiness
attracts the Fates' anger.
They are sisters, savages—
in the end, they have
no emotion but envy.

A PRECEDENT

In the same way as she'd prepare for the others,
my mother planned for the child that died.

Bureaus of soft clothes.
Little jackets neatly folded.
Each one almost fit in the palm of a hand.

In the same way, she wondered
which day would be its birthday.
And as each passed, she knew a day as common
would become a symbol of joy.

Because death hadn't touched my mother's life,
she was thinking of something else,
dreaming, the way you do when a child's coming.

LOST LOVE

My sister spent a whole life in the earth.
She was born, she died.
In between,
not one alert look, not one sentence.

She did what babies do,
she cried. But she didn't want to be fed.
Still, my mother held her, trying to change
first fate, then history.

Something did change: when my sister died,
my mother's heart became
very cold, very rigid,
like a tiny pendant of iron.

Then it seemed to me my sister's body
was a magnet. I could feel it draw
my mother's heart into the earth,
so it would grow.

LULLABY

My mother's an expert in one thing:
sending people she loves into the other world.
The little ones, the babies—these
she rocks, whispering or singing quietly. I can't say
what she did for my father;
whatever it was, I'm sure it was right.

It's the same thing, really, preparing a person
for sleep, for death. The lullabies—they all say
don't be afraid, that's how they paraphrase
the heartbeat of the mother.
So the living slowly grow calm; it's only
the dying who can't, who refuse.

The dying are like tops, like gyroscopes—
they spin so rapidly they seem to be still.
Then they fly apart: in my mother's arms,
my sister was a cloud of atoms, of particles—that's the difference.
When a child's asleep, it's still whole.

My mother's seen death; she doesn't talk about the soul's integrity.
She's held an infant, an old man, as by comparison the dark grew
solid around them, finally changing to earth.

The soul's like all matter:
why would it stay intact, stay faithful to its one form,
when it could be free?

MOUNT ARARAT

Nothing's sadder than my sister's grave
unless it's the grave of my cousin, next to her.
To this day, I can't bring myself to watch
my aunt and my mother,
though the more I try to escape
seeing their suffering, the more it seems
the fate of our family:
each branch donates one girl child to the earth.

In my generation, we put off marrying, put off having children.
When we did have them, we each had one;
for the most part, we had sons, not daughters.

We don't discuss this ever.
But it's always a relief to bury an adult,
someone remote, like my father.
It's a sign that maybe the debt's finally been paid.

In fact, no one believes this.
Like the earth itself, every stone here
is dedicated to the Jewish god
who doesn't hesitate to take
a son from a mother.

APPEARANCES

When we were children, my parents had our portraits painted,
then hung them side by side, over the mantel,
where we couldn't fight.
I'm the dark one, the older one. My sister's blond,
the one who looks angry because she can't talk.

It never bothered me, not talking.
That hasn't changed much. My sister's still blond, not different
from the portrait. Except we're adults now, we've been analyzed:
we understand our expressions.

My mother tried to love us equally,
dressed us in the same dresses; she wanted us
perceived as sisters.
That's what she wanted from the portraits:
you need to see them hanging together, facing one another—
separated, they don't make the same statement.
You wouldn't know what the eyes were fixed on;
they'd seem to be staring into space.

This was the summer we went to Paris, the summer I was seven.
Every morning, we went to the convent.
Every afternoon, we sat still, having the portraits painted,
wearing green cotton dresses, the square neck marked with a ruffle.
Monsieur Davanzo added the flesh tones: my sister's ruddy; mine, faintly bluish
To amuse us, Madame Davanzo hung cherries over our ears.

It was something I was good at: sitting still, not moving.
I did it to be good, to please my mother, to distract her from the child that
    died.
I wanted to be child enough. I'm still the same,
like a toy that can stop and go, but not change direction.

Anyone can love a dead child, love an absence.
My mother's strong; she doesn't do what's easy.
She's like her mother: she believes in family, in order.
She doesn't change her house, just freshens the paint occasionally.
Sometimes something breaks, gets thrown away, but that's all.
She likes to sit there, on the blue couch, looking up at her daughters,
at the two who lived. She can't remember how it really was,
how anytime she ministered to one child, loved that child,
she damaged the other. You could say
she's like an artist with a dream, a vision.
Without that, she'd have been torn apart.

We were like the portraits, always together: you had to shut out
one child to see the other.
That's why only the painter noticed: a face already so controlled, so withdrawn,
and too obedient, the clear eyes saying
If you want me to be a nun, I'll be a nun.

THE UNTRUSTWORTHY SPEAKER

Don't listen to me; my heart's been broken.
I don't see anything objectively.

I know myself; I've learned to hear like a psychiatrist.
When I speak passionately,
that's when I'm least to be trusted.

It's very sad, really: all my life, I've been praised
for my intelligence, my powers of language, of insight.
In the end, they're wasted—

I never see myself,
standing on the front steps, holding my sister's hand.
That's why I can't account
for the bruises on her arm, where the sleeve ends.

In my own mind, I'm invisible: that's why I'm dangerous.
People like me, who seem selfless,
we're the cripples, the liars;
we're the ones who should be factored out
in the interest of truth.

When I'm quiet, that's when the truth emerges.
A clear sky, the clouds like white fibers.
Underneath, a little gray house, the azaleas
red and bright pink.

If you want the truth, you have to close yourself
to the older daughter, block her out:
when a living thing is hurt like that,
in its deepest workings,
all function is altered.

That's why I'm not to be trusted.
Because a wound to the heart
is also a wound to the mind.

A FABLE

Two women with
the same claim
came to the feet of
the wise king. Two women,
but only one baby.
The king knew
someone was lying.
What he said was
Let the child be
cut in half; that way
no one will go
empty-handed. He
drew his sword.
Then, of the two
women, one
renounced her share:
this was
the sign, the lesson.
Suppose
you saw your mother
torn between two daughters:
what could you do
to save her but be
willing to destroy
yourself—she would know
who was the rightful child,
the one who couldn't bear
to divide the mother.

NEW WORLD

As I saw it,
all my mother's life, my father
held her down, like
lead strapped to her ankles.

She was
buoyant by nature;
she wanted to travel,
go to theater, go to museums.
What he wanted
was to lie on the couch
with the *Times*
over his face,
so that death, when it came,
wouldn't seem a significant change.

In couples like this,
where the agreement
is to do things together,
it's always the active one
who concedes, who gives.
You can't go to museums
with someone who won't
open his eyes.

I thought my father's death
would free my mother.
In a sense, it has:
she takes trips, looks at
great art. But she's floating.
Like some child's balloon
that gets lost the minute
it isn't held.
Or like an astronaut
who somehow loses the ship

and has to drift in space
knowing, however long it lasts,
this is what's left of being alive: she's free
in that sense.
Without relation to earth.

BIRTHDAY

Every year, on her birthday, my mother got twelve roses
from an old admirer. Even after he died, the roses kept coming:
the way some people leave paintings and furniture,
this man left bulletins of flowers,
his way of saying that the legend of my mother's beauty
had simply gone underground.

At first, it seemed bizarre.
Then we got used to it: every December, the house suddenly
filling with flowers. They even came to set
a standard of courtesy, of generosity—

After ten years, the roses stopped.
But all that time I thought
the dead could minister to the living;
I didn't realize
this was the anomaly; that for the most part
the dead were like my father.

My mother doesn't mind, she doesn't need
displays from my father.
Her birthday comes and goes; she spends it
sitting by a grave.

She's showing him she understands,
that she accepts his silence.
He hates deception: she doesn't want him making
signs of affection when he can't feel.

BROWN CIRCLE

My mother wants to know
why, if I hate
family so much,
I went ahead and
had one. I don't
answer my mother.
What I hated
was being a child,
having no choice about
what people I loved.

I don't love my son
the way I meant to love him.
I thought I'd be
the lover of orchids who finds
red trillium growing
in the pine shade, and doesn't
touch it, doesn't need
to possess it. What I am
is the scientist,
who comes to that flower
with a magnifying glass
and doesn't leave, though
the sun burns a brown
circle of grass around
the flower. Which is
more or less the way
my mother loved me.

I must learn
to forgive my mother,
now that I'm helpless
to spare my son.

CHILDREN COMING HOME FROM SCHOOL

I.

If you live in a city, it's different: someone has to meet
the child at the bus stop. There's a reason. A child all alone
can disappear, get lost, maybe forever.

My sister's daughter wants to walk home alone; she thinks she's old
    enough.
My sister thinks it's too soon for such a big change;
the best her daughter gets
is the option to walk without holding hands.

That's what they do; they compromise, which anyone
can manage for a few blocks. My niece gets one hand
totally free; my sister says
if she's old enough to walk this way, she's old enough
to hold her own violin.

2.

My son accuses me
of his unhappiness, not
in words, but in the way
he stares at the ground, inching
slowly up the driveway: he knows
I'm watching. That's why
he greets the cat,
to show he's capable
of open affection.
My father used
the dog in the same way.
My son and I, we're the living
experts in silence.
Snow's sweeping the sky;
it shifts directions, going
first steadily down, then sideways.

3.

One thing you learn, growing up with my sister:
you learn that rules don't mean anything.
Sooner or later, whatever you're waiting to hear will get itself said.
It doesn't matter what it is: *I love you* or *I'll never speak to you again*.
It all gets said, often in the same night.

Then you slip in, you take advantage. There are ways
to hold a person to what's been said; for example, by using the word *promise*.
But you have to have patience; you have to be able to wait, to listen.

My niece knows that in time, with intelligence, she'll get everything she wants.
It's not a bad life. Of course, she has those gifts,
time and intelligence.

ANIMALS

My sister and I reached
the same conclusion:
the best way
to love us was to not
spend time with us.
It seemed that
we appealed
chiefly to strangers.
We had good clothes, good
manners in public.

In private, we were
always fighting. Usually
the big one finished
sitting on the little one
and pinching her.
The little one
bit: in forty years
she never learned
the advantage in not
leaving a mark.

The parents
had a credo: they didn't
believe in anger.
The truth was, for different reasons,
they couldn't bring themselves
to inflict pain. You should only hurt
something you can give
your whole heart to. They preferred
tribunals: the child
most in the wrong could choose
her own punishment.

My sister and I
never became allies,
never turned on our parents.
We had
other obsessions: for example,
we both felt there were
too many of us
to survive.

We were like animals
trying to share a dry pasture.
Between us, one tree, barely
strong enough to sustain
a single life.

We never moved
our eyes from each other
nor did either touch
one thing that could
feed her sister.

SAINTS

In our family, there were two saints,
my aunt and my grandmother.
But their lives were different.

My grandmother's was tranquil, even at the end.
She was like a person walking in calm water;
for some reason
the sea couldn't bring itself to hurt her.
When my aunt took the same path,
the waves broke over her, they attacked her,
which is how the Fates respond
to a true spiritual nature.

My grandmother was cautious, conservative:
that's why she escaped suffering.
My aunt's escaped nothing;
each time the sea retreats, someone she loves is taken away.

Still, she won't experience
the sea as evil. To her, it is what it is:
where it touches land, it must turn to violence.

YELLOW DAHLIA

My sister's like a sun, like a yellow dahlia.
Daggers of gold hair around the face.
Gray eyes, full of spirit.

I made an enemy of a flower:
now, I'm ashamed.

We were supposed to be opposites:
one fair, like daylight.
One different, negative.

If there are two things
then one must be better,
isn't that true? I know now
we both thought that, if what children do
can really be called thinking.

I look at my sister's daughter,
a child so like her,
and I'm ashamed: nothing justifies
the impulse to destroy
a smaller, a dependent life.

I guess I knew that always.
That's why I had to hurt
myself instead:
I believed in justice.

We were like day and night,
one act of creation.
I couldn't separate
the two halves,
one child from the other.

My son's very graceful; he has perfect balance.
He's not competitive, like my sister's daughter.

Day and night, she's always practicing.
Today, it's hitting softballs into the copper beech,
retrieving them, hitting them again.
After a while, no one even watches her.
If she were any stronger, the tree would be bald.

My son won't play with her; he won't even ride bicycles with her.
She accepts that; she's used to playing by herself.
The way she sees it, it isn't personal:
whoever won't play doesn't like losing.

It's not that my son's inept, that he doesn't do things well.
I've watched him race: he's natural, effortless—
right from the first, he takes the lead.
And then he stops. It's as though he was born rejecting
the solitude of the victor.

My sister's daughter doesn't have that problem.
She may as well be first; she's already alone.

PARADISE

I grew up in a village: now
it's almost a city.
People came from the city, wanting
something simple, something
better for the children.
Clean air; nearby
a little stable.
All the streets
named after sweethearts or girl children.

Our house was gray, the sort of place
you buy to raise a family.
My mother's still there, all alone.
When she's lonely, she watches television.

The houses get closer together,
the old trees die or get taken down.

In some ways, my father's
close, too; we call
a stone by his name.
Now, above his head, the grass blinks,
in spring, when the snow has melted.
Then the lilac blooms, heavy, like clusters of grapes.

They always said
I was like my father, the way he showed
contempt for emotion.
They're the emotional ones,
my sister and my mother.

More and more
my sister comes from the city,
weeds, tidies the garden. My mother
lets her take over: she's the one

who cares, the one who does the work.
To her, it looks like country—
the clipped lawns, strips of colored flowers.
She doesn't know what it once was.

But I know. Like Adam,
I was the firstborn.
Believe me, you never heal,
you never forget the ache in your side,
the place where something was taken away
to make another person.

CHILD CRYING OUT

You're asleep now,
your eyelids quiver.
What son of mine
could be expected
to rest quietly, to live
even one moment
free of wariness?

The night's cold;
you've pushed the covers away.
As for your thoughts, your dreams—

I'll never understand
the claim of a mother
on a child's soul.

So many times
I made that mistake
in love, taking
some wild sound to be
the soul exposing itself—

But not with you,
even when I held you constantly.
You were born, you were far away.

Whatever those cries meant,
they came and went
whether I held you or not,
whether I was there or not.

The soul is silent.
If it speaks at all
it speaks in dreams.

SNOW

Late December: my father and I
are going to New York, to the circus.
He holds me
on his shoulders in the bitter wind:
scraps of white paper
blow over the railroad ties.

My father liked
to stand like this, to hold me
so he couldn't see me.
I remember
staring straight ahead
into the world my father saw;
I was learning
to absorb its emptiness,
the heavy snow
not falling, whirling around us.

When I saw my father for the last time, we both did the same thing.
He was standing in the doorway to the living room,
waiting for me to get off the telephone.
That he wasn't also pointing to his watch
was a signal he wanted to talk.

Talk for us always meant the same thing.
He'd say a few words. I'd say a few back.
That was about it.

It was the end of August, very hot, very humid.
Next door, workmen dumped new gravel on the driveway.

My father and I avoided being alone;
we didn't know how to connect, to make small talk—
there didn't seem to be
any other possibilities.
So this was special: when a man's dying,
he has a subject.

It must have been early morning. Up and down the street
sprinklers started coming on. The gardener's truck
appeared at the end of the block,
then stopped, parking.

My father wanted to tell me what it was like to be dying.
He told me he wasn't suffering.
He said he kept expecting pain, waiting for it, but it never came.
All he felt was a kind of weakness.
I said I was glad for him, that I thought he was lucky.

Some of the husbands were getting in their cars, going to work.
Not people we knew anymore. New families,
families with young children.
The wives stood on the steps, gesturing or calling.

We said goodbye in the usual way,
no embrace, nothing dramatic.
When the taxi came, my parents watched from the front door,
arm in arm, my mother blowing kisses as she always does,
because it frightens her when a hand isn't being used.
But for a change, my father didn't just stand there.
This time, he waved.

That's what I did, at the door to the taxi.
Like him, waved to disguise my hand's trembling.

LAMENT

Suddenly, after you die, those friends
who never agreed about anything
agree about your character.
They're like a houseful of singers rehearsing
the same score:
you were just, you were kind, you lived a fortunate life.
No harmony. No counterpoint. Except
they're not performers;
real tears are shed.

Luckily, you're dead; otherwise
you'd be overcome with revulsion.
But when that's passed,
when the guests begin filing out, wiping their eyes
because, after a day like this,
shut in with orthodoxy,
the sun's amazingly bright,
though it's late afternoon, September—
when the exodus begins,
that's when you'd feel
pangs of envy.

Your friends the living embrace one another,
gossip a little on the sidewalk
as the sun sinks, and the evening breeze
ruffles the women's shawls—
this, this, is the meaning of
"a fortunate life": it means
to exist in the present.

MIRROR IMAGE

Tonight I saw myself in the dark window as
the image of my father, whose life
was spent like this,
thinking of death, to the exclusion
of other sensual matters,
so in the end that life
was easy to give up, since
it contained nothing: even
my mother's voice couldn't make him
change or turn back
as he believed
that once you can't love another human being
you have no place in the world.

CHILDREN COMING HOME FROM SCHOOL

The year I started school, my sister couldn't walk long distances.
Every day, my mother strapped her in the stroller; then,
they'd walk to the corner.
That way, when school was over, I could see them; I could see my mother,
first a blur, then a shape with arms.
I walked very slowly, to appear to need nothing.
That's why my sister envied me—she didn't know
you can lie with your face, your body.

She didn't see we were both in false positions.
She wanted freedom. Whereas I continued, in pathetic ways,
to covet the stroller. Meaning
all my life.

And, in that sense, it was lost on me: all the waiting, all my mother's
effort to restrain my sister, all the calling, the waving,
since, in that sense, I had no home any longer.

AMAZONS

End of summer: the spruces put out a few green shoots.
Everything else is gold—that's how you know the end of the growing season.
A kind of symmetry between what's dying, what's just coming to bloom.

It's always been a sensitive time in this family.
We're dying out, too, the whole tribe.
My sister and I, we're the end of something.

Now the windows darken.
And the rain comes, steady and heavy.

In the dining room, the children draw.
That's what we did: when we couldn't see,
we made pictures.

I can see the end: it's the name that's going.
When we're done with it, it's finished, it's a dead language.
That's how language dies, because it doesn't need to be spoken.

My sister and I, we're like amazons,
a tribe without a future.
I watch the children draw: my son, her daughter.
We used soft chalk, the disappearing medium.

I have a friend who still believes in heaven.
Not a stupid person, yet with all she knows, she literally talks to god,
she thinks someone listens in heaven.
On earth, she's unusually competent.
Brave, too, able to face unpleasantness.

We found a caterpillar dying in the dirt, greedy ants crawling over it.
I'm always moved by weakness, by disaster, always eager to oppose vitality.
But timid, also, quick to shut my eyes.
Whereas my friend was able to watch, to let events play out
according to nature. For my sake, she intervened,
brushing a few ants off the torn thing, and set it down across the road.

My friend says I shut my eyes to god, that nothing else explains
my aversion to reality. She says I'm like the child who buries her head in
the pillow
so as not to see, the child who tells herself
that light causes sadness—
My friend is like the mother. Patient, urging me
to wake up an adult like herself, a courageous person—

In my dreams, my friend reproaches me. We're walking
on the same road, except it's winter now;
she's telling me that when you love the world you hear celestial music:
look up, she says. When I look up, nothing.
Only clouds, snow, a white business in the trees
like brides leaping to a great height—
Then I'm afraid for her; I see her
caught in a net deliberately cast over the earth—

In reality, we sit by the side of the road, watching the sun set;
from time to time, the silence pierced by a birdcall.
It's this moment we're both trying to explain, the fact
that we're at ease with death, with solitude.
My friend draws a circle in the dirt; inside, the caterpillar doesn't move.

She's always trying to make something whole, something beautiful, an image
capable of life apart from her.
We're very quiet. It's peaceful sitting here, not speaking, the composition
fixed, the road turning suddenly dark, the air
going cool, here and there the rocks shining and glittering—
it's this stillness that we both love.
The love of form is a love of endings.

FIRST MEMORY

Long ago, I was wounded. I lived
to revenge myself
against my father, not
for what he was—
for what I was: from the beginning of time,
in childhood, I thought
that pain meant
I was not loved.
It meant I loved.

THE WILD IRIS

(1992)

FOR

KATHRYN DAVIS
MEREDITH HOPPIN
DAVID LANGSTON

FOR

JOHN AND NOAH

At the end of my suffering
there was a door.

Hear me out: that which you call death
I remember.

Overhead, noises, branches of the pine shifting.
Then nothing. The weak sun
flickered over the dry surface.

It is terrible to survive
as consciousness
buried in the dark earth.

Then it was over: that which you fear, being
a soul and unable
to speak, ending abruptly, the stiff earth
bending a little. And what I took to be
birds darting in low shrubs.

You who do not remember
passage from the other world
I tell you I could speak again: whatever
returns from oblivion returns
to find a voice:

from the center of my life came
a great fountain, deep blue
shadows on azure seawater.

The sun shines; by the mailbox, leaves
of the divided birch tree folded, pleated like fins.
Underneath, hollow stems of the white daffodils, Ice Wings, Cantatrice; dark
leaves of the wild violet. Noah says
depressives hate the spring, imbalance
between the inner and the outer world. I make
another case—being depressed, yes, but in a sense passionately
attached to the living tree, my body
actually curled in the split trunk, almost at peace, in the evening rain
almost able to feel
sap frothing and rising: Noah says this is
an error of depressives, identifying
with a tree, whereas the happy heart
wanders the garden like a falling leaf, a figure for
the part, not the whole.

MATINS

Unreachable father, when we were first
exiled from heaven, you made
a replica, a place in one sense
different from heaven, being
designed to teach a lesson: otherwise
the same—beauty on either side, beauty
without alternative— Except
we didn't know what was the lesson. Left alone,
we exhausted each other. Years
of darkness followed; we took turns
working the garden, the first tears
filling our eyes as earth
misted with petals, some
dark red, some flesh colored—
We never thought of you
whom we were learning to worship.
We merely knew it wasn't human nature to love
only what returns love.

When I woke up I was in a forest. The dark
seemed natural, the sky through the pine trees
thick with many lights.

I knew nothing; I could do nothing but see.
And as I watched, all the lights of heaven
faded to make a single thing, a fire
burning through the cool firs.
Then it wasn't possible any longer
to stare at heaven and not be destroyed.

Are there souls that need
death's presence, as I require protection?
I think if I speak long enough
I will answer that question, I will see
whatever they see, a ladder
reaching through the firs, whatever
calls them to exchange their lives—

Think what I understand already.
I woke up ignorant in a forest;
only a moment ago, I didn't know my voice
if one were given me
would be so full of grief, my sentences
like cries strung together.
I didn't even know I felt grief
until that word came, until I felt
rain streaming from me.

LAMIUM

This is how you live when you have a cold heart.
As I do: in shadows, trailing over cool rock,
under the great maple trees.

The sun hardly touches me.
Sometimes I see it in early spring, rising very far away.
Then leaves grow over it, completely hiding it. I feel it
glinting through the leaves, erratic,
like someone hitting the side of a glass with a metal spoon.

Living things don't all require
light in the same degree. Some of us
make our own light: a silver leaf
like a path no one can use, a shallow
lake of silver in the darkness under the great maples.

But you know this already.
You and the others who think
you live for truth and, by extension, love
all that is cold.

SNOWDROPS

Do you know what I was, how I lived? You know
what despair is; then
winter should have meaning for you.

I did not expect to survive,
earth suppressing me. I didn't expect
to waken again, to feel
in damp earth my body
able to respond again, remembering
after so long how to open again
in the cold light
of earliest spring—

afraid, yes, but among you again
crying yes risk joy

in the raw wind of the new world.

CLEAR MORNING

I've watched you long enough,
I can speak to you any way I like—

I've submitted to your preferences, observing patiently
the things you love, speaking

through vehicles only, in
details of earth, as you prefer,

tendrils
of blue clematis, light

of early evening—
you would never accept

a voice like mine, indifferent
to the objects you busily name,

your mouths
small circles of awe—

And all this time
I indulged your limitation, thinking

you would cast it aside yourselves sooner or later,
thinking matter could not absorb your gaze forever—

obstacle of the clematis painting
blue flowers on the porch window—

I cannot go on
restricting myself to images

because you think it is your right
to dispute my meaning:

I am prepared now to force
clarity upon you.

SPRING SNOW

Look at the night sky:
I have two selves, two kinds of power.

I am here with you, at the window,
watching you react. Yesterday
the moon rose over moist earth in the lower garden.
Now the earth glitters like the moon,
like dead matter crusted with light.

You can close your eyes now.
I have heard your cries, and cries before yours,
and the demand behind them.
I have shown you what you want:
not belief, but capitulation
to authority, which depends on violence.

END OF WINTER

Over the still world, a bird calls
waking solitary among black boughs.

You wanted to be born; I let you be born.
When has my grief ever gotten
in the way of your pleasure?

Plunging ahead
into the dark and light at the same time
eager for sensation

as though you were some new thing, wanting
to express yourselves

all brilliance, all vivacity

never thinking
this would cost you anything,
never imagining the sound of my voice
as anything but part of you—

you won't hear it in the other world,
not clearly again,
not in birdcall or human cry,

not the clear sound, only
persistent echoing
in all sound that means goodbye, goodbye—

the one continuous line
that binds us to each other.

MATINS

Forgive me if I say I love you: the powerful
are always lied to since the weak are always
driven by panic. I cannot love
what I can't conceive, and you disclose
virtually nothing: are you like the hawthorn tree,
always the same thing in the same place,
or are you more the foxglove, inconsistent, first springing up
a pink spike on the slope behind the daisies,
and the next year, purple in the rose garden? You must see
it is useless to us, this silence that promotes belief
you must be all things, the foxglove and the hawthorn tree,
the vulnerable rose and tough daisy—we are left to think
you couldn't possibly exist. Is this
what you mean us to think, does this explain
the silence of the morning,
the crickets not yet rubbing their wings, the cats
not fighting in the yard?

MATINS

I see it is with you as with the birches:
I am not to speak to you
in the personal way. Much
has passed between us. Or
was it always only
on the one side? I am
at fault, at fault, I asked you
to be human—I am no needier
than other people. But the absence
of all feeling, of the least
concern for me—I might as well go on
addressing the birches,
as in my former life: let them
do their worst, let them
bury me with the Romantics,
their pointed yellow leaves
falling and covering me.

SCILLA

Not I, you idiot, not self, but we, we—waves
of sky blue like
a critique of heaven: why
do you treasure your voice
when to be one thing
is to be next to nothing?
Why do you look up? To hear
an echo like the voice
of god? You are all the same to us,
solitary, standing above us, planning
your silly lives: you go
where you are sent, like all things,
where the wind plants you,
one or another of you forever
looking down and seeing some image
of water, and hearing what? Waves,
and over waves, birds singing.

When I made you, I loved you.
Now I pity you.

I gave you all you needed:
bed of earth, blanket of blue air—

As I get further away from you
I see you more clearly.
Your souls should have been immense by now,
not what they are,
small talking things—

I gave you every gift,
blue of the spring morning,
time you didn't know how to use—
you wanted more, the one gift
reserved for another creation.

Whatever you hoped,
you will not find yourselves in the garden,
among the growing plants.
Your lives are not circular like theirs:

your lives are the bird's flight
which begins and ends in stillness—
which *begins* and *ends*, in form echoing
this arc from the white birch
to the apple tree.

THE GARDEN

I couldn't do it again,
I can hardly bear to look at it—

in the garden, in light rain
the young couple planting
a row of peas, as though
no one has ever done this before,
the great difficulties have never as yet
been faced and solved—

They cannot see themselves,
in fresh dirt, starting up
without perspective,
the hills behind them pale green, clouded with flowers—

She wants to stop;
he wants to get to the end,
to stay with the thing—

Look at her, touching his cheek
to make a truce, her fingers
cool with spring rain;
in thin grass, bursts of purple crocus—

even here, even at the beginning of love,
her hand leaving his face makes
an image of departure

and they think
they are free to overlook
this sadness.

Side by side, not
hand in hand: I watch you
walking in the summer garden—things
that can't move
learn to see; I do not need
to chase you through
the garden; human beings leave
signs of feeling
everywhere, flowers
scattered on the dirt path, all
white and gold, some
lifted a little by
the evening wind; I do not need
to follow where you are now,
deep in the poisonous field, to know
the cause of your flight, human
passion or rage: for what else
would you let drop
all you have gathered?

LOVE IN MOONLIGHT

Sometimes a man or woman forces his despair
on another person, which is called
baring the heart, alternatively, baring the soul—
meaning for this moment they acquired souls—
outside, a summer evening, a whole world
thrown away on the moon: groups of silver forms
which might be buildings or trees, the narrow garden
where the cat hides, rolling on its back in the dust,
the rose, the coreopsis, and, in the dark, the gold
    dome of the capitol
converted to an alloy of moonlight, shape
without detail, the myth, the archetype, the soul
filled with fire that is moonlight really, taken
from another source, and briefly
shining as the moon shines: stone or not,
the moon is still that much of a living thing.

APRIL

No one's despair is like my despair—

You have no place in this garden
thinking such things, producing
the tiresome outward signs; the man
pointedly weeding an entire forest,
the woman limping, refusing to change clothes
or wash her hair.

Do you suppose I care
if you speak to one another?
But I mean you to know
I expected better of two creatures
who were given minds: if not
that you would actually care for each other
at least that you would understand
grief is distributed
between you, among all your kind, for me
to know you, as deep blue
marks the wild scilla, white
the wood violet.

VIOLETS

Because in our world
something is always hidden,
small and white,
small and what you call
pure, we do not grieve
as you grieve, dear
suffering master; you
are no more lost
than we are, under
the hawthorn tree, the hawthorn holding
balanced trays of pearls: what
has brought you among us
who would teach you, though
you kneel and weep,
clasping your great hands,
in all your greatness knowing
nothing of the soul's nature,
which is never to die: poor sad god,
either you never have one
or you never lose one.

WITCHGRASS

Something
comes into the world unwelcome
calling disorder, disorder—

If you hate me so much
don't bother to give me
a name: do you need
one more slur
in your language, another
way to blame
one tribe for everything—

as we both know,
if you worship
one god, you only need
one enemy—

I'm not the enemy.
Only a ruse to ignore
what you see happening
right here in this bed,
a little paradigm
of failure. One of your precious flowers
dies here almost every day
and you can't rest until
you attack the cause, meaning
whatever is left, whatever
happens to be sturdier
than your personal passion—

It was not meant
to last forever in the real world.
But why admit that, when you can go on
doing what you always do,
mourning and laying blame,
always the two together.

I don't need your praise
to survive. I was here first,
before you were here, before
you ever planted a garden.
And I'll be here when only the sun and moon
are left, and the sea, and the wide field.

I will constitute the field.

Trapped in the earth,
wouldn't you too want to go
to heaven? I live
in a lady's garden. Forgive me, lady;
longing has taken my grace. I am
not what you wanted. But
as men and women seem
to desire each other, I too desire
knowledge of paradise—and now
your grief, a naked stem
reaching the porch window.
And at the end, what? A small blue flower
like a star. Never
to leave the world! Is this
not what your tears mean?

MATINS

You want to know how I spend my time?
I walk the front lawn, pretending
to be weeding. You ought to know
I'm never weeding, on my knees, pulling
clumps of clover from the flower beds: in fact
I'm looking for courage, for some evidence
my life will change, though
it takes forever, checking
each clump for the symbolic
leaf, and soon the summer is ending, already
the leaves turning, always the sick trees
going first, the dying turning
brilliant yellow, while a few dark birds perform
their curfew of music. You want to see my hands?
As empty now as at the first note.
Or was the point always
to continue without a sign?

What is my heart to you
that you must break it over and over
like a plantsman testing
his new species? Practice
on something else: how can I live
in colonies, as you prefer, if you impose
a quarantine of affliction, dividing me
from healthy members of
my own tribe: you do not do this
in the garden, segregate
the sick rose; you let it wave its sociable
infested leaves in
the faces of the other roses, and the tiny aphids
leap from plant to plant, proving yet again
I am the lowest of your creatures, following
the thriving aphid and the trailing rose— Father,
as agent of my solitude, alleviate
at least my guilt; lift
the stigma of isolation, unless
it is your plan to make me
sound forever again, as I was
sound and whole in my mistaken childhood,
or if not then, under the light weight
of my mother's heart, or if not then,
in dream, first
being that would never die.

SONG

Like a protected heart,
the blood-red
flower of the wild rose begins
to open on the lowest branch,
supported by the netted
mass of a large shrub:
it blooms against the dark
which is the heart's constant
backdrop, while flowers
higher up have wilted or rotted;
to survive
adversity merely
deepens its color. But John
objects, he thinks
if this were not a poem but
an actual garden, then
the red rose would be
required to resemble
nothing else, neither
another flower nor
the shadowy heart, at
earth level pulsing
half maroon, half crimson.

FIELD FLOWERS

What are you saying? That you want
eternal life? Are your thoughts really
as compelling as all that? Certainly
you don't look at us, don't listen to us,
on your skin
stain of sun, dust
of yellow buttercups: I'm talking
to you, you staring through
bars of high grass shaking
your little rattle— O
the soul! the soul! Is it enough
only to look inward? Contempt
for humanity is one thing, but why
disdain the expansive
field, your gaze rising over the clear heads
of the wild buttercups into what? Your poor
idea of heaven: absence
of change. Better than earth? How
would you know, who are neither
here nor there, standing in our midst?

THE RED POPPY

The great thing
is not having
a mind. Feelings:
oh, I have those; they
govern me. I have
a lord in heaven
called the sun, and open
for him, showing him
the fire of my own heart, fire
like his presence.
What could such glory be
if not a heart? Oh my brothers and sisters,
were you like me once, long ago,
before you were human? Did you
permit yourselves
to open once, who would never
open again? Because in truth
I am speaking now
the way you do. I speak
because I am shattered.

CLOVER

What is dispersed
among us, which you call
the sign of blessedness
although it is, like us,
a weed, a thing
to be rooted out—

by what logic
do you hoard
a single tendril
of something you want
dead?

If there is any presence among us
so powerful, should it not
multiply, in service
of the adored garden?

You should be asking
these questions yourself,
not leaving them
to your victims. You should know
that when you swagger among us
I hear two voices speaking,
one your spirit, one
the acts of your hands.

MATINS

Not the sun merely but the earth
itself shines, white fire
leaping from the showy mountains
and the flat road
shimmering in early morning: is this
for us only, to induce
response, or are you
stirred also, helpless
to control yourself
in earth's presence—I am ashamed
at what I thought you were,
distant from us, regarding us
as an experiment: it is
a bitter thing to be
the disposable animal,
a bitter thing. Dear friend,
dear trembling partner, what
surprises you most in what you feel,
earth's radiance or your own delight?
For me, always
the delight is the surprise.

HEAVEN AND EARTH

Where one finishes, the other begins.
On top, a band of blue; underneath,
a band of green and gold, green and deep rose.

John stands at the horizon: he wants
both at once, he wants
everything at once.

The extremes are easy. Only
the middle is a puzzle. Midsummer—
everything is possible.

Meaning: never again will life end.

How can I leave my husband
standing in the garden
dreaming this sort of thing, holding
his rake, triumphantly
preparing to announce this discovery

as the fire of the summer sun
truly does stall
being entirely contained by
the burning maples
at the garden's border.

THE DOORWAY

I wanted to stay as I was,
still as the world is never still,
not in midsummer but the moment before
the first flower forms, the moment
nothing is as yet past—

not midsummer, the intoxicant,
but late spring, the grass not yet
high at the edge of the garden, the early tulips
beginning to open—

like a child hovering in a doorway, watching the others,
the ones who go first,
a tense cluster of limbs, alert to
the failures of others, the public falterings

with a child's fierce confidence of imminent power
preparing to defeat
these weaknesses, to succumb
to nothing, the time directly

prior to flowering, the epoch of mastery

before the appearance of the gift,
before possession.

MIDSUMMER

How can I help you when you all want
different things—sunlight and shadow,
moist darkness, dry heat—

Listen to yourselves, vying with one another—

And you wonder
why I despair of you,
you think something could fuse you into a whole—

the still air of high summer
tangled with a thousand voices

each calling out
some need, some absolute

and in that name continually
strangling each other
in the open field—

For what? For space and air?
The privilege of being
single in the eyes of heaven?

You were not intended
to be unique. You were
my embodiment, all diversity

not what you think you see
searching the bright sky over the field,
your incidental souls
fixed like telescopes on some
enlargement of yourselves—

Why would I make you if I meant
to limit myself
to the ascendant sign,
the star, the fire, the fury?

VESPERS

Once I believed in you; I planted a fig tree.
Here, in Vermont, country
of no summer. It was a test: if the tree lived,
it would mean you existed.

By this logic, you do not exist. Or you exist
exclusively in warmer climates,
in fervent Sicily and Mexico and California,
where are grown the unimaginable
apricot and fragile peach. Perhaps
they see your face in Sicily; here, we barely see
the hem of your garment. I have to discipline myself
to share with John and Noah the tomato crop.

If there is justice in some other world, those
like myself, whom nature forces
into lives of abstinence, should get
the lion's share of all things, all
objects of hunger, greed being
praise of you. And no one praises
more intensely than I, with more
painfully checked desire, or more deserves
to sit at your right hand, if it exists, partaking
of the perishable, the immortal fig,
which does not travel.

VESPERS

In your extended absence, you permit me
use of earth, anticipating
some return on investment. I must report
failure in my assignment, principally
regarding the tomato plants.
I think I should not be encouraged to grow
tomatoes. Or, if I am, you should withhold
the heavy rains, the cold nights that come
so often here, while other regions get
twelve weeks of summer. All this
belongs to you: on the other hand,
I planted the seeds, I watched the first shoots
like wings tearing the soil, and it was my heart
broken by the blight, the black spot so quickly
multiplying in the rows. I doubt
you have a heart, in our understanding of
that term. You who do not discriminate
between the dead and the living, who are, in consequence,
immune to foreshadowing, you may not know
how much terror we bear, the spotted leaf,
the red leaves of the maple falling
even in August, in early darkness: I am responsible
for these vines.

More than you love me, very possibly
you love the beasts of the field, even,
possibly, the field itself, in August dotted
with wild chicory and aster:
I know. I have compared myself
to those flowers, their range of feeling
so much smaller and without issue; also to white sheep,
actually gray: I am uniquely
suited to praise you. Then why
torment me? I study the hawkweed,
the buttercup protected from the grazing herd
by being poisonous: is pain
your gift to make me
conscious in my need of you, as though
I must need you to worship you,
or have you abandoned me
in favor of the field, the stoic lambs turning
silver in twilight; waves of wild aster and chicory shining
pale blue and deep blue, since you already know
how like your raiment it is.

DAISIES

Go ahead: say what you're thinking. The garden
is not the real world. Machines
are the real world. Say frankly what any fool
could read in your face: it makes sense
to avoid us, to resist
nostalgia. It is
not modern enough, the sound the wind makes
stirring a meadow of daisies: the mind
cannot shine following it. And the mind
wants to shine, plainly, as
machines shine, and not
grow deep, as, for example, roots. It is very touching,
all the same, to see you cautiously
approaching the meadow's border in early morning,
when no one could possibly
be watching you. The longer you stand at the edge,
the more nervous you seem. No one wants to hear
impressions of the natural world: you will be
laughed at again; scorn will be piled on you.
As for what you're actually
hearing this morning: think twice
before you tell anyone what was said in this field
and by whom.

END OF SUMMER

After all things occurred to me,
the void occurred to me.

There is a limit
to the pleasure I had in form—

I am not like you in this,
I have no release in another body,

I have no need
of shelter outside myself—

My poor inspired
creation, you are
distractions, finally,
mere curtailment; you are
too little like me in the end
to please me.

And so adamant—
you want to be paid off
for your disappearance,
all paid in some part of the earth,
some souvenir, as you were once
rewarded for labor,
the scribe being paid
in silver, the shepherd in barley

although it is not earth
that is lasting, not
these small chips of matter—

If you would open your eyes
you would see me, you would see
the emptiness of heaven
mirrored on earth, the fields
vacant again, lifeless, covered with snow—

then white light
no longer disguised as matter.

VESPERS

I don't wonder where you are anymore.
You're in the garden; you're where John is,
in the dirt, abstracted, holding his green trowel.
This is how he gardens: fifteen minutes of intense effort,
fifteen minutes of ecstatic contemplation. Sometimes
I work beside him, doing the shade chores,
weeding, thinning the lettuces; sometimes I watch
from the porch near the upper garden until twilight makes
lamps of the first lilies: all this time,
peace never leaves him. But it rushes through me,
not as sustenance the flower holds
but like bright light through the bare tree.

Even as you appeared to Moses, because
I need you, you appear to me, not
often, however. I live essentially
in darkness. You are perhaps training me to be
responsive to the slightest brightening. Or, like the poets,
are you stimulated by despair, does grief
move you to reveal your nature? This afternoon,
in the physical world to which you commonly
contribute your silence, I climbed
the small hill above the wild blueberries, metaphysically
descending, as on all my walks: did I go deep enough
for you to pity me, as you have sometimes pitied
others who suffer, favoring those
with theological gifts? As you anticipated,
I did not look up. So you came down to me:
at my feet, not the wax
leaves of the wild blueberry but your fiery self, a whole
pasture of fire, and beyond, the red sun neither falling nor rising—
I was not a child; I could take advantage of illusions.

You thought we didn't know. But we knew once,
children know these things. Don't turn away now—we inhabited
a lie to appease you. I remember
sunlight of early spring, embankments
netted with dark vinca. I remember
lying in a field, touching my brother's body.
Don't turn away now; we denied
memory to console you. We mimicked you, reciting
the terms of our punishment. I remember
some of it, not all of it: deceit
begins as forgetting. I remember small things, flowers
growing under the hawthorn tree, bells
of the wild scilla. Not all, but enough
to know you exist: who else had reason to create
mistrust between a brother and sister but the one
who profited, to whom we turned in solitude? Who else
would so envy the bond we had then
as to tell us it was not earth
but heaven we were losing?

EARLY DARKNESS

How can you say
earth should give me joy? Each thing
born is my burden; I cannot succeed
with all of you.

And you would like to dictate to me,
you would like to tell me
who among you is most valuable,
who most resembles me.
And you hold up as an example
the pure life, the detachment
you struggle to achieve—

How can you understand me
when you cannot understand yourselves?
Your memory is not
powerful enough, it will not
reach back far enough—

Never forget you are my children.
You are not suffering because you touched each other
but because you were born,
because you required life
separate from me.

HARVEST

It grieves me to think of you in the past—

Look at you, blindly clinging to earth
as though it were the vineyards of heaven
while the fields go up in flames around you—

Ah, little ones, how unsubtle you are:
it is at once the gift and the torment.

If what you fear in death
is punishment beyond this, you need not
fear death:

how many times must I destroy my own creation
to teach you
this is your punishment:

with one gesture I established you
in time and in paradise.

THE WHITE ROSE

This is the earth? Then
I don't belong here.

Who are you in the lighted window,
shadowed now by the flickering leaves
of the wayfarer tree?
Can you survive where I won't last
beyond the first summer?

All night the slender branches of the tree
shift and rustle at the bright window.
Explain my life to me, you who make no sign,

though I call out to you in the night:
I am not like you, I have only
my body for a voice; I can't
disappear into silence—

And in the cold morning
over the dark surface of the earth
echoes of my voice drift,
whiteness steadily absorbed into darkness

as though you were making a sign after all
to convince me you too couldn't survive here

or to show me you are not the light I called to
but the blackness behind it.

IPOMOEA

What was my crime in another life,
as in this life my crime
is sorrow, that I am not to be
permitted to ascend ever again,
never in any sense
permitted to repeat my life,
wound in the hawthorn, all
earthly beauty my punishment
as it is yours—
Source of my suffering, why
have you drawn from me
these flowers like the sky, except
to mark me as a part
of my master: I am
his cloak's color, my flesh giveth
form to his glory.

PRESQUE ISLE

In every life, there's a moment or two.
In every life, a room somewhere, by the sea or in the mountains.

On the table, a dish of apricots. Pits in a white ashtray.

Like all images, these were the conditions of a pact:
on your cheek, tremor of sunlight,
my finger pressing your lips.
The walls blue-white; paint from the low bureau flaking a little.

That room must still exist, on the fourth floor,
with a small balcony overlooking the ocean.
A square white room, the top sheet pulled back over the edge of the bed.
It hasn't dissolved back into nothing, into reality.
Through the open window, sea air, smelling of iodine.

Early morning: a man calling a small boy back from the water.
That small boy—he would be twenty now.

Around your face, rushes of damp hair, streaked with auburn.
Muslin, flicker of silver. Heavy jar filled with white peonies.

You were like very young children,
always waiting for a story.
And I'd been through it all too many times;
I was tired of telling stories.
So I gave you the pencil and paper.
I gave you pens made of reeds
I had gathered myself, afternoons in the dense meadows.
I told you, write your own story.

After all those years of listening
I thought you'd know
what a story was.

All you could do was weep.
You wanted everything told to you
and nothing thought through yourselves.

Then I realized you couldn't think
with any real boldness or passion;
you hadn't had your own lives yet,
your own tragedies.
So I gave you lives, I gave you tragedies,
because apparently tools alone weren't enough.

You will never know how deeply
it pleases me to see you sitting there
like independent beings,
to see you dreaming by the open window,
holding the pencils I gave you
until the summer morning disappears into writing.

Creation has brought you
great excitement, as I knew it would,
as it does in the beginning.
And I am free to do as I please now,
to attend to other things, in confidence
you have no need of me anymore.

VESPERS

I know what you planned, what you meant to do, teaching me
to love the world, making it impossible
to turn away completely, to shut it out completely ever again—
it is everywhere; when I close my eyes,
birdsong, scent of lilac in early spring, scent of summer roses:
you mean to take it away, each flower, each connection with earth—
why would you wound me, why would you want me
desolate in the end, unless you wanted me so starved for hope
I would refuse to see that finally
nothing was left to me, and would believe instead
in the end you were left to me.

VESPERS: PAROUSIA

Love of my life, you
are lost and I am
young again.

A few years pass.
The air fills
with girlish music;
in the front yard
the apple tree is
studded with blossoms.

I try to win you back,
that is the point
of the writing.
But you are gone forever,
as in Russian novels, saying
a few words I don't remember—

How lush the world is,
how full of things that don't belong to me—

I watch the blossoms shatter,
no longer pink,
but old, old, a yellowish white—
the petals seem
to float on the bright grass,
fluttering slightly.

What a nothing you were,
to be changed so quickly
into an image, an odor—
you are everywhere, source
of wisdom and anguish.

VESPERS

Your voice is gone now; I hardly hear you.
Your starry voice all shadow now
and the earth dark again
with your great changes of heart.

And by day the grass going brown in places
under the broad shadows of the maple trees.
Now, everywhere I am talked to by silence

so it is clear I have no access to you;
I do not exist for you, you have drawn
a line through my name.

In what contempt do you hold us
to believe only loss can impress
your power on us,

the first rains of autumn shaking the white lilies—

When you go, you go absolutely,
deducting visible life from all things

but not all life,
lest we turn from you.

VESPERS

End of August. Heat
like a tent over
John's garden. And some things
have the nerve to be getting started,
clusters of tomatoes, stands
of late lilies—optimism
of the great stalks—imperial
gold and silver: but why
start anything
so close to the end?
Tomatoes that will never ripen, lilies
winter will kill, that won't
come back in spring. Or
are you thinking
I spend too much time
looking ahead, like
an old woman wearing
sweaters in summer;
are you saying I can
flourish, having
no hope
of enduring? Blaze of the red cheek, glory
of the open throat, white,
spotted with crimson.

SUNSET

My great happiness
is the sound your voice makes
calling to me even in despair; my sorrow
that I cannot answer you
in speech you accept as mine.

You have no faith in your own language.
So you invest
authority in signs
you cannot read with any accuracy.

And yet your voice reaches me always.
And I answer constantly,
my anger passing
as winter passes. My tenderness
should be apparent to you
in the breeze of the summer evening
and in the words that become
your own response.

LULLABY

Time to rest now; you have had
enough excitement for the time being.

Twilight, then early evening. Fireflies
in the room, flickering here and there, here and there,
and summer's deep sweetness filling the open window.

Don't think of these things anymore.
Listen to my breathing, your own breathing
like the fireflies, each small breath
a flare in which the world appears.

I've sung to you long enough in the summer night.
I'll win you over in the end; the world can't give you
this sustained vision.

You must be taught to love me. Human beings must be taught to love
silence and darkness.

The nights have grown cool again, like the nights
of early spring, and quiet again. Will
speech disturb you? We're
alone now; we have no reason for silence.

Can you see, over the garden—the full moon rises.
I won't see the next full moon.

In spring, when the moon rose, it meant
time was endless. Snowdrops
opened and closed, the clustered
seeds of the maples fell in pale drifts.
White over white, the moon rose over the birch tree.
And in the crook, where the tree divides,
leaves of the first daffodils, in moonlight
soft greenish-silver.

We have come too far together toward the end now
to fear the end. These nights, I am no longer even certain
I know what the end means. And you, who've been with a man—

after the first cries,
doesn't joy, like fear, make no sound?

SEPTEMBER TWILIGHT

I gathered you together,
I can dispense with you—

I'm tired of you, chaos
of the living world—
I can only extend myself
for so long to a living thing.

I summoned you into existence
by opening my mouth, by lifting
my little finger, shimmering

blues of the wild
aster, blossom
of the lily, immense,
gold-veined—

you come and go; eventually
I forget your names.

You come and go, every one of you
flawed in some way,
in some way compromised: you are worth
one life, no more than that.

I gathered you together;
I can erase you
as though you were a draft to be thrown away,
an exercise

because I've finished you, vision
of deepest mourning.

THE GOLD LILY

As I perceive
I am dying now and know
I will not speak again, will not
survive the earth, be summoned
out of it again, not
a flower yet, a spine only, raw dirt
catching my ribs, I call you,
father and master: all around,
my companions are failing, thinking
you do not see. How
can they know you see
unless you save us?
In the summer twilight, are you
close enough to hear
your child's terror? Or
are you not my father,
you who raised me?

THE WHITE LILIES

As a man and woman make
a garden between them like
a bed of stars, here
they linger in the summer evening
and the evening turns
cold with their terror: it
could all end, it is capable
of devastation. All, all
can be lost, through scented air
the narrow columns
uselessly rising, and beyond,
a churning sea of poppies—

Hush, beloved. It doesn't matter to me
how many summers I live to return:
this one summer we have entered eternity.
I felt your two hands
bury me to release its splendor.

MEADOWLANDS

(1996)

Let's play choosing music. Favorite form.
Opera.

Favorite work.
Figaro. No. Figaro and Tannhauser. Now it's your turn:
sing one for me.

PENELOPE'S SONG

Little soul, little perpetually undressed one,
do now as I bid you, climb
the shelf-like branches of the spruce tree;
wait at the top, attentive, like
a sentry or look-out. He will be home soon;
it behooves you to be
generous. You have not been completely
perfect either; with your troublesome body
you have done things you shouldn't
discuss in poems. Therefore
call out to him over the open water, over the bright water
with your dark song, with your grasping,
unnatural song—passionate,
like Maria Callas. Who
wouldn't want you? Whose most demonic appetite
could you possibly fail to answer? Soon
he will return from wherever he goes in the meantime,
suntanned from his time away, wanting
his grilled chicken. Ah, you must greet him,
you must shake the boughs of the tree
to get his attention,
but carefully, carefully, lest
his beautiful face be marred
by too many falling needles.

CANA

What can I tell you that you don't know
that will make you tremble again?

Forsythia
by the roadside, by
wet rocks, on the embankments
underplanted with hyacinth—

For ten years I was happy.
You were there; in a sense,
you were always with me, the house, the garden
constantly lit,
not with light as we have in the sky
but with those emblems of light
which are more powerful, being
implicitly some earthly
thing transformed—

And all of it vanished,
reabsorbed into impassive process. Then
what will we see by,
now that the yellow torches have become
green branches?

QUIET EVENING

You take my hand; then we're alone
in the life-threatening forest. Almost immediately

we're in a house; Noah's
grown and moved away; the clematis after ten years
suddenly flowers white.

More than anything in the world
I love these evenings when we're together,
the quiet evenings in summer, the sky still light at this hour.

So Penelope took the hand of Odysseus,
not to hold him back but to impress
this peace on his memory:

from this point on, the silence through which you move
is my voice pursuing you.

I stopped liking artichokes when I stopped eating
butter. Fennel
I never liked.

One thing I've always hated
about you: I hate that you refuse
to have people at the house. Flaubert
had more friends and Flaubert
was a recluse.

> Flaubert was crazy: he lived
> with his mother.

Living with you is like living
at boarding school:
chicken Monday, fish Tuesday.

> I have deep friendships.
> I have friendships
> with other recluses.

> Why do you call it rigidity?
> Can't you call it a taste
> for ceremony? Or is your hunger for beauty
> completely satisfied by your own person?

Another thing: name one other person
who doesn't have furniture.

> We have fish Tuesday
> because it's fresh Tuesday. If I could drive
> we could have it different days.

If you're so desperate
for precedent, try
Stevens. Stevens
never traveled; that doesn't mean
he didn't know pleasure.

Pleasure maybe but not
joy. When you make artichokes,
make them for yourself.

PARABLE OF THE KING

The great king looking ahead
saw not fate but simply
dawn glittering over
the unknown island: as a king
he thought in the imperative—best
not to reconsider direction, best
to keep going forward
over the radiant water. Anyway,
what is fate but a strategy for ignoring
history, with its moral
dilemmas, a way of regarding
the present, where decisions
are made, as the necessary
link between the past (images of the king
as a young prince) and the glorious future (images
of slave girls). Whatever
it was ahead, why did it have to be
so blinding? Who could have known
that wasn't the usual sun
but flames rising over a world
about to become extinct?

MOONLESS NIGHT

A lady weeps at a dark window.
Must we say what it is? Can't we simply say
a personal matter? It's early summer;
next door the Lights are practicing klezmer music.
A good night: the clarinet is in tune.

As for the lady—she's going to wait forever;
there's no point in watching longer.
After awhile, the streetlight goes out.

But is waiting forever
always the answer? Nothing
is always the answer; the answer
depends on the story.

Such a mistake to want
clarity above all things. What's
a single night, especially
one like this, now so close to ending?
On the other side, there could be anything,
all the joy in the world, the stars fading,
the streetlight becoming a bus stop.

DEPARTURE

The night isn't dark; the world is dark.
Stay with me a little longer.

Your hands on the back of the chair—
that's what I'll remember.
Before that, lightly stroking my shoulders.
Like a man training himself to avoid the heart.

In the other room, the maid discreetly
putting out the light I read by.

That room with its chalk walls—
how will it look to you I wonder
once your exile begins? I think your eyes will seek out
its light as opposed to the moon.
Apparently, after so many years, you need
distance to make plain its intensity.

Your hands on the chair, stroking
my body and the wood in exactly the same way.
Like a man who wants to feel longing again,
who prizes longing above all other emotion.

On the beach, voices of the Greek farmers,
impatient for sunrise.
As though dawn will change them
from farmers into heroes.

And before that, you are holding me because you are going away—
these are statements you are making,
not questions needing answers.

How can I know you love me
unless I see you grieve over me?

ITHACA

The beloved doesn't
need to live. The beloved
lives in the head. The loom
is for the suitors, strung up
like a harp with white shroud-thread.

He was two people.
He was the body and voice, the easy
magnetism of a living man, and then
the unfolding dream or image
shaped by the woman working the loom,
sitting there in a hall filled
with literal-minded men.

As you pity
the deceived sea that tried
to take him away forever
and took only the first,
the actual husband, you must
pity these men: they don't know
what they're looking at;
they don't know that when one loves this way
the shroud becomes a wedding dress.

TELEMACHUS' DETACHMENT

When I was a child looking
at my parents' lives, you know
what I thought? I thought
heartbreaking. Now I think
heartbreaking, but also
insane. Also
very funny.

PARABLE OF THE HOSTAGES

The Greeks are sitting on the beach
wondering what to do when the war ends. No one
wants to go home, back
to that bony island; everyone wants a little more
of what there is in Troy, more
life on the edge, that sense of every day as being
packed with surprises. But how to explain this
to the ones at home to whom
fighting a war is a plausible
excuse for absence, whereas
exploring one's capacity for diversion
is not. Well, this can be faced
later; these
are men of action, ready to leave
insight to the women and children.
Thinking things over in the hot sun, pleased
by a new strength in their forearms, which seem
more golden than they did at home, some
begin to miss their families a little,
to miss their wives, to want to see
if the war has aged them. And a few grow
slightly uneasy: what if war
is just a male version of dressing up,
a game devised to avoid
profound spiritual questions? Ah,
but it wasn't only the war. The world had begun
calling them, an opera beginning with the war's
loud chords and ending with the floating aria of the sirens.
There on the beach, discussing the various
timetables for getting home, no one believed
it could take ten years to get back to Ithaca;
no one foresaw that decade of insoluble dilemmas—oh unanswerable
affliction of the human heart: how to divide
the world's beauty into acceptable
and unacceptable loves! On the shores of Troy,

how could the Greeks know
they were hostage already: who once
delays the journey is
already enthralled; how could they know
that of their small number
some would be held forever by the dreams of pleasure,
some by sleep, some by music?

RAINY MORNING

You don't love the world.
If you loved the world you'd have
images in your poems.

John loves the world. He has
a motto: judge not
lest ye be judged. Don't

argue this point
on the theory it isn't possible
to love what one refuses
to know: to refuse

speech is not
to suppress perception.

Look at John, out in the world,
running even on a miserable day
like today. Your
staying dry is like the cat's pathetic
preference for hunting dead birds: completely

consistent with your tame spiritual themes,
autumn, loss, darkness, etc.

We can all write about suffering
with our eyes closed. You should show people
more of yourself; show them your clandestine
passion for red meat.

PARABLE OF THE TRELLIS

A clematis grew at the foot of a great trellis.
Despite being
modeled on a tree, the trellis
was a human invention; every year, in May,
the green wires of the struggling vine
climbed the straightforward
trellis, and after many years
white flowers burst from the brittle wood, like
a star shower from the heart of the garden.

Enough of that ruse. We both know
how the vine grows without
the trellis, how it sneaks
along the ground; we have both seen it
flower there, the white blossoms
like headlights growing out of a snake.

This isn't what the vine wants.
Remember, to the vine, the trellis
was never an image of confinement:
this is not
diminishment or tragedy.

The vine has a dream of light:
what is life in the dirt
with its dark freedoms
compared to supported ascent?

And for a time,
every summer we could see the vine
relive this decision, thus
obscuring the wood, structure
beautiful in itself, like
a harbor or willow tree.

TELEMACHUS' GUILT

Patience of the sort my mother
practiced on my father
(which in his self-
absorption he mistook
for tribute though it was in fact
a species of rage—didn't he
ever wonder why he was
so blocked in expressing
his native abandon?): it infected
my childhood. Patiently
she fed me; patiently
she supervised the kindly
slaves who attended me, regardless
of my behavior, an assumption
I tested with increasing
violence. It seemed clear to me
that from her perspective
I didn't exist, since
my actions had
no power to disturb her: I was
the envy of my playmates.
In the decades that followed
I was proud of my father
for staying away
even if he stayed away for
the wrong reasons;
I used to smile
when my mother wept.
I hope now she could
forgive that cruelty; I hope
she understood how like
her own coldness it was,
a means of remaining
separate from what
one loves deeply.

ANNIVERSARY

I said you could snuggle. That doesn't mean
your cold feet all over my dick.

Someone should teach you how to act in bed.
What I think is you should
keep your extremities to yourself.

Look what you did—
you made the cat move.

   But I didn't want your hand there.
   I wanted your hand here.

   You should pay attention to my feet.
   You should picture them
   the next time you see a hot fifteen year old.
   Because there's a lot more where those feet come from.

MEADOWLANDS I

I wish we went on walks
like Steven and Kathy; then
we'd be happy. You can even see it
in the dog.

> We don't have a dog.
> We have a hostile cat.

> I think Sam's
> intelligent; he
> resents being a pet.

> Why is it always family with you?
> Can't we ever be two adults?

Look how happy Captain is, how
at peace in the world. Don't you love
how he sits on the lawn, staring up at the birds? He thinks
because he's white they can't see him.

You know why they're happy? They take
the children. And you know why they can go
on walks with children? Because
they *have* children.

> They're nothing like us; they don't
> travel. That's why they have a dog.

Have you noticed how Alissa always comes back from the walks
holding something, bringing nature
into the house? Flowers in spring,
sticks in winter.

I bet they're still taking the dog
when the children are grown up.
He's a young dog, practically
a puppy.

If we don't expect
Sam to follow, couldn't we
take him along?
You could hold him.

TELEMACHUS' KINDNESS

When I was younger I felt
sorry for myself
compulsively; in practical terms,
I had no father; my mother
lived at her loom hypothesizing
her husband's erotic life; gradually
I realized no child on that island had
a different story; my trials
were the general rule, common
to all of us, a bond
among us, therefore
with humanity: what
a life my mother had, without
compassion for my father's
suffering, for a soul
ardent by nature, thus
ravaged by choice, nor had my father
any sense of her courage, subtly
expressed as inaction, being
himself prone to dramatizing,
to acting out: I found
I could share these perceptions
with my closest friends, as they shared
theirs with me, to test them,
to refine them: as a grown man
I can look at my parents
impartially and pity them both: I hope
always to be able to pity them.

PARABLE OF THE BEAST

The cat circles the kitchen
with the dead bird,
its new possession.

Someone should discuss
ethics with the cat as it
inquires into the limp bird:

in this house
we do not experience
will in this manner.

Tell that to the animal,
its teeth already
deep in the flesh of another animal.

MIDNIGHT

Speak to me, aching heart: what
ridiculous errand are you inventing for yourself
weeping in the dark garage
with your sack of garbage: it is not your job
to take out the garbage, it is your job
to empty the dishwasher. You are showing off again,
exactly as you did in childhood—where
is your sporting side, your famous
ironic detachment? A little moonlight hits
the broken window, a little summer moonlight, tender
murmurs from the earth with its ready sweetnesses—
is this the way you communicate
with your husband, not answering
when he calls, or is this the way the heart
behaves when it grieves: it wants to be
alone with the garbage? If I were you,
I'd think ahead. After fifteen years,
his voice could be getting tired; some night
if you don't answer, someone else will answer.

SIREN

I became a criminal when I fell in love.
Before that I was a waitress.

I didn't want to go to Chicago with you.
I wanted to marry you, I wanted
your wife to suffer.

I wanted her life to be like a play
in which all the parts are sad parts.

Does a good person
think this way? I deserve

credit for my courage—

I sat in the dark on your front porch.
Everything was clear to me:
if your wife wouldn't let you go
that proved she didn't love you.
If she loved you
wouldn't she want you happy?

I think now
if I felt less I would be
a better person. I was
a good waitress,
I could carry eight drinks.

I used to tell you my dreams.
Last night I saw a woman sitting in a dark bus—
in the dream, she's weeping, the bus she's on
is moving away. With one hand
she's waving; the other strokes
an egg carton full of babies.

The dream doesn't rescue the maiden.

Alissa isn't bringing back
sticks for the house; the sticks
belong to the dog.

MARINA

My heart was a stone wall
you broke through anyway.

My heart was an island garden
about to be trampled by you.

You didn't want my heart;
you were on your way to my body.

None of it was my fault.
You were everything to me,
not just beauty and money.
When we made love
the cat went to another bedroom.

Then you forgot me.

Not for no reason
did the stones
tremble around the walled garden:

there's nothing there now
except the wildness people call nature,
the chaos that takes over.

You took me to a place
where I could see the evil in my character
and left me there.

The abandoned cat
wails in the empty bedchamber.

PARABLE OF THE DOVE

A dove lived in a village.
When it opened its mouth
sweetness came out, sound
like a silver light around
the cherry bough. But
the dove wasn't satisfied.

It saw the villagers
gathered to listen under
the blossoming tree.
It didn't think: I
am higher than they are.
It wanted to walk among them,
to experience the violence of human feeling,
in part for its song's sake.

So it became human.
It found passion, it found violence,
first conflated, then
as separate emotions
and these were not
contained by music. Thus
its song changed,
the sweet notes of its longing to be human
soured and flattened. Then

the world drew back; the mutant
fell from love
as from the cherry branch,
it fell stained with the bloody
fruit of the tree.

So it is true after all, not merely
a rule of art:
change your form and you change your nature.
And time does this to us.

TELEMACHUS' DILEMMA

I can never decide
what to write on
my parents' tomb. I know
what he wants: he wants
beloved, which is
certainly to the point, particularly
if we count all
the women. But
that leaves my mother
out in the cold. She tells me
this doesn't matter to her
in the least; she prefers
to be represented by
her own achievement. It seems
tactless to remind them
that one does not
honor the dead by perpetuating
their vanities, their
projections of themselves.
My own taste dictates
accuracy without
garrulousness; they are
my parents, consequently
I see them together,
sometimes inclining to
husband and wife, other times
to *opposing forces*.

MEADOWLANDS 3

How could the Giants name
that place the Meadowlands? It has
about as much in common with a pasture
as would the inside of an oven.

New Jersey
was rural. They want you
to remember that.

Simms
was not a thug. LT
was not a thug.

What I think is we should
look at our surroundings
realistically, for what they are
in the present.

That's what
I tell you about the house.

No giant
would talk the way you talk.
You'd be a nicer person
if you were a fan of something.
When you do that with your mouth
you look like your mother.

You know what they are?
Kings among men.

So what king
fired Simms?

Insignia
of the earth's
terrible recesses, spirit
of darkness, of
the criminal mind, I feel
certain there is within you
something human, to be
approached in speech. How else
did you approach Eve
with your addictive
information? I have paid
bitterly for her
lapse, therefore
attend to me. Tell me
how you live in hell,
what is required in hell,
for I would send
my beloved there. Not
of course forever:
I may want him
back sometime, not
permanently harmed but
severely chastened,
as he has not been, here
on the surface. What
shall I give him for
protection, what
shield that will not
wholly screen him? You must be
his guide and master: help him
shed his skin
as you do, though in this case
we want him
older underneath, maybe
a little mousy. I feel confident

you understand these
subtleties—you seem
so interested, you do not
slide back under your rock! Oh
I am sure we are somehow related
even if you are not
human; perhaps I have
the soul of a reptile after all.

CIRCE'S POWER

I never turned anyone into a pig.
Some people are pigs; I make them
look like pigs.

I'm sick of your world
that lets the outside disguise the inside.

Your men weren't bad men;
undisciplined life
did that to them. As pigs,

under the care of
me and my ladies, they
sweetened right up.

Then I reversed the spell,
showing you my goodness
as well as my power. I saw

we could be happy here,
as men and women are
when their needs are simple. In the same breath,

I foresaw your departure,
your men with my help braving
the crying and pounding sea. You think

a few tears upset me? My friend,
every sorceress is
a pragmatist at heart; nobody
sees essence who can't
face limitation. If I wanted only to hold you

I could hold you prisoner.

TELEMACHUS' FANTASY

Sometimes I wonder about my father's
years on those islands: why
was he so attractive
to women? He was in straits then, I suppose
desperate. I believe
women like to see a man
still whole, still standing, but
about to go to pieces: such
disintegration reminds them
of passion. I think of them as living
their whole lives
completely undressed. It must have
dazzled him, I think, women
so much younger than he was
evidently wild for him, ready
to do anything he wished. Is it
fortunate to encounter circumstances
so responsive to one's own will, to live
so many years
unquestioned, unthwarted? One
would have to believe oneself
entirely good or worthy. I
suppose in time either
one becomes a monster or
the beloved sees what one is. I never
wish for my father's life
nor have I any idea
what he sacrificed
to survive that moment. Less dangerous
to believe he was drawn to them
and so stayed
to see who they were. I think, though,
as an imaginative man
to some extent he
became who they were.

PARABLE OF FLIGHT

A flock of birds leaving the side of the mountain.
Black against the spring evening, bronze in early summer,
rising over blank lake water.

Why is the young man disturbed suddenly,
his attention slipping from his companion?
His heart is no longer wholly divided; he's trying to think
how to say this compassionately.

Now we hear the voices of the others, moving through the library
toward the veranda, the summer porch; we see them
taking their usual places on the various hammocks and chairs,
the white wood chairs of the old house, rearranging
the striped cushions.

Does it matter where the birds go? Does it even matter
what species they are?
They leave here, that's the point,
first their bodies, then their sad cries.
And from that moment, cease to exist for us.

You must learn to think of our passion that way.
Each kiss was real, then
each kiss left the face of the earth.

ODYSSEUS' DECISION

The great man turns his back on the island.
Now he will not die in paradise
nor hear again
the lutes of paradise among the olive trees,
by the clear pools under the cypresses. Time

begins now, in which he hears again
that pulse which is the narrative
sea, at dawn when its pull is strongest.
*What has brought us here
will lead us away; our ship
sways in the tinted harbor water.*

Now the spell is ended.
Give him back his life,
sea that can only move forward.

There was an apple tree in the yard—
this would have been
forty years ago—behind,
only meadow. Drifts
of crocus in the damp grass.
I stood at that window:
late April. Spring
flowers in the neighbor's yard.
How many times, really, did the tree
flower on my birthday,
the exact day, not
before, not after? Substitution
of the immutable
for the shifting, the evolving.
Substitution of the image
for relentless earth. What
do I know of this place,
the role of the tree for decades
taken by a bonsai, voices
rising from the tennis courts—
Fields. Smell of the tall grass, new cut.
As one expects of a lyric poet.
We look at the world once, in childhood.
The rest is memory.

THE BUTTERFLY

Look, a butterfly. Did you make a wish?

You don't wish on butterflies.

You do so. Did you make one?

Yes.

It doesn't count.

CIRCE'S TORMENT

I regret bitterly
the years of loving you in both
your presence and absence, regret
the law, the vocation
that forbid me to keep you, the sea
a sheet of glass, the sun-bleached
beauty of the Greek ships: how
could I have power if
I had no wish
to transform you: as
you loved my body,
as you found there
passion we held above
all other gifts, in that single moment
over honor and hope, over
loyalty, in the name of that bond
I refuse you
such feeling for your wife
as will let you
rest with her, I refuse you
sleep again
if I cannot have you.

CIRCE'S GRIEF

In the end, I made myself
known to your wife as
a god would, in her own house, in
Ithaca, a voice
without a body: she
paused in her weaving, her head turning
first to the right, then left
though it was hopeless of course
to trace that sound to any
objective source: I doubt
she will return to her loom
with what she knows now. When
you see her again, tell her
this is how a god says goodbye:
if I am in her head forever
I am in your life forever.

PENELOPE'S STUBBORNNESS

A bird comes to the window. It's a mistake
to think of them
as birds, they are so often
messengers. That is why, once they
plummet to the sill, they sit
so perfectly still, to mock
patience, lifting their heads to sing
poor lady, poor lady, their three-note
warning, later flying
like a dark cloud from the sill to the olive grove.
But who would send such a weightless being
to judge my life? My thoughts are deep
and my memory long; why would I envy such freedom
when I have humanity? Those
with the smallest hearts have
the greatest freedom.

TELEMACHUS' CONFESSION

They
were not better off
when he left; ultimately
I was better off. This
amazed me, not because I was convinced
I needed them both but because
long into adulthood I retained
something of the child's
hunger for ritual. How else address
that sense of being
insufficiently loved? Possibly
all children are
insufficiently loved; I
wouldn't know. But all along
they each wanted something
different from me: having
to fabricate the being
each required in any
given moment was
less draining than
having to be
two people. And after awhile
I realized I *was*
actually a person; I had
my own voice, my own perceptions, though
I came to them late. I no longer regret
the terrible moment in the fields,
the ploy that took
my father away. My mother
grieves enough for us all.

VOID

I figured out why you won't buy furniture.
You won't buy furniture because you're depressed.

I'll tell you what's wrong with you: you're not
gregarious. You should
look at yourself; the only time you're totally happy
is when you cut up a chicken.

Why can't we talk about what I want to talk about?
Why do you always change the subject?

You hurt my feelings. I do *not* mistake
reiteration for analysis.

You should take one of those chemicals,
maybe you'd write more.
Maybe you have some kind of void syndrome.

You know why you cook? Because
you like control. A person who cooks is a person who likes
to create debt.

Actual people! Actual human beings
sitting on our chairs in our living room!
I'll tell you what: I'll learn
bridge.

Don't think of them as guests, think of them
as extra chickens. You'd like it.
If we had more furniture
you'd have more control.

TELEMACHUS' BURDEN

Nothing
was exactly difficult because
routines develop, compensations
for perceived
absences and omissions. My mother
was the sort of woman
who let you know she was suffering and then
denied that suffering since in her view
suffering was what slaves did; when
I tried to console her,
to relieve her misery, she
rejected me. I now realize
if she'd been capable of honesty
she would have been
a Stoic. Unfortunately
she was a queen, she wanted it understood
at every moment she had chosen
her own destiny. She would have had to be
insane to choose that destiny. Well,
good luck to my father, in my opinion
a stupid man if he expects
his return to diminish
her isolation; perhaps
he came back for that.

PARABLE OF THE SWANS

On a small lake off
the map of the world, two
swans lived. As swans,
they spent eighty percent of the day studying
themselves in the attentive water and
twenty percent ministering to the beloved
other. Thus
their fame as lovers stems
chiefly from narcissism, which leaves
so little leisure for
more general cruising. But
fate had other plans: after ten years, they hit
slimy water; whatever the filth was, it
clung to the male's plumage, which turned
instantly gray; simultaneously,
the true purpose of his neck's
flexible design revealed itself. So much
action on the flat lake, so much
he's missed! Sooner or later in a long
life together, every couple encounters
some emergency like this, some
drama which results
in harm. This
occurs for a reason: to test
love and to demand
fresh articulation of its complex terms.
So it came to light that the male and female
flew under different banners: whereas
the male believed that love
was what one felt in one's heart
the female believed
love was what one did. But this is not
a little story about the male's
inherent corruption, using as evidence the swan's
sleazy definition of purity. It is

a story of guile and innocence. For ten years
the female studied the male; she dallied
when he slept or when he was
conveniently absorbed in the water,
while the spontaneous male
acted casually, on
the whim of the moment. On the muddy water
they bickered awhile, in the fading light,
until the bickering grew
slowly abstract, becoming
part of their song
after a little longer.

PURPLE BATHING SUIT

I like watching you garden
with your back to me in your purple bathing suit:
your back is my favorite part of you,
the part furthest away from your mouth.

You might give some thought to that mouth.
Also to the way you weed, breaking
the grass off at ground level
when you should pull it up by the roots.

How many times do I have to tell you
how the grass spreads, your little
pile notwithstanding, in a dark mass which
by smoothing over the surface you have finally
fully obscured? Watching you

stare into space in the tidy
rows of the vegetable garden, ostensibly
working hard while actually
doing the worst job possible, I think

you are a small irritating purple thing
and I would like to see you walk off the face of the earth
because you are all that's wrong with my life
and I need you and I claim you.

PARABLE OF FAITH

Now, in twilight, on the palace steps
the king asks forgiveness of his lady.

He is not
duplicitous; he has tried to be
true to the moment; is there another way of being
true to the self?

The lady
hides her face, somewhat
assisted by shadows. She weeps
for her past; when one has a secret life,
one's tears are never explained.

Yet gladly would the king bear
the grief of his lady: his
is the generous heart,
in pain as in joy.

Do you know
what forgiveness means? It means
the world has sinned, the world
must be pardoned—

REUNION

When Odysseus has returned at last
unrecognizable to Ithaca and killed
the suitors swarming the throne room,
very delicately he signals to Telemachus
to depart: as he stood twenty years ago,
he stands now before Penelope.
On the palace floor, wide bands of sunlight turning
from gold to red. He tells her
nothing of those years, choosing to speak instead
exclusively of small things, as would be
the habit of a man and woman long together:
once she sees who he is, she will know what he's done.
And as he speaks, ah,
tenderly he touches her forearm.

THE DREAM

I had the weirdest dream. I dreamed we were married again.

You talked a lot. You kept saying things like *this is realistic.*
When I woke up, I started reading all my old diaries.

I thought you hated diaries.

I keep them when I'm miserable. Anyway,
all those years I thought we were so happy
I had a lot of diaries.

Do you ever think about it? Do you ever wonder
if the whole thing was a mistake? Actually,
half the guests said that at the wedding.

I'll tell you something I never told you:
I took a valium that night.

I kept thinking of how we used to watch television,
how I would put my feet in your lap. The cat would sit
on top of them. Doesn't that still seem
an image of contentment, of well-being? So
why couldn't it go on longer?

Because it was a dream.

A beautiful morning; nothing
died in the night.
The Lights are putting up their bean tepees.
Rebirth! Renewal! And across the yard,
very quietly, someone is playing Otis Redding.

Now the great themes
come together again: I am twenty-three, riding the subways
in pursuit of Chassler, of my lost love, clutching
my own record, because I have to hear
this exact sound no matter where I land, no matter
whose apartment—whose apartments
did I visit that summer? I have no idea
where I'm going, about to leave New York, to live
in paradise, as I have then
no concept of change, no slightest sense of what would
happen to Chassler, to obsessive need, my one thought being
the only grief that touched mine was Otis' grief.

Look, the tepees
are standing: Steven
has balanced them the first try.
Now the seeds go in, there is Anna
sitting in the dirt with the open packet.

This is the end, isn't it?
And you are here with me again, listening with me: *the sea
no longer torments me; the self
I wished to be is the self I am.*

THE WISH

Remember that time you made the wish?

    I make a lot of wishes.

The time I lied to you
about the butterfly. I always wondered
what you wished for.

    What do you think I wished?

I don't know. That I'd come back,
that we'd somehow be together in the end.

    I wished for what I always wish for.
    I wished for another poem.

PARABLE OF THE GIFT

My friend gave me
a fuchsia plant, expecting
much of me, in cold April
judgment not to leave it
overnight in nature, deep
pink in its plastic
basket—I have
killed my gift, exposed
flowers in a mass of leaves,
mistaking it
for part of nature with
its many stems: what
do I do with you now,
former living thing
that last night still
resembled my friend, abundant
leaves like her fluffy hair
although the leaves had
a reddish cast: I see her
climbing the stone steps in spring dusk
holding the quivering
present in her hands, with
Eric and Daphne following
close behind, each
bearing a towel of lettuce leaves:
so much, so much to celebrate
tonight, as though she were saying
here is the world, that should be
enough to make you happy.

I want to do two things:
I want to order meat from Lobel's
and I want to have a party.

You hate parties. You hate
any group bigger than four.

If I hate it
I'll go upstairs. Also
I'm only inviting people who can cook.
Good cooks and all my old lovers.
Maybe even your ex-girlfriends, except
the exhibitionists.

If I were you,
I'd start with the meat order.

We'll have buglights in the garden.
When you look into people's faces
you'll see how happy they are.
Some are dancing, maybe
Jasmine in her Himalayan anklet.
When she gets tired, the bells drag.

It will be spring again; all
the tulips will be opening.

The point isn't whether or not
the guests are happy.

The point is whether or not
they're dead.

Trust me: no one's
going to be hurt again.

For one night, affection
will triumph over passion. The passion
will all be in the music.

If you can hear the music
you can imagine the party.
I have it all planned: first
violent love, then
sweetness. First *Norma*
then maybe the Lights will play.

VITA NOVA

(1999)

The master said *You must write what you see.*
But what I see does not move me.
The master answered *Change what you see.*

You saved me, you should remember me.

The spring of the year; young men buying tickets for the ferryboats.
Laughter, because the air is full of apple blossoms.

When I woke up, I realized I was capable of the same feeling.

I remember sounds like that from my childhood,
laughter for no cause, simply because the world is beautiful,
something like that.

Lugano. Tables under the apple trees.
Deckhands raising and lowering the colored flags.
And by the lake's edge, a young man throws his hat into the water;
perhaps his sweetheart has accepted him.

Crucial
sounds or gestures like
a track laid down before the larger themes

and then unused, buried.

Islands in the distance. My mother
holding out a plate of little cakes—

as far as I remember, changed
in no detail, the moment
vivid, intact, having never been
exposed to light, so that I woke elated, at my age
hungry for life, utterly confident—

By the tables, patches of new grass, the pale green
pieced into the dark existing ground.

Surely spring has been returned to me, this time
not as a lover but a messenger of death, yet
it is still spring, it is still meant tenderly.

AUBADE

The world was very large. Then
the world was small. O
very small, small enough
to fit in a brain.

It had no color, it was all
interior space: nothing
got in or out. But time
seeped in anyway, that
was the tragic dimension.

I took time very seriously in those years,
if I remember accurately.

A room with a chair, a window.
A small window, filled with the patterns light makes.
In its emptiness the world

was whole always, not
a chip of something, with
the self at the center.

And at the center of the self,
grief I thought I couldn't survive.

A room with a bed, a table. Flashes
of light on the naked surfaces.

I had two desires: desire
to be safe and desire to feel. As though

the world were making
a decision against white
because it disdained potential
and wanted in its place substance:

panels
of gold where the light struck.
In the window, reddish
leaves of the copper beech tree.

Out of the stasis, facts, objects
blurred or knitted together: somewhere

time stirring, time
crying to be touched, to be
palpable,

the polished wood
shimmering with distinctions—

and then I was once more
a child in the presence of riches
and I didn't know what the riches were made of.

THE QUEEN OF CARTHAGE

Brutal to love,
more brutal to die.
And brutal beyond the reaches of justice
to die of love.

In the end, Dido
summoned her ladies in waiting
that they might see
the harsh destiny inscribed for her by the Fates.

She said, "Aeneas
came to me over the shimmering water;
I asked the Fates
to permit him to return my passion,
even for a short time. What difference
between that and a lifetime: in truth, in such moments,
they are the same, they are both eternity.

I was given a great gift
which I attempted to increase, to prolong.
Aeneas came to me over the water: the beginning
blinded me.

Now the Queen of Carthage
will accept suffering as she accepted favor:
to be noticed by the Fates
is some distinction after all.

Or should one say, to have honored hunger,
since the Fates go by that name also."

My mother made my need,
my father my conscience.
De mortuis nil nisi bonum.

Therefore it will cost me
bitterly to lie,
to prostrate myself
at the edge of a grave.

I say to the earth
be kind to my mother,
now and later.
Save, with your coldness,
the beauty we all envied.

I became an old woman.
I welcomed the dark
I used so to fear.
De mortuis nil nisi bonum.

UNWRITTEN LAW

Interesting how we fall in love:
in my case, absolutely. Absolutely, and, alas, often—
so it was in my youth.
And always with rather boyish men—
unformed, sullen, or shyly kicking the dead leaves:
in the manner of Balanchine.
Nor did I see them as versions of the same thing.
I, with my inflexible Platonism,
my fierce seeing of only one thing at a time:
I ruled against the indefinite article.
And yet, the mistakes of my youth
made me hopeless, because they repeated themselves,
as is commonly true.
But in you I felt something beyond the archetype—
a true expansiveness, a buoyance and love of the earth
utterly alien to my nature. To my credit,
I blessed my good fortune in you.
Blessed it absolutely, in the manner of those years.
And you in your wisdom and cruelty
gradually taught me the meaninglessness of that term.

THE BURNING HEART

". . . No sadness
is greater than in misery to rehearse
memories of joy . . ."

Ask her if she regrets anything.

I was
promised to another—
I lived with someone.
You forget these things when you're touched.

Ask her how he touched her.

His gaze touched me
before his hands touched me.

Ask her how he touched her.

I didn't ask for anything;
everything was given.

Ask her what she remembers.

We were hauled into the underworld.

I thought
we were not responsible
any more than we were responsible
for being alive. I was
a young girl, rarely subject to censure:

then a pariah. Did I change that much
from one day to the next?
If I didn't change, wasn't my action
in the character of that young girl?

Ask her what she remembers.

I noticed nothing. I noticed
I was trembling.

Ask her if the fire hurts.

I remember
we were together.
And gradually I understood
that though neither of us ever moved
we were not together but profoundly separate.

Ask her if the fire hurts.

You expect to live forever with your husband
in fire more durable than the world.
I suppose this wish was granted,
where we are now being both
fire and eternity.

Do you regret your life?

Even before I was touched, I belonged to you;
you had only to look at me.

ROMAN STUDY

He felt at first
he should have been born
to Aphrodite, not Venus,
that too little was left to do,
to accomplish, after the Greeks.

And he resented light,
to which Greece has
the greatest claim.

He cursed his mother
(privately, discreetly),
she who could have arranged all of this.

And then it occurred to him
to examine these responses
in which, finally, he recognized
a new species of thought entirely,
more worldly, more ambitious
and politic, in what we now call
human terms.

And the longer he thought
the more he experienced
faint contempt for the Greeks,
for their austerity, the eerie
balance of even the great tragedies—
thrilling at first, then
faintly predictable, routine.

And the longer he thought
the more plain to him how much
still remained to be experienced,
and written down, a material world heretofore
hardly dignified.

And he recognized in exactly this reasoning
the scope and trajectory of his own
watchful nature.

I slept the sleep of the just,
later the sleep of the unborn
who come into the world
guilty of many crimes.
And what these crimes are
nobody knows at the beginning.
Only after many years does one know.
Only after long life is one prepared
to read the equation.

I begin now to perceive
the nature of my soul, the soul
I inhabit as punishment.
Inflexible, even in hunger.

I have been in my other lives
too hasty, too eager,
my haste a source of pain in the world.
Swaggering as a tyrant swaggers;
for all my amorousness,
cold at heart, in the manner of the superficial.

I slept the sleep of the just;
I lived the life of a criminal
slowly repaying an impossible debt.
And I died having answered for
one species of ruthlessness.

FORMAGGIO

The world
was whole because
it shattered. When it shattered,
then we knew what it was.

It never healed itself.
But in the deep fissures, smaller worlds appeared:
it was a good thing that human beings made them;
human beings know what they need,
better than any god.

On Huron Avenue they became
a block of stores; they became
Fishmonger, Formaggio. Whatever
they were or sold, they were
alike in their function: they were
visions of safety. Like
a resting place. The salespeople
were like parents; they appeared
to live there. On the whole,
kinder than parents.

Tributaries
feeding into a large river: I had
many lives. In the provisional world,
I stood where the fruit was,
flats of cherries, clementines,
under Hallie's flowers.

I had many lives. Feeding
into a river, the river
feeding into a great ocean. If the self
becomes invisible has it disappeared?

I thrived. I lived
not completely alone, alone
but not completely, strangers
surging around me.

That's what the sea is:
we exist in secret.

I had lives before this, stems
of a spray of flowers: they became
one thing, held by a ribbon at the center, a ribbon
visible under the hand. Above the hand,
the branching future, stems
ending in flowers. And the gripped fist—
that would be the self in the present.

TIMOR MORTIS

Why are you afraid?

A man in a top hat passed under the bedroom window.
I couldn't have been
more than four at the time.

It was a dream: I saw him
when I was high up, where I should have been
safe from him.

Do you remember your childhood?

When the dream ended
terror remained. I lay in my bed—
my crib maybe.

I dreamed I was kidnapped. That means
I knew what love was,
how it places the soul in jeopardy.
I knew. I substituted my body.

But you were hostage?

I was afraid of love, of being taken away.
Everyone afraid of love is afraid of death.

I pretended indifference
even in the presence of love, in the presence of hunger.
And the more deeply I felt
the less able I was to respond.

Do you remember your childhood?

I understood that the magnitude of these gifts
was balanced by the scope of my rejection.

Do you remember your childhood?

I lay in the forest.
Still, more still than any living creature.
Watching the sun rise.

And I remember once my mother turning away from me
in great anger. Or perhaps it was grief.
Because for all she had given me,
for all her love, I failed to show gratitude.
And I made no sign of understanding.

For which I was never forgiven.

LUTE SONG

No one wants to be the muse;
in the end, everyone wants to be Orpheus.

Valiantly reconstructed
(out of terror and pain)
and then overwhelmingly beautiful;

restoring, ultimately,
not Eurydice, the lamented one,
but the ardent
spirit of Orpheus, made present

not as a human being, rather
as pure soul rendered
detached, immortal,
through deflected narcissism.

I made a harp of disaster
to perpetuate the beauty of my last love.
Yet my anguish, such as it is,
remains the struggle for form

and my dreams, if I speak openly,
less the wish to be remembered
than the wish to survive,
which is, I believe, the deepest human wish.

ORFEO

"J'ai perdu mon Eurydice . . ."

I have lost my Eurydice,
I have lost my lover,
and suddenly I am speaking French
and it seems to me I have never been in better voice;
it seems these songs
are songs of a high order.

And it seems one is somehow expected to apologize
for being an artist,
as though it were not entirely human to notice these fine points.
And who knows, perhaps the gods never spoke to me in Dis,
never singled me out,
perhaps it was all illusion.

O Eurydice, you who married me for my singing,
why do you turn on me, wanting human comfort?
Who knows what you'll tell the furies
when you see them again.

Tell them I have lost my beloved;
I am completely alone now.
Tell them there is no music like this
without real grief.

In Dis, I sang to them; they will remember me.

DESCENT TO THE VALLEY

I found the years of the climb upward
difficult, filled with anxiety.
I didn't doubt my capacities:
rather, as I moved toward it,
I feared the future, the shape of which
I perceived. I saw
the shape of a human life:
on the one side, always upward and forward
into the light; on the other side,
downward into the mists of uncertainty.
All eagerness undermined by knowledge.

I have found it otherwise.
The light of the pinnacle, the light that was,
theoretically, the goal of the climb,
proves to have been poignantly abstract:
my mind, in its ascent,
was entirely given over to detail, never
perception of form; my eyes
nervously attending to footing.

How sweet my life now
in its descent to the valley,
the valley itself not mist-covered
but fertile and tranquil.
So that for the first time I find myself
able to look ahead, able to look at the world,
even to move toward it.

THE GARMENT

My soul dried up.
Like a soul cast into fire, but not completely,
not to annihilation. Parched,
it continued. Brittle,
not from solitude but from mistrust,
the aftermath of violence.

Spirit, invited to leave the body,
to stand exposed a moment,
trembling, as before
your presentation to the divine—
spirit lured out of solitude
by the promise of grace,
how will you ever again believe
the love of another being?

My soul withered and shrank.
The body became for it too large a garment.

And when hope was returned to me
it was another hope entirely.

CONDO

I lived in a tree. The dream specified
pine, as though it thought I needed
prompting to keep mourning. I hate
when your own dreams treat you as stupid.

Inside, it was
my apartment in Plainfield, twenty years ago,
except I'd added a commercial stove.
Deep-rooted

passion for the second floor! Just because
the past is longer than the future
doesn't mean there is no future.

The dream confused them, mistaking
one for the other: repeated

scenes of the gutted house—Vera was there,
talking about the light.
And certainly there was a lot of light, since
there were no walls.

I thought: this is where the bed would be,
where it was in Plainfield.
And deep serenity flooded through me,
such as you feel when the world can't touch you.
Beyond the invisible bed, light
of late summer in the little street,
between flickering ash trees.

Which the dream changed, adding, you could say,
a dimension of hope. It was
a beautiful dream, my life was small and sweet, the world
broadly visible because remote.

The dream showed me how to have it again
by being safe from it. It showed me
sleeping in my old bed, first stars
shining through bare ash trees.

I have been lifted and carried far away
into a luminous city. Is this what having means,
to look down on? Or is this dreaming still?
I was right, wasn't I, choosing
against the ground?

IMMORTAL LOVE

Like a door
the body opened and
the soul looked out.
Timidly at first, then
less timidly
until it was safe.
Then in hunger it ventured.
Then in brazen hunger,
then at the invitation
of any desire.

Promiscuous one, how will you find
god now? How will you
ascertain the divine?
Even in the garden you were told
to live in the body, not
outside it, and suffer in it
if that comes to be necessary.
How will god find you
if you are never in one place
long enough, never
in the home he gave you?

Or do you believe
you have no home, since god
never meant to contain you?

EARTHLY LOVE

Conventions of the time
held them together.
It was a period
(very long) in which
the heart once given freely
was required, as a formal gesture,
to forfeit liberty: a consecration
at once moving and hopelessly doomed.

As to ourselves:
fortunately we diverged
from these requirements,
as I reminded myself
when my life shattered.
So that what we had for so long
was, more or less,
voluntary, alive.
And only long afterward
did I begin to think otherwise.

We are all human—
we protect ourselves
as well as we can
even to the point of denying
clarity, the point
of self-deception. As in
the consecration to which I alluded.

And yet, within this deception,
true happiness occurred.
So that I believe I would
repeat these errors exactly.
Nor does it seem to me
crucial to know
whether or not such happiness

is built on illusion:
it has its own reality.
And in either case, it will end.

EURYDICE

Eurydice went back to hell.
What was difficult
was the travel, which,
on arrival, is forgotten.

Transition
is difficult.
And moving between two worlds
especially so;
the tension is very great.

A passage
filled with regret, with longing,
to which we have, in the world,
some slight access or memory.

Only for a moment
when the dark of the underworld
settled around her again
(gentle, respectful),
only for a moment could
an image of earth's beauty
reach her again, beauty
for which she grieved.

But to live with human faithlessness
is another matter.

CASTILE

Orange blossoms blowing over Castile
children begging for coins

I met my love under an orange tree
or was it an acacia tree
or was he not my love?

I read this, then I dreamed this:
can waking take back what happened to me?
Bells of San Miguel
ringing in the distance
his hair in the shadows blond-white

I dreamed this,
does that mean it didn't happen?
Does it have to happen in the world to be real?

I dreamed everything, the story
became my story:

he lay beside me,
my hand grazed the skin of his shoulder

Mid-day, then early evening:
in the distance, the sound of a train

But it was not the world:
in the world, a thing happens finally, absolutely,
the mind cannot reverse it.

Castile: nuns walking in pairs through the dark garden.
Outside the walls of the Holy Angels
children begging for coins

When I woke I was crying,
has that no reality?

I met my love under an orange tree:
I have forgotten
only the facts, not the inference—
there were children somewhere, crying, begging for coins

I dreamed everything, I gave myself
completely and for all time

And the train returned us
first to Madrid
then to the Basque country

MUTABLE EARTH

Are you healed or do you only think you're healed?

I told myself
from nothing
nothing could be taken away.

But can you love anyone yet?

When I feel safe, I can love.

But will you touch anyone?

I told myself
if I had nothing
the world couldn't touch me.

In the bathtub, I examine my body.
We're supposed to do that.

And your face too?
Your face in the mirror?

I was vigilant: when I touched myself
I didn't feel anything.

Were you safe then?

I was never safe, even when I was most hidden.
Even then I was waiting.

So you couldn't protect yourself?

The absolute
erodes; the boundary, the wall
around the self erodes.
If I was waiting I had been
invaded by time.

But do you think you're free?

I think I recognize the patterns of my nature.

But do you think you're free?

I had nothing
and I was still changed.
Like a costume, my numbness
was taken away. Then
hunger was added.

THE WINGED HORSE

Here is my horse Abstraction,
silver-white, color of the page,
of the unwritten.

Come, Abstraction,
by Will out of Demonic Ambition:
carry me lightly into the regions of the immortal.

I am weary of my other mount,
by Instinct out of Reality,
color of dust, of disappointment,
notwithstanding
the saddle that went with him
and the bronze spurs, the bit
of indestructible metal.

I am weary of the world's gifts, the world's
stipulated limits.

And I am weary of being opposed
and weary of being constantly contradicted by the material, as by
a massive wall where all I say can be
checked up on.

Then come, Abstraction,
take me where you have taken so many others,
far from here, to the void, the star pasture.

Bear me quickly,
Dream out of Blind Hope.

EARTHLY TERROR

I stood at the gate of a rich city.
I had everything the gods required;
I was ready; the burdens
of preparation had been long.
And the moment was the right moment,
the moment assigned to me.

Why were you afraid?

The moment was the right moment;
response must be ready.
On my lips,
the words trembled that were
the right words. Trembled—

and I knew that if I failed to answer
quickly enough, I would be turned away.

THE GOLDEN BOUGH

Even the goddess of love
fights for her children, her vanity
notwithstanding: more than other heroes,
Aeneas flourished; even the road back upward from hell
was simplified. And the sacrifice of love
less painful than for the other heroes.
His mind was clear: even as he endured sacrifice,
he saw its practical purpose. His mind was clear,
and in its clarity, fortified against despair,
even as grief made more human a heart
that might otherwise have seemed immutable. And beauty
ran in his veins: he had no need
for more of it. He conceded to other visions
the worlds of art and science, those paths that lead
only to torment, and instead gathered
the diverse populations of earth
into an empire, a conception
of justice through submission, an intention "to spare the humble
and to crush the proud": subjective,
necessarily, as judgments necessarily are.
Beauty ran in his veins; he had no need for more of it.
That and his taste for empire:
that much can be verified.

EVENING PRAYERS

I believe my sin
to be entirely common:
the request for help
masking request for favor
and the plea for pity
thinly veiling complaint.

So little at peace in the spring evening,
I pray for strength, for direction,
but I also ask
to survive my illness
(the immediate one)—never mind
anything in the future.
I make this a special point,
this unconcern for the future,
also the courage I will have acquired by then
to meet my suffering alone
but with heightened fortitude.

Tonight, in my unhappiness,
I wonder what qualities this presumes
in the one who listens.
And as the breeze stirs
the leaves of the little birch tree,
I construct a presence
wholly skeptical and wholly tender,
thus incapable of surprise.

I believe my sin is common, therefore
intended; I can feel
the leaves stir, sometimes

with words, sometimes without,
as though the highest form of pity
could be irony.

Bedtime, they whisper.
Time to begin lying.

RELIC

Where would I be without my sorrow,
sorrow of my beloved's making,
without some sign of him, this song
of all gifts the most lasting?

How would you like to die
while Orpheus was singing?
A long death; all the way to Dis
I heard him.

Torment of earth
Torment of mortal passion—

I think sometimes
too much is asked of us;
I think sometimes
our consolations are the costliest thing.

All the way to Dis
I heard my husband singing,
much as you now hear me.
Perhaps it was better that way,
my love fresh in my head
even at the moment of death.

Not the first response—
that was terror—
but the last.

NEST

A bird was making its nest.
In the dream, I watched it closely:
in my life, I was trying to be
a witness not a theorist.

The place you begin doesn't determine
the place you end: the bird

took what it found in the yard,
its base materials, nervously
scanning the bare yard in early spring;
in debris by the south wall pushing
a few twigs with its beak.

Image
of loneliness: the small creature
coming up with nothing. Then
dry twigs. Carrying, one by one,
the twigs to the hideout.
Which is all it was then.

It took what there was:
the available material. Spirit
wasn't enough.

And then it wove like the first Penelope
but toward a different end.
How did it weave? It weaved,
carefully but hopelessly, the few twigs
with any suppleness, any flexibility,
choosing these over the brittle, the recalcitrant.

Early spring, late desolation.
The bird circled the bare yard making
efforts to survive
on what remained to it.

It had its task:
to imagine the future. Steadily flying around,
patiently bearing small twigs to the solitude
of the exposed tree in the steady coldness
of the outside world.

I had nothing to build with.
It was winter: I couldn't imagine
anything but the past. I couldn't even
imagine the past, if it came to that.

And I didn't know how I came here.
Everyone else much farther along.
I was back at the beginning
at a time in life we can't remember beginnings.

The bird
collected twigs in the apple tree, relating
each addition to existing mass.
But when was there suddenly *mass*?

It took what it found after the others
were finished.
The same materials—why should it matter
to be finished last? The same materials, the same
limited good. Brown twigs,
broken and fallen. And in one,
a length of yellow wool.

Then it was spring and I was inexplicably happy.
I knew where I was: on Broadway with my bag of groceries.
Spring fruit in the stores: first
cherries at Formaggio. Forsythia
beginning.

First I was at peace.
Then I was contented, satisfied.
And then flashes of joy.
And the season changed—for all of us,
of course.

And as I peered out my mind grew sharper.
And I remember accurately
the sequence of my responses,
my eyes fixing on each thing
from the shelter of the hidden self:

first, *I love it*.
Then, *I can use it*.

Spring
descended. Or should one say
rose? Should one say rose up?
At the Butlers' house,
witch hazel in bloom.

So it would have been
late February.

Pale
yellow of the new year,
unpracticed color. Sheen
of ice over the dull ground.

I thought: *stop now*, meaning
stop here.
Speaking of my life.

The spring of the year: yellow-
green of forsythia, the Commons
planted with new grass—

the new
protected always, the new thing
given its explicit shield, its metal
plaque of language, bordered
with white rope.

Because we wish it to live,
a pale green
hemming the dark existing shapes.

Late
winter sun. Or spring?
The spring sun
so early? Screened
by dense forsythia. I looked
directly into it or almost into it—

Across the street, a small boy
threw his hat into the air: the new

ascending always, the fresh
unsteady colors climbing and rising,
alternating
blue and gold:

Ellsworth Avenue.
A striped
abstraction of the human head
triumphant over dead shrubs.

      Spring
descended. Or should one say
rose up again? Or should one say
broke from earth?

INFERNO

Why did you move away?

I walked out of the fire alive;
how can that be?

How much was lost?

Nothing was lost: it was all
destroyed. Destruction
is the result of action.

Was there a real fire?

I remember going back into the house twenty years ago,
trying to save what we could.
Porcelain and so on. The smell of smoke
on everything.

In my dream, I built a funeral pyre.
For myself, you understand.
I thought I had suffered enough.

I thought this was the end of my body: fire
seemed the right end for hunger;
they were the same thing.

And yet you didn't die?

It was a dream; I thought I was going home.
I remember telling myself
it wouldn't work; I remember thinking
my soul was too stubborn to die.
I thought soul was the same as consciousness—
probably everyone thinks that.

Why did you move away?

I woke up in another world.
As simple as that.

Why did you move away?

The world changed. I walked out of the fire
into a different world—maybe
the world of the dead, for all I know.
Not the end of need but need
raised to the highest power.

SEIZURE

You saved me, you should remember me.

You came to me; twice
I saw you in the garden.
When I woke I was on the ground.

I didn't know who I was anymore;
I didn't know what trees were.

Twice in the garden; many times
before that. Why should it be
kept secret?

The raspberries were very thick;
I hadn't pruned them, I hadn't weeded anything.

I didn't know where I was.
Only: there was a fire near me—no,
above me. In the distance,
the sound of a river.

It was never focus that was missing,
it was meaning.

There was a crown,
a circle over my head.
My hands were covered with dirt,
not from labor.

Why should I lie: that life
is over now.
Why shouldn't I
use what I know?

You changed me, you should remember me.

I remember I had gone out
to walk in the garden. As before into
the streets of the city, into
the bedroom of that first apartment.

And yes, I was alone;
how could I not be?

THE MYSTERY

I became a creature of light.
I sat in a driveway in California;
the roses were hydrant-color; a baby
rolled by in its yellow stroller, making
bubbling fishlike sounds.

I sat in a folding chair
reading Nero Wolfe for the twentieth time,
a mystery that has become restful.
I know who the innocent are; I have acquired in some measure
the genius of the master, in whose supple mind
time moves in two directions: backward
from the act to the motive
and forward to just resolution.

Fearless heart, never tremble again:
the only shadow is the narrow palm's
that cannot enclose you absolutely.
Not like the shadows of the east.

My life took me many places,
many of them very dark.
It took me without my volition,
pushing me from behind,
from one world to another, like
the fishlike baby.
And it was all entirely arbitrary,
without discernible form.

The passionate threats and questions,
the old search for justice,
must have been entirely deluded.

And yet I saw amazing things.
I became almost radiant at the end;
I carried my book everywhere,
like an eager student
clinging to these simple mysteries

so that I might silence in myself
the last accusations:

Who are you and what is your purpose?

LAMENT

A terrible thing is happening—my love
is dying again, my love who has died already:
died and been mourned. And music continues,
music of separation: the trees
become instruments.

How cruel the earth, the willows shimmering,
the birches bending and sighing.
How cruel, how profoundly tender.

My love is dying; my love
not only a person, but an idea, a life.

What will I live for?
Where will I find him again
if not in grief, dark wood
from which the lute is made.

Once is enough. Once is enough
to say goodbye on earth.
And to grieve, that too, of course.
Once is enough to say goodbye forever.

The willows shimmer by the stone fountain,
paths of flowers abutting.

Once is enough: why is he living again?
And so briefly, and only in dream.

My love is dying; parting has started again.
And through the veils of the willows
sunlight rising and glowing,
not the light we knew.
And the birds singing again, even the mourning dove.

Ah, I have sung this song. By the stone fountain
the willows are singing again
with unspeakable tenderness, trailing their leaves
in the radiant water.

Clearly they know, they know. He is dying again,
and the world also. Dying the rest of my life,
so I believe.

In the splitting-up dream
we were fighting over who would keep
the dog,
Blizzard. You tell me
what that name means. He was
a cross between
something big and fluffy
and a dachshund. Does this have to be
the male and female
genitalia? Poor Blizzard,
why was he a dog? He barely touched
the hummus in his dogfood dish.
Then there was something else,
a sound. Like
gravel being moved. Or sand?
The sands of time? Then it was
Erica with her maracas,
like the sands of time
personified. Who will
explain this to
the dog? Blizzard,
Daddy needs you; Daddy's heart is empty,
not because he's leaving Mommy but because
the kind of love he wants Mommy
doesn't have, Mommy's
too ironic—Mommy wouldn't do
the rhumba in the driveway. Or
is this wrong. Supposing
I'm the dog, as in
my child-self, unconsolable because
completely pre-verbal? With
anorexia! O Blizzard,
be a brave dog—this is
all material; you'll wake up
in a different world,

you will eat again, you will grow up into a poet!
Life is very weird, no matter how it ends,
very filled with dreams. Never
will I forget your face, your frantic human eyes
swollen with tears.
I thought my life was over and my heart was broken.
Then I moved to Cambridge.

THE SEVEN AGES

(2001)

Thou earth, thou, Speak.
    —THE TEMPEST

In my first dream the world appeared
the salt, the bitter, the forbidden, the sweet
In my second I descended

I was human, I couldn't just see a thing
beast that I am

I had to touch, to contain it

I hid in the groves,
I worked in the fields until the fields were bare—

time
that will never come again—
the dry wheat bound, caskets
of figs and olives

I even loved a few times in my disgusting human way

and like everyone I called that accomplishment
erotic freedom,
absurd as it seems

The wheat gathered and stored, the last
fruit dried: time

that is hoarded, that is never used
does it also end?

In my first dream the world appeared
the sweet, the forbidden
but there was no garden, only
raw elements

I was human:
I had to beg to descend

the salt, the bitter, the demanding, the preemptive

And like everyone, I took, I was taken
I dreamed

I was betrayed:

Earth was given to me in a dream
In a dream I possessed it

MOONBEAM

The mist rose with a little sound. Like a thud.
Which was the heart beating. And the sun rose, briefly diluted.
And after what seemed years, it sank again
and twilight washed over the shore and deepened there.
And from out of nowhere lovers came,
people who still had bodies and hearts. Who still had
arms, legs, mouths, although by day they might be
housewives and businessmen.

The same night also produced people like ourselves.
You are like me, whether or not you admit it.
Unsatisfied, meticulous. And your hunger is not for experience
but for understanding, as though it could be had in the abstract.

Then it's daylight again and the world goes back to normal.
The lovers smooth their hair; the moon resumes its hollow existence.
And the beach belongs again to mysterious birds
soon to appear on postage stamps.

But what of our memories, the memories of those who depend on images?
Do they count for nothing?

The mist rose, taking back proof of love.
Without which we have only the mirror, you and I.

I call to you across a monstrous river or chasm
to caution you, to prepare you.

Earth will seduce you, slowly, imperceptibly,
subtly, not to say with connivance.

I was not prepared: I stood in my grandmother's kitchen,
holding out my glass. Stewed plums, stewed apricots—

the juice poured off into the glass of ice.
And the water added, patiently, in small increments,

the various cousins discriminating, tasting
with each addition—

aroma of summer fruit, intensity of concentration:
the colored liquid turning gradually lighter, more radiant,

more light passing through it.
Delight, then solace. My grandmother waiting,

to see if more was wanted. Solace, then deep immersion.
I loved nothing more: deep privacy of the sensual life,

the self disappearing into it or inseparable from it,
somehow suspended, floating, its needs

fully exposed, awakened, fully alive—
Deep immersion, and with it

mysterious safety. Far away, the fruit glowing in its glass bowls.
Outside the kitchen, the sun setting.

I was not prepared: sunset, end of summer. Demonstrations
of time as a continuum, as something coming to an end,

not a suspension; the senses wouldn't protect me.
I caution you as I was never cautioned:

you will never let go, you will never be satiated.
You will be damaged and scarred, you will continue to hunger.

Your body will age, you will continue to need.
You will want the earth, then more of the earth—

Sublime, indifferent, it is present, it will not respond.
It is encompassing, it will not minister.

Meaning, it will feed you, it will ravish you,
it will not keep you alive.

MOTHER AND CHILD

We're all dreamers; we don't know who we are.

Some machine made us; machine of the world, the constricting family.
Then back to the world, polished by soft whips.

We dream; we don't remember.

Machine of the family: dark fur, forests of the mother's body.
Machine of the mother: white city inside her.

And before that: earth and water.
Moss between rocks, pieces of leaves and grass.

And before, cells in a great darkness.
And before that, the veiled world.

This is why you were born: to silence me.
Cells of my mother and father, it is your turn
to be pivotal, to be the masterpiece.

I improvised; I never remembered.
Now it's your turn to be driven;
you're the one who demands to know:

Why do I suffer? Why am I ignorant?
Cells in a great darkness. Some machine made us;
it is your turn to address it, to go back asking
what am I for? What am I for?

FABLE

We had, each of us, a set of wishes.
The number changed. And what we wished—
that changed also. Because
we had, all of us, such different dreams.

The wishes were all different, the hopes all different.
And the disasters and catastrophes, always different.

In great waves they left the earth,
even the one that is always wasted.

Waves of despair, waves of hopeless longing and heartache.
Waves of the mysterious wild hungers of youth, the dreams of childhood.
Detailed, urgent; once in a while, selfless.

All different, except of course
the wish to go back. Inevitably
last or first, repeated
over and over—

So the echo lingered. And the wish
held us and tormented us
though we knew in our own bodies
it was never granted.

We knew, and on dark nights, we acknowledged this.
How sweet the night became then,
once the wish released us,
how utterly silent.

Each year, on this same date, the summer solstice comes.
Consummate light: we plan for it,
the day we tell ourselves
that time is very long indeed, nearly infinite.
And in our reading and writing, preference is given
to the celebratory, the ecstatic.

There is in these rituals something apart from wonder:
there is also a kind of preening,
as though human genius had participated in these arrangements
and we found the results satisfying.

What follows the light is what precedes it:
the moment of balance, of dark equivalence.

But tonight we sit in the garden in our canvas chairs
so late into the evening—
why should we look either forward or backward?
Why should we be forced to remember:
it is in our blood, this knowledge.
Shortness of the days; darkness, coldness of winter.
It is in our blood and bones; it is in our history.
It takes genius to forget these things.

STARS

I'm awake; I am in the world—
I expect
no further assurance.
No protection, no promise.

Solace of the night sky,
the hardly moving
face of the clock.

I'm alone—all
my riches surround me.
I have a bed, a room.
I have a bed, a vase
of flowers beside it.
And a nightlight, a book.

I'm awake; I am safe.
The darkness like a shield, the dreams
put off, maybe
vanished forever.

And the day—
the unsatisfying morning that says
I am your future,
here is your cargo of sorrow:

Do you reject me? Do you mean
to send me away because I am not
full, in your word,
because you see
the black shape already implicit?

I will never be banished. I am the light,
your personal anguish and humiliation.
Do you dare
send me away as though
you were waiting for something better?

There is no better.
Only (for a short space)
the night sky like
a quarantine that sets you
apart from your task.

Only (softly, fiercely)
the stars shining. Here,
in the room, the bedroom.
Saying *I was brave, I resisted,
I set myself on fire.*

My sister and I at two ends of the sofa,
reading (I suppose) English novels.
The television on; various schoolbooks open,
or places marked with sheets of lined paper.
Euclid, Pythagoras. As though we had looked into
the origin of thought and preferred novels.

Sad sounds of our growing up—
twilight of cellos. No trace
of a flute, a piccolo. And it seemed at the time
almost impossible to conceive of any of it
as evolving or malleable.

Sad sounds. Anecdotes
that were really still lives.
The pages of the novels turning;
the two dogs snoring quietly.

And from the kitchen,
sounds of our mother,
smell of rosemary, of lamb roasting.

A world in process
of shifting, of being made or dissolved,
and yet we didn't live that way;
all of us lived our lives
as the simultaneous ritualized enactment
of a great principle, something
felt but not understood.
And the remarks we made were like lines in a play,
spoken with conviction but not from choice.

A principle, a terrifying familial will
that implied opposition to change, to variation,
a refusal even to ask questions—

Now that world begins
to shift and eddy around us, only now
when it no longer exists.
It has become the present: unending and without form.

Not one animal, but two.
Not one plate, dwarfed by cutlery,
but a pair of plates, a tablecloth.
And in the market, the little cart
neither poignantly empty nor
desperately full. And in the dark theater,
the two hands seeking each other.

Parts of a shrine, like a shrine in church,
blurred by candles.

And whose idea is this? Who is kneeling there
if not the child who doesn't belong,
the blemished one for whom
recess is the ordeal.

Later, bent over his work
while the others are passing notes,
earnestly applying what his teacher calls
his good mind to his assignment—
what is he protecting? Is it his heart again,
completely lost
in the margin at the edge of the notebook?

With what do you fill an empty life?
Amorous figures, the self
in a dream, the self
replicated in another self, the two
stacked together, though the arms and legs
are always perfectly shaded
as in an urn or bas relief.

Inside, ashes of the actual life.
Ashes, disappointment—

And all he asks
is to complete his work, to be
suspended in time like
an orange slice in an ice cube—

Shadows on the dark grass. The wind
suddenly still. And time, which is so impatient,
which wants to go on, lying quietly there, like an animal.
And the lovers lying there in each other's arms,
their shattered hearts mended again, as in life of course
they will never be, the moment
of consummate delight, of union, able to be sustained—
Is it vivid to them? He has seen them.
He has seen, in his singlemindedness, his apparent abstraction,
neither distracted nor frightened away
by all the writhing, the crying out—

And he has understood; he has restored it all,
exalted figure of the poet, figure of the dreamer.

REUNION

It is discovered, after twenty years, they like each other,
despite enormous differences (one a psychiatrist, one a city official),
differences that could have been, that were, predicted:
differences in tastes, in inclinations, and, now, in wealth
(the one literary, the one entirely practical and yet
deliciously wry; the two wives cordial and mutually curious).
And this discovery is, also, discovery of the self, of new capacities:
they are, in this conversation, like the great sages,
the philosophers they used to read (never together), men
of worldly accomplishment and wisdom, speaking
with all the charm and ebullience and eager openness for which
youth is so unjustly famous. And to these have been added
a broad tolerance and generosity, a movement away from any contempt or
    wariness.
It is a pleasure, now, to speak of the ways in which
their lives have developed, alike in some ways, in others
profoundly different (though each with its core of sorrow, either
implied or disclosed): to speak of the difference now,
to speak of everything that had been, once, part
of a kind of hovering terror, is to lay claim to a subject. Insofar
as theme elevates and shapes a dialogue, this one calls up in them (in its
    grandeur)
kindness and good will of a sort neither had seemed, before,
to possess. Time has been good to them, and now
they can discuss it together from within, so to speak,
which, before, they could not.

RADIUM

When summer ended, my sister was going to school.
No more staying at home with the dogs,
waiting to catch up. No more
playing house with my mother. She was growing up,
she could join the carpool.

No one wanted to stay home. Real life
was the world: you discovered radium,
you danced the swan queen. Nothing

explained my mother. Nothing explained
putting aside radium because you realized finally
it was more interesting to make beds,
to have children like my sister and me.

My sister watched the trees; the leaves
couldn't turn fast enough. She kept asking
was it fall, was it cold enough?

But it was still summer. I lay in bed,
listening to my sister breathe.
I could see her blond hair in the moonlight;
under the white sheet, her little elf's body.
And on the bureau, I could see my new notebook.
It was like my brain: clean, empty. In six months
what was written there would be in my head also.

I watched my sister's face, one side buried in her stuffed bear.
She was being stored in my head, as memory,
like facts in a book.

I didn't want to sleep. I never wanted to sleep
these days. Then I didn't want to wake up. I didn't want
the leaves turning, the nights turning dark early.
I didn't want to love my new clothes, my notebook.

I knew what they were: a bribe, a distraction.
Like the excitement of school: the truth was
time was moving in one direction, like a wave lifting
the whole house, the whole village.

I turned the light on, to wake my sister.
I wanted my parents awake and vigilant; I wanted them
to stop lying. But nobody woke. I sat up
reading my Greek myths in the nightlight.

The nights were cold, the leaves fell.
My sister was tired of school, she missed being home.
But it was too late to go back, too late to stop.
Summer was gone, the nights were dark. The dogs
wore sweaters to go outside.

And then fall was gone, the year was gone.
We were changing, we were growing up. But
it wasn't something you decided to do;
it was something that happened, something
you couldn't control.

Time was passing. Time was carrying us
faster and faster toward the door of the laboratory,
and then beyond the door into the abyss, the darkness.
My mother stirred the soup. The onions,
by a miracle, became part of the potatoes.

BIRTHDAY

Amazingly, I can look back
fifty years. And there, at the end of the gaze,
a human being already entirely recognizable,
the hands clutched in the lap, the eyes
staring into the future with the combined
terror and hopelessness of a soul expecting annihilation.

Entirely familiar, though still, of course, very young.
Staring blindly ahead, the expression of someone staring into utter
    darkness.
And thinking—which meant, I remember, the attempts of the mind
to prevent change.

Familiar, recognizable, but much more deeply alone, more despondent.
She does not, in her view, meet the definition
of child, a person with everything to look forward to.

This is how the others look; this is, therefore, what they are.
Constantly making friends
with the camera, many of them actually
smiling with real conviction—

I remember that age. Riddled with self-doubt, self-loathing,
and at the same time suffused
with contempt for the communal, the ordinary; forever
consigned to solitude, the bleak solace of perception, to a future
completely dominated by the tragic, with no use for the immense will
but to fend it off—

That is the problem of silence:
one cannot test one's ideas.
Because they are not ideas, they are the truth.

All the defenses, the spiritual rigidity, the insistent
unmasking of the ordinary to reveal the tragic,
were actually innocence of the world.

Meaning the partial, the shifting, the mutable—
all that the absolute excludes. I sat in the dark, in the living room.
The birthday was over. I was thinking, naturally, about time.
I remember how, in almost the same instant,
my heart would leap up exultant and collapse
in desolate anguish. The leaping up—the half I didn't count—
that was happiness; that is what the word meant.

ANCIENT TEXT

How deeply fortunate my life, my every prayer
heard by the angels.

I asked for the earth; I received earth, like so much
mud in the face.

I prayed for relief from suffering; I received suffering.
Who can say my prayers were not heard? They were

translated, edited—and if certain
of the important words were left out or misunderstood, a crucial

article deleted, still they were taken in, studied like ancient texts.
Perhaps they *were* ancient texts, re-created

in the vernacular of a particular period.
And as my life was, in a sense, increasingly given over to prayer,

so the task of the angels was, I believe, to master this language
in which they were not as yet entirely fluent or confident.

And if I felt, in my youth, rejected, abandoned,
I came to feel, in the end, that we were, all of us,

intended as teachers, possibly
teachers of the deaf, kind helpers whose virtuous patience

is sustained by an abiding passion.
I understood at last! We were the aides and helpers,

our masterpieces strangely useful, like primers.
How simple life became then; how clear, in the childish errors,

the perpetual labor: night and day, angels were
discussing my meanings. Night and day, I revised my appeals,

making each sentence better and clearer, as though one might
elude forever all misconstruction. How flawless they became—

impeccable, beautiful, continuously misread. If I was, in a sense,
an obsessive staggering through time, in another sense

I was a winged obsessive, my moonlit
feathers were paper. I lived hardly at all among men and women;

I spoke only to angels. How fortunate my days,
how charged and meaningful the nights' continuous silence and opacity.

FROM A JOURNAL

I had a lover once,
I had a lover twice,
easily three times I loved.
And in between
my heart reconstructed itself perfectly
like a worm.
And my dreams also reconstructed themselves.

After a time, I realized I was living
a completely idiotic life.
Idiotic, wasted—
And sometime later, you and I
began to correspond, inventing
an entirely new form.

Deep intimacy over great distance!
Keats to Fanny Brawne, Dante to Beatrice—

One cannot invent
a new form in
an old character. The letters I sent remained
immaculately ironic, aloof
yet forthright. Meanwhile, I was writing
different letters in my head,
some of which became poems.

So much genuine feeling!
So many fierce declarations
of passionate longing!

I loved once, I loved twice,
and suddenly
the form collapsed: I was
unable to sustain ignorance.

How sad to have lost you, to have lost
any chance of actually knowing you
or remembering you over time
as a real person, as someone I could have grown
deeply attached to, maybe
the brother I never had.

And how sad to think
of dying before finding out
anything. And to realize
how ignorant we all are most of the time,
seeing things
only from the one vantage, like a sniper.

And there were so many things
I never got to tell you about myself,
things which might have swayed you.
And the photo I never sent, taken
the night I looked almost splendid.

I wanted you to fall in love. But the arrow
kept hitting the mirror and coming back.
And the letters kept dividing themselves
with neither half totally true.

And sadly, you never figured out
any of this, though you always wrote back
so promptly, always the same elusive letter.

I loved once, I loved twice,
and even though in our case
things never got off the ground
it was a good thing to have tried.
And I still have the letters, of course.
Sometimes I will take a few years' worth

to reread in the garden,
with a glass of iced tea.

And I feel, sometimes, part of something
very great, wholly profound and sweeping.

I loved once, I loved twice,
easily three times I loved.

ISLAND

The curtains parted. Light
coming in. Moonlight, then sunlight.
Not changing because time was passing
but because the one moment had many aspects.

White lisianthus in a chipped vase.
Sound of the wind. Sound
of lapping water. And hours passing, the white sails
luminous, the boat rocking at anchor.

Motion not yet channeled in time.
The curtains shifting or stirring; the moment
shimmering, a hand moving
backward, then forward. Silence. And then

one word, a name. And then another word:
again, again. And time
salvaged, like a pulse between
stillness and change. Late afternoon. The soon to be lost

becoming memory; the mind closing around it. The room
claimed again, as a possession. Sunlight,
then moonlight. The eyes glazed over with tears.
And then the moon fading, the white sails flexing.

THE DESTINATION

We had only a few days, but they were very long,
the light changed constantly.
A few days, spread out over several years,
over the course of a decade.

And each meeting charged with a sense of exactness,
as though we had traveled, separately,
some great distance; as though there had been,
through all the years of wandering,
a destination, after all.
Not a place, but a body, a voice.

A few days. Intensity
that was never permitted to develop
into tolerance or sluggish affection.

And I believed for many years this was a great marvel;
in my mind, I returned to those days repeatedly,
convinced they were the center of my amorous life.

The days were very long, like the days now.
And the intervals, the separations, exalted,
suffused with a kind of passionate joy that seemed, somehow,
to extend those days, to be inseparable from them.
So that a few hours could take up a lifetime.

A few hours, a world that neither unfolded nor diminished,
that could, at any point, be entered again—

So that long after the end I could return to it without difficulty,
I could live almost completely in imagination.

THE BALCONY

It was a night like this, at the end of summer.

We had rented, I remember, a room with a balcony.
How many days and nights? Five, perhaps—no more.

Even when we weren't touching we were making love.
We stood on our little balcony in the summer night.
And off somewhere, the sounds of human life.

We were the soon to be anointed monarchs,
well disposed to our subjects. Just beneath us,
sounds of a radio playing, an aria we didn't in those years know.

Someone dying of love. Someone from whom time had taken
the only happiness, who was alone now,
impoverished, without beauty.

The rapturous notes of an unendurable grief, of isolation and terror,
the nearly impossible to sustain slow phrases of the ascending figures—
they drifted out over the dark water
like an ecstasy.

Such a small mistake. And many years later,
the only thing left of that night, of the hours in that room.

COPPER BEECH

Why is the earth angry at heaven?
If there's a question, is there an answer?

On Dana Street, a copper beech.
Immense, like the tree of my childhood,
but with a violence I wasn't ready to see then.

I was a child like a pointed finger,
then an explosion of darkness;
my mother could do nothing with me.
Interesting, isn't it,
the language she used.

The copper beech rearing like an animal.

Frustration, rage, the terrible wounded pride
of rebuffed love—I remember

rising from the earth to heaven. I remember
I had two parents,
one harsh, one invisible. Poor
clouded father, who worked
only in gold and silver.

STUDY OF MY SISTER

We respect, here in America,
what is concrete, visible. We ask
What is it for? What does it lead to?

My sister
put her fork down. She felt, she said,
as though she should jump off a cliff.

A crime has been committed
against a human soul

as against the small child
who spends all day entertaining herself
with the colored blocks

so that she looks up
radiant at the end,
presenting herself,
giving herself back to her parents

and they say
What did you build?
and then, because she seems
so blank, so confused,
they repeat the question.

AUGUST

My sister painted her nails fuchsia,
a color named after a fruit.
All the colors were named after foods:
coffee frost, tangerine sherbet.
We sat in the backyard, waiting for our lives to resume
the ascent summer interrupted:
triumphs, victories, for which school
was a kind of practice.

The teachers smiled down at us, pinning on the blue ribbons.
And in our heads, we smiled down at the teachers.

Our lives were stored in our heads.
They hadn't begun; we were both sure
we'd know when they did.
They certainly weren't this.

We sat in the backyard, watching our bodies change:
first bright pink, then tan.
I dribbled baby oil on my legs; my sister
rubbed polish remover on her left hand,
tried another color.

We read, we listened to the portable radio.
Obviously this wasn't life, this sitting around
in colored lawn chairs.

Nothing matched up to the dreams.
My sister kept trying to find a color she liked:
it was summer, they were all frosted.
Fuchsia, orange, mother-of-pearl.
She held her left hand in front of her eyes,
moved it from side to side.

Why was it always like this—
the colors so intense in the glass bottles,
so distinct, and on the hand
almost exactly alike,
a film of weak silver.

My sister shook the bottle. The orange
kept sinking to the bottom; maybe
that was the problem.
She shook it over and over, held it up to the light,
studied the words in the magazine.

The world was a detail, a small thing not yet
exactly right. Or like an afterthought, somehow
still crude or approximate.
What was real was the idea:

My sister added a coat, held her thumb
to the side of the bottle.
We kept thinking we would see
the gap narrow, though in fact it persisted.
The more stubbornly it persisted,
the more fiercely we believed.

SUMMER AT THE BEACH

Before we started camp, we went to the beach.

Long days, before the sun was dangerous.
My sister lay on her stomach, reading mysteries.
I sat in the sand, watching the water.

You could use the sand to cover
parts of your body that you didn't like.
I covered my feet, to make my legs longer;
the sand climbed over my ankles.

I looked down at my body, away from the water.
I was what the magazines told me to be:
coltish. I was a frozen colt.

My sister didn't bother with these adjustments.
When I told her to cover her feet, she tried a few times,
but she got bored; she didn't have enough willpower
to sustain a deception.

I watched the sea; I listened to the other families.
Babies everywhere: what went on in their heads?
I couldn't imagine myself as a baby;
I couldn't picture myself not thinking.

I couldn't imagine myself as an adult either.
They all had terrible bodies: lax, oily, completely
committed to being male and female.

The days were all the same.
When it rained, we stayed home.
When the sun shone, we went to the beach with my mother.

My sister lay on her stomach, reading her mysteries.
I sat with my legs arranged to resemble
what I saw in my head, what I believed was my true self.

Because it *was* true: when I didn't move I was perfect.

RAIN IN SUMMER

We were supposed to be, all of us,
a circle, a line at every point
equally weighted or tensed, equally
close to the center. I saw it
differently. In my mind, my parents
were the circle; my sister and I
were trapped inside.

Long Island. Terrible
storms off the Atlantic, summer rain
hitting the gray shingles. I watched
the copper beech, the dark leaves turning
a sort of lacquered ebony. It seemed to be
secure, as secure as the house.

It made sense to be housebound.
We were anyway: we couldn't change who we were.
We couldn't change even the smallest facts:
our long hair parted in the center,
secured with two barrettes. We embodied
those ideas of my mother's
not appropriate to adult life.

Ideas of childhood: how to look, how to act.
Ideas of spirit: what gifts to claim, to develop.
Ideas of character: how to be driven, how to prevail,
how to triumph in the true manner of greatness
without seeming to lift a finger.

It was all going on much too long:
childhood, summer. But we were safe;
we lived in a closed form.

Piano lessons. Poems, drawings. Summer rain
hammering at the circle. And the mind
developing within fixed conditions
a few tragic assumptions: we felt safe,
meaning we saw the world as dangerous.
We would prevail or conquer, meaning
we saw homage as love.

My sister and I stared out
into the violence of the summer rain.
It was obvious to us two people couldn't
prevail at the same time. My sister
took my hand, reaching across the flowered cushions.

Neither of us could see, yet,
the cost of any of this.
But she was frightened, she trusted me.

CIVILIZATION

It came to us very late:
perception of beauty, desire for knowledge.
And in the great minds, the two often configured as one.

To perceive, to speak, even on subjects inherently cruel—
to speak boldly even when the facts were, in themselves, painful or dire—
seemed to introduce among us some new action,
having to do with human obsession, human passion.

And yet something, in this action, was being conceded.
And this offended what remained in us of the animal:
it was enslavement speaking, assigning
power to forces outside ourselves.
Therefore the ones who spoke were exiled and silenced,
scorned in the streets.

But the facts persisted. They were among us,
isolated and without pattern; they were among us,
shaping us—

Darkness. Here and there a few fires in doorways,
wind whipping around the corners of buildings—

Where were the silenced, who conceived these images?
In the dim light, finally summoned, resurrected.
As the scorned were praised, who had brought
these truths to our attention, who had felt their presence,
who had perceived them clearly in their blackness and horror
and had arranged them to communicate
some vision of their substance, their magnitude—

In which the facts themselves were suddenly
serene, glorious. They were among us,

not singly, as in chaos, but woven
into relationship or set in order, as though life on earth
could, in this one form, be apprehended deeply
though it could never be mastered.

DECADE

What joy touches
the solace of ritual? A void

appears in the life.
A shock so deep, so terrible,
its force
levels the perceived world. You were

a beast at the edge of its cave, only
waking and sleeping. Then
the minute shift; the eye

taken by something.
Spring: the unforeseen
flooding the abyss.

And the life
filling again. And finally
a place
found for everything.

THE EMPTY GLASS

I asked for much; I received much.
I asked for much; I received little, I received
next to nothing.

And between? A few umbrellas opened indoors.
A pair of shoes by mistake on the kitchen table.

O wrong, wrong—it was my nature. I was
hard-hearted, remote. I was
selfish, rigid to the point of tyranny.

But I was always that person, even in early childhood.
Small, dark-haired, dreaded by the other children.
I never changed. Inside the glass, the abstract
tide of fortune turned
from high to low overnight.

Was it the sea? Responding, maybe,
to celestial force? To be safe,
I prayed. I tried to be a better person.
Soon it seemed to me that what began as terror
and matured into moral narcissism
might have become in fact
actual human growth. Maybe
this is what my friends meant, taking my hand,
telling me they understood
the abuse, the incredible shit I accepted,
implying (so I once thought) I was a little sick
to give so much for so little.
Whereas they meant I was *good* (clasping my hand intensely)—
a good friend and person, not a creature of pathos.

I was not pathetic! I was writ large,
like a great queen or saint.

Well, it all makes for interesting conjecture.
And it occurs to me that what is crucial is to believe
in effort, to believe some good will come of simply *trying*,
a good completely untainted by the corrupt initiating impulse
to persuade or seduce—

What are we without this?
Whirling in the dark universe,
alone, afraid, unable to influence fate—

What do we have really?
Sad tricks with ladders and shoes,
tricks with salt, impurely motivated recurring
attempts to build character.
What do we have to appease the great forces?

And I think in the end this was the question
that destroyed Agamemnon, there on the beach,
the Greek ships at the ready, the sea
invisible beyond the serene harbor, the future
lethal, unstable: he was a fool, thinking
it could be controlled. He should have said
I have nothing, I am at your mercy.

QUINCE TREE

We had, in the end, only the weather for a subject.
Luckily, we lived in a world with seasons—
we felt, still, access to variety:
darkness, euphoria, various kinds of waiting.

I suppose, in the true sense, our exchanges
couldn't be called conversation, being
dominated by accord, by repetition.

And yet it would be wrong to imagine
we had neither sense of one another nor
deep response to the world, as it would be wrong to believe
our lives were narrow, or empty.

We had great wealth.
We had, in fact, everything we could see
and while it is true we could see
neither great distance nor fine detail,
what we were able to discern we grasped
with a hunger the young can barely conceive,
as though all experience had been channeled into
these few perceptions.

Channeled without memory.
Because the past was lost to us as referent,
lost as image, as narrative. What had it contained?
Was there love? Had there been, once,
sustained labor? Or fame, had there ever been
something like that?

In the end, we didn't need to ask. Because
we felt the past; it was, somehow,
in these things, the front lawn and back lawn,
suffusing them, giving the little quince tree
a weight and meaning almost beyond enduring.

Utterly lost and yet strangely alive, the whole of our human existence—
it would be wrong to think
because we never left the yard
that what we felt there was somehow shrunken or partial.
In its grandeur and splendor, the world
was finally present.

And it was always this we discussed or alluded to
when we were moved to speak.
The weather. The quince tree.
You, in your innocence, what do you know of this world?

THE TRAVELER

At the top of the tree was what I wanted.
Fortunately I had read books:
I knew I was being tested.

I knew nothing would work—
not to climb that high, not to force
the fruit down. One of three results must follow:
the fruit isn't what you imagined,
or it is but fails to satiate.
Or it is damaged in falling
and as a shattered thing torments you forever.

But I refused to be
bested by fruit. I stood under the tree,
waiting for my mind to save me.
I stood, long after the fruit rotted.

And after many years, a traveler passed by me
where I stood, and greeted me warmly,
as one would greet a brother. And I asked why,
why was I so familiar to him,
having never seen him?

And he said, "Because I am like you,
therefore I recognize you. I treated all experience
as a spiritual or intellectual trial
in which to exhibit or prove my superiority
to my predecessors. I chose
to live in hypothesis; longing sustained me.

In fact, what I needed most was longing, which you seem
to have achieved in stasis,
but which I have found in change, in departure."

We had the problem of age, the problem of wishing to linger.
Not needing, anymore, even to make a contribution.
Merely wishing to linger: to be, to be here.

And to stare at things, but with no real avidity.
To browse, to purchase nothing.
But there were many of us; we took up time. We crowded out
our own children, and the children of friends. We did great damage,
meaning no harm.

We continued to plan; to fix things as they broke.
To repair, to improve. We traveled, we put in gardens.
And we continued brazenly to plant trees and perennials.

We asked so little of the world. We understood
the offense of advice, of holding forth. We checked ourselves:
we were correct, we were silent.
But we could not cure ourselves of desire, not completely.
Our hands, folded, reeked of it.

How did we do so much damage, merely sitting and watching,
strolling, on fine days, the grounds of the park, the arboretum,
or sitting on benches in front of the public library,
feeding pigeons out of a paper bag?

We were correct, and yet desire pursued us.
Like a great force, a god. And the young
were offended; their hearts
turned cold in reaction. We asked

so little of the world; small things seemed to us
immense wealth. Merely to smell once more the early roses
in the arboretum: we asked
so little, and we claimed nothing. And the young
withered nevertheless.

Or they became like stones in the arboretum: as though
our continued existence, our asking so little for so many years, meant
we asked everything.

DREAM OF LUST

After one of those nights, a day:
the mind dutiful, waking, putting on its slippers,
and the spirit restive, muttering
I'd rather, I'd rather—

Where did it come from,
so sudden, so fierce,
an unexpected animal? Who
was the mysterious figure?
You are ridiculously young, I told him.

The day tranquil, beautiful, expecting attention.
The night distracting and barred—
and I cannot return,
not even for information.

Roses in bloom, penstemon, the squirrels
preoccupied for the moment.
And suddenly I don't live here, I live in a mystery.

He had an odd lumbering gaucheness
that became erotic grace.

It is what I thought and not what I thought:
the world is not my world, the human body
makes an impasse, an obstacle.

Clumsy, in jeans, then suddenly
doing the most amazing things
as though they were entirely his idea—

But the afterward at the end of the timeless:
coffee, dark bread, the sustaining rituals
going on now so far away—

the human body a compulsion, a magnet,
the dream itself obstinately
clinging, the spirit
helpless to let it go—

it is still not worth
losing the world.

GRACE

We were taught, in those years,
never to speak of good fortune.
To not speak, to not feel—
it was the smallest step for a child
of any imagination.

And yet an exception was made
for the language of faith;
we were trained in the rudiments of this language
as a precaution.

Not to speak swaggeringly in the world
but to speak in homage, abjectly, privately—

And if one lacked faith?
If one believed, even in childhood, only in chance—

such powerful words they used, our teachers!
Disgrace, punishment: many of us
preferred to remain mute, even in the presence of the divine.

Ours were the voices raised in lament
against the cruel vicissitudes.
Ours were the dark libraries, the treatises
on affliction. In the dark, we recognized one another;
we saw, each in the other's gaze,
experience never manifested in speech.

The miraculous, the sublime, the undeserved;
the relief merely of waking once more in the morning—
only now, with old age nearly beginning,
do we dare to speak of such things, or confess, with gusto,
even to the smallest joys. Their disappearance
approaches, in any case: ours are the lives
this knowledge enters as a gift.

FABLE

The weather grew mild, the snow melted.
The snow melted, and in its place
flowers of early spring:
mertensia, chionodoxa. The earth
turned blue by mistake.

Urgency, there was so much urgency—

to change, to escape the past.

It was cold, it was winter:
I was frightened for my life—

Then it was spring, the earth
turning a surprising blue.

The weather grew mild, the snow melted—
spring overtook it.
And then summer. And time stopped
because we stopped waiting.

And summer lasted. It lasted
because we were happy.

The weather grew mild, like
the past circling back
intending to be gentle, like
a form of the everlasting.

Then the dream ended. The everlasting began.

The windows shut, the sun rising.
Sounds of a few birds;
the garden filmed with a light moisture.
And the insecurity of great hope
suddenly gone.
And the heart still alert.

And a thousand small hopes stirring,
not new but newly acknowledged.
Affection, dinner with friends.
And the structure of certain
adult tasks.

The house clean, silent.
The trash not needing to be taken out.

It is a kingdom, not an act of imagination:
and still very early,
the white buds of the penstemon open.

Is it possible we have finally paid
bitterly enough?
That sacrifice is not to be required,
that anxiety and terror have been judged sufficient?

A squirrel racing along the telephone wire,
a crust of bread in its mouth.

And darkness delayed by the season.
So that it seems
part of a great gift
not to be feared any longer.

The day unfurling, but very gradually, a solitude
not to be feared, the changes
faint, barely perceived—

the penstemon open.
The likelihood
of seeing it through to the end.

RIPE PEACH

1.

There was a time
only certainty gave me
any joy. Imagine—
certainty, a dead thing.

2.

And then the world,
the experiment.
The obscene mouth
famished with love—
it is like love:
the abrupt, hard
certainty of the end—

3.

In the center of the mind,
the hard pit,
the conclusion. As though
the fruit itself
never existed, only
the end, the point
midway between
anticipation and nostalgia—

4.

So much fear.
So much terror of the physical world.
The mind frantic
guarding the body from
the passing, the temporary,
the body straining against it—

5.

A peach on the kitchen table.
A replica. It is the earth,
the same
disappearing sweetness
surrounding the stone end,
and like the earth
available—

6.

An opportunity
for happiness: earth
we cannot possess
only experience— And now
sensation: the mind
silenced by fruit—

7.

They are not
reconciled. The body
here, the mind
separate, not
merely a warden:
it has separate joys.
It is the night sky,
the fiercest stars are its
immaculate distinctions—

8.

Can it survive? Is there
light that survives the end

in which the mind's enterprise
continues to live: thought
darting about the room,
above the bowl of fruit—

9.

Fifty years. The night sky
filled with shooting stars.
Light, music
from far away—I must be
nearly gone. I must be
stone, since the earth
surrounds me—

10.

There was
a peach in a wicker basket.
There was a bowl of fruit.
Fifty years. Such a long walk
from the door to the table.

UNPAINTED DOOR

Finally, in middle age,
I was tempted to return to childhood.

The house was the same, but
the door was different.
Not red anymore—unpainted wood.
The trees were the same: the oak, the copper beech.
But the people—all the inhabitants of the past—
were gone: lost, dead, moved away.
The children from across the street
old men and women.

The sun was the same, the lawns
parched brown in summer.
But the present was full of strangers.

And in some way it was all exactly right,
exactly as I remembered: the house, the street,
the prosperous village—

Not to be reclaimed or re-entered
but to legitimize
silence and distance,
distance of place, of time,
bewildering accuracy of imagination and dream—

I remember my childhood as a long wish to be elsewhere.
This is the house; this must be
the childhood I had in mind.

MITOSIS

No one actually remembers them
as not divided. Whoever says he does—
that person is lying.

No one remembers. And somehow
everyone knows:

they had to be, in the beginning, equally straightforward,
committed to a direct path.
In the end, only the body continued
implacably moving ahead, as it had to,
to stay alive.

But at some point the mind lingered.
It wanted more time by the sea, more time in the fields
gathering wildflowers. It wanted
more nights sleeping in its own bed; it wanted
its own nightlight, its favorite drink.
And more mornings—it wanted these
possibly most of all. More
of the first light, the penstemon blooming, the alchemilla
still covered with its evening jewels, the night rain
still clinging to it.

And then, more radically, it wanted to go back.
It wished simply to repeat the whole passage,
like the exultant conductor, who feels only that
the violin might have been a little softer, more plangent.

And through all this, the body
continues like the path of an arrow
as it has to, to live.

And if that means to get to the end
(the mind buried like an arrowhead), what choice does it have,
what dream except the dream of the future?

Limitless world! The vistas clear, the clouds risen.
The water azure, the sea plants bending and sighing
among the coral reefs, the sullen mermaids
all suddenly angels, or like angels. And music
rising over the open sea—

Exactly like the dream of the mind.
The same sea, the same shimmering fields.
The plate of fruit, the identical
violin (in the past and the future) but
softer now, finally
sufficiently sad.

I had drawn my chair to the hotel window, to watch the rain.

I was in a kind of dream or trance—
in love, and yet
I wanted nothing.

It seemed unnecessary to touch you, to see you again.
I wanted only this:
the room, the chair, the sound of the rain falling,
hour after hour, in the warmth of the spring night.

I needed nothing more; I was utterly sated.
My heart had become small; it took very little to fill it.
I watched the rain falling in heavy sheets over the darkened city—

You were not concerned; I could let you
live as you needed to live.

At dawn the rain abated. I did the things
one does in daylight, I acquitted myself,
but I moved like a sleepwalker.

It was enough and it no longer involved you.
A few days in a strange city.
A conversation, the touch of a hand.
And afterward, I took off my wedding ring.

That was what I wanted: to be naked.

THE RUSE

They sat far apart
deliberately, to experience, daily,
the sweetness of seeing each other across
great distance. They understood

instinctively that erotic passion
thrives on distance, either
actual (one is married, one
no longer loves the other) or
spurious, deceptive, a ruse

miming the subordination
of passion to social convention,
but a ruse, so that it demonstrated
not the power of convention but rather

the power of eros to annihilate
objective reality. The world, time, distance—
withering like dry fields before
the fire of the gaze—

Never before. Never with anyone else.
And after the eyes, the hands.
Experienced as glory, as consecration—

Sweet. And after so many years,
completely unimaginable.

Never before. Never with anyone else.
And then the whole thing
repeated exactly with someone else.
Until it was finally obvious

that the only constant
was distance, the servant of need.
Which was used to sustain
whatever fire burned in each of us.

The eyes, the hands—less crucial
than we believed. In the end
distance was sufficient, by itself.

TIME

There was too much, always, then too little.
Childhood: sickness.
By the side of the bed I had a little bell—
at the other end of the bell, my mother.

Sickness, gray rain. The dogs slept through it. They slept on the bed,
at the end of it, and it seemed to me they understood
about childhood: best to remain unconscious.

The rain made gray slats on the windows.
I sat with my book, the little bell beside me.
Without hearing a voice, I apprenticed myself to a voice.
Without seeing any sign of the spirit, I determined
to live in the spirit.

The rain faded in and out.
Month after month, in the space of a day.
Things became dreams; dreams became things.

Then I was well; the bell went back to the cupboard.
The rain ended. The dogs stood at the door,
panting to go outside.

I was well, then I was an adult.
And time went on—it was like the rain,
so much, so much, as though it was a weight that couldn't be moved.

I was a child, half sleeping.
I was sick; I was protected.
And I lived in the world of the spirit,
the world of the gray rain,
the lost, the remembered.

Then suddenly the sun was shining.
And time went on, even when there was almost none left.
And the perceived became the remembered,
the remembered, the perceived.

MEMOIR

I was born cautious, under the sign of Taurus.
I grew up on an island, prosperous,
in the second half of the twentieth century;
the shadow of the Holocaust
hardly touched us.

I had a philosophy of love, a philosophy
of religion, both based on
early experience within a family.

And if when I wrote I used only a few words
it was because time always seemed to me short
as though it could be stripped away
at any moment.

And my story, in any case, wasn't unique
though, like everyone else, I had a story,
a point of view.

A few words were all I needed:
nourish, sustain, attack.

When I was seven, I had a vision:
I believed I would die. I would die
at ten, of polio. I saw my death:
it was a vision, an insight—
it was what Joan had, to save France.

I grieved bitterly. Cheated
of earth, cheated
of a whole childhood, of the great dreams of my heart
which would never be manifest.

No one knew any of this.
And then I lived.

I kept being alive
when I should have been burning:
I was Joan, I was Lazarus.

Monologue
of childhood, of adolescence.
I was Lazarus, the world given to me again.
Nights I lay in my bed, waiting to be found out.
And the voices returned, but the world
refused to withdraw.

I lay awake, listening.
Fifty years ago, in my childhood.
And of course now.
What was it, speaking to me? Terror
of death, terror of gradual loss;
fear of sickness in its bridal whites—

When I was seven, I believed I would die:
only the dates were wrong. I heard
a dark prediction
rising in my own body.

I gave you your chance.
I listened to you, I believed in you.
I will not let you have me again.

AUBADE

There was one summer
that returned many times over
there was one flower unfurling
taking many forms

Crimson of the monarda, pale gold of the late roses

There was one love
There was one love, there were many nights

Smell of the mock orange tree
Corridors of jasmine and lilies
Still the wind blew

There were many winters but I closed my eyes
The cold air white with dissolved wings

There was one garden when the snow melted
Azure and white; I couldn't tell
my solitude from love—

There was one love; he had many voices
There was one dawn; sometimes
we watched it together

I was here
I was here

There was one summer returning over and over
there was one dawn
I grew old watching

SCREENED PORCH

The stars were foolish, they were not worth waiting for.
The moon was shrouded, fragmentary.
Twilight like silt covered the hills.
The great drama of human life was nowhere evident—
but for that, you don't go to nature.

The terrible harrowing story of a human life,
the wild triumph of love: they don't belong
to the summer night, panorama of hills and stars.

We sat on our terraces, our screened porches,
as though we expected to gather, even now,
fresh information or sympathy. The stars
glittered a bit above the landscape, the hills
suffused still with a faint retroactive light.
Darkness. Luminous earth. We stared out, starved for knowledge,
and we felt, in its place, a substitute:
indifference that appeared benign.

Solace of the natural world. Panorama
of the eternal. The stars
were foolish, but somehow soothing. The moon
presented itself as a curved line.
And we continued to project onto the glowing hills
qualities we needed: fortitude, the potential
for spiritual advancement.

Immunity to time, to change. Sensation
of perfect safety, the sense of being
protected from what we loved—

And our intense need was absorbed by the night
and returned as sustenance.

SUMMER NIGHT

Orderly, and out of long habit, my heart continues to beat.
I hear it, nights when I wake, over the mild sound of the air conditioner.
As I used to hear it over the beloved's heart, or
variety of hearts, owing to there having been several.
And as it beats, it continues to drum up ridiculous emotion.

So many passionate letters never sent!
So many urgent journeys conceived of on summer nights,
surprise visits to men who were nearly complete strangers.
The tickets never bought, the letters never stamped.
And pride spared. And the life, in a sense, never completely lived.
And the art always in some danger of growing repetitious.

Why not? Why not? Why should my poems not imitate my life?
Whose lesson is not the apotheosis but the pattern, whose meaning
is not in the gesture but in the inertia, the reverie.

Desire, loneliness, wind in the flowering almond—
surely these are the great, the inexhaustible subjects
to which my predecessors apprenticed themselves.
I hear them echo in my own heart, disguised as convention.

Balm of the summer night, balm of the ordinary,
imperial joy and sorrow of human existence,
the dreamed as well as the lived—
what could be dearer than this, given the closeness of death?

FABLE

Then I looked down and saw
the world I was entering, that would be my home.
And I turned to my companion, and I said *Where are we?*
And he replied *Nirvana.*
And I said again *But the light will give us no peace.*

AVERNO

(2006)

FOR NOAH

Averno. Ancient name Avernus. A small crater lake, ten miles west of Naples, Italy; regarded by the ancient Romans as the entrance to the underworld.

THE NIGHT MIGRATIONS

This is the moment when you see again
the red berries of the mountain ash
and in the dark sky
the birds' night migrations.

It grieves me to think
the dead won't see them—
these things we depend on,
they disappear.

What will the soul do for solace then?
I tell myself maybe it won't need
these pleasures anymore;
maybe just not being is simply enough,
hard as that is to imagine.

I

OCTOBER

1.

Is it winter again, is it cold again,
didn't Frank just slip on the ice,
didn't he heal, weren't the spring seeds planted

didn't the night end,
didn't the melting ice
flood the narrow gutters

wasn't my body
rescued, wasn't it safe

didn't the scar form, invisible
above the injury

terror and cold,
didn't they just end, wasn't the back garden
harrowed and planted—

I remember how the earth felt, red and dense,
in stiff rows, weren't the seeds planted,
didn't vines climb the south wall

I can't hear your voice
for the wind's cries, whistling over the bare ground

I no longer care
what sound it makes

when was I silenced, when did it first seem
pointless to describe that sound

what it sounds like can't change what it is—

didn't the night end, wasn't the earth
safe when it was planted

didn't we plant the seeds,
weren't we necessary to the earth,

the vines, were they harvested?

2.

Summer after summer has ended,
balm after violence:
it does me no good
to be good to me now;
violence has changed me.

Daybreak. The low hills shine
ochre and fire, even the fields shine.
I know what I see; sun that could be
the August sun, returning
everything that was taken away—

You hear this voice? This is my mind's voice;
you can't touch my body now.
It has changed once, it has hardened,
don't ask it to respond again.

A day like a day in summer.
Exceptionally still. The long shadows of the maples
nearly mauve on the gravel paths.
And in the evening, warmth. Night like a night in summer.

It does me no good; violence has changed me.
My body has grown cold like the stripped fields;
now there is only my mind, cautious and wary,
with the sense it is being tested.

Once more, the sun rises as it rose in summer;
bounty, balm after violence.
Balm after the leaves have changed, after the fields
have been harvested and turned.

Tell me this is the future,
I won't believe you.
Tell me I'm living,
I won't believe you.

3.

Snow had fallen. I remember
music from an open window.

Come to me, said the world.
This is not to say
it spoke in exact sentences
but that I perceived beauty in this manner.

Sunrise. A film of moisture
on each living thing. Pools of cold light
formed in the gutters.

I stood
at the doorway,
ridiculous as it now seems.

What others found in art,
I found in nature. What others found
in human love, I found in nature.
Very simple. But there was no voice there.

Winter was over. In the thawed dirt,
bits of green were showing.

Come to me, said the world. I was standing
in my wool coat at a kind of bright portal—
I can finally say
long ago; it gives me considerable pleasure. Beauty

the healer, the teacher—

death cannot harm me
more than you have harmed me,
my beloved life.

4.

The light has changed;
middle C is tuned darker now.
And the songs of morning sound over-rehearsed.

This is the light of autumn, not the light of spring.
The light of autumn: *you will not be spared*.

The songs have changed; the unspeakable
has entered them.

This is the light of autumn, not the light that says
I am reborn.

Not the spring dawn: *I strained, I suffered, I was delivered.*
This is the present, an allegory of waste.

So much has changed. And still, you are fortunate:
the ideal burns in you like a fever.
Or not like a fever, like a second heart.

The songs have changed, but really they are still quite beautiful.
They have been concentrated in a smaller space, the space of the mind.
They are dark, now, with desolation and anguish.

And yet the notes recur. They hover oddly
in anticipation of silence.
The ear gets used to them.
The eye gets used to disappearances.

You will not be spared, nor will what you love be spared.

A wind has come and gone, taking apart the mind;
it has left in its wake a strange lucidity.

How privileged you are, to be still passionately
clinging to what you love;
the forfeit of hope has not destroyed you.

Maestoso, doloroso:

This is the light of autumn; it has turned on us.
Surely it is a privilege to approach the end
still believing in something.

5.

It is true there is not enough beauty in the world.
It is also true that I am not competent to restore it.
Neither is there candor, and here I may be of some use.

I am
at work, though I am silent.

The bland

misery of the world
bounds us on either side, an alley

lined with trees; we are

companions here, not speaking,
each with his own thoughts;

behind the trees, iron
gates of the private houses,
the shuttered rooms

somehow deserted, abandoned,

as though it were the artist's
duty to create
hope, but out of what? what?

the word itself
false, a device to refute
perception— At the intersection,

ornamental lights of the season.

I was young here. Riding
the subway with my small book
as though to defend myself against

this same world:

you are not alone,
the poem said,
in the dark tunnel.

6.

The brightness of the day becomes
the brightness of the night;
the fire becomes the mirror.

My friend the earth is bitter; I think
sunlight has failed her.
Bitter or weary, it is hard to say.

Between herself and the sun,
something has ended.
She wants, now, to be left alone;
I think we must give up
turning to her for affirmation.

Above the fields,
above the roofs of the village houses,
the brilliance that made all life possible
becomes the cold stars.

Lie still and watch:
they give nothing but ask nothing.

From within the earth's
bitter disgrace, coldness and barrenness

my friend the moon rises:
she is beautiful tonight, but when is she not beautiful?

PERSEPHONE THE WANDERER

In the first version, Persephone
is taken from her mother
and the goddess of the earth
punishes the earth—this is
consistent with what we know of human behavior,

that human beings take profound satisfaction
in doing harm, particularly
unconscious harm:

we may call this
negative creation.

Persephone's initial
sojourn in hell continues to be
pawed over by scholars who dispute
the sensations of the virgin:

did she cooperate in her rape,
or was she drugged, violated against her will,
as happens so often now to modern girls.

As is well known, the return of the beloved
does not correct
the loss of the beloved: Persephone

returns home
stained with red juice like
a character in Hawthorne—

I am not certain I will
keep this word: is earth
"home" to Persephone? Is she at home, conceivably,
in the bed of the god? Is she
at home nowhere? Is she
a born wanderer, in other words
an existential
replica of her own mother, less
hamstrung by ideas of causality?

You are allowed to like
no one, you know. The characters
are not people.
They are aspects of a dilemma or conflict.

Three parts: just as the soul is divided,
ego, superego, id. Likewise

the three levels of the known world,
a kind of diagram that separates
heaven from earth from hell.

You must ask yourself:
where is it snowing?

White of forgetfulness,
of desecration—

It is snowing on earth; the cold wind says

Persephone is having sex in hell.
Unlike the rest of us, she doesn't know
what winter is, only that
she is what causes it.

She is lying in the bed of Hades.
What is in her mind?
Is she afraid? Has something
blotted out the idea
of mind?

She does know the earth
is run by mothers, this much
is certain. She also knows
she is not what is called
a girl any longer. Regarding
incarceration, she believes

she has been a prisoner since she has been a daughter.

The terrible reunions in store for her
will take up the rest of her life.
When the passion for expiation
is chronic, fierce, you do not choose
the way you live. You do not live;
you are not allowed to die.

You drift between earth and death
which seem, finally,
strangely alike. Scholars tell us

that there is no point in knowing what you want
when the forces contending over you
could kill you.

White of forgetfulness,
white of safety—

They say
there is a rift in the human soul
which was not constructed to belong
entirely to life. Earth

asks us to deny this rift, a threat
disguised as suggestion—
as we have seen
in the tale of Persephone
which should be read

as an argument between the mother and the lover—
the daughter is just meat.

When death confronts her, she has never seen
the meadow without the daisies.
Suddenly she is no longer
singing her maidenly songs
about her mother's
beauty and fecundity. Where
the rift is, the break is.

Song of the earth,
song of the mythic vision of eternal life—

My soul
shattered with the strain
of trying to belong to earth—

What will you do,
when it is your turn in the field with the god?

PRISM

1.

Who can say what the world is? The world
is in flux, therefore
unreadable, the winds shifting,
the great plates invisibly shifting and changing—

2.

Dirt. Fragments
of blistered rock. On which
the exposed heart constructs
a house, memory: the gardens
manageable, small in scale, the beds
damp at the sea's edge—

3.

As one takes in
an enemy, through these windows
one takes in
the world:

here is the kitchen, here the darkened study.

Meaning: I am master here.

4.

When you fall in love, my sister said,
it's like being struck by lightning.

She was speaking hopefully,
to draw the attention of the lightning.

I reminded her that she was repeating exactly
our mother's formula, which she and I

had discussed in childhood, because we both felt
that what we were looking at in the adults

were the effects not of lightning
but of the electric chair.

5.

Riddle:
Why was my mother happy?

Answer:
She married my father.

6.

"You girls," my mother said, "should marry
someone like your father."

That was one remark. Another was,
"There is no one like your father."

7.

From the pierced clouds, steady lines of silver.

Unlikely
yellow of the witch hazel, veins
of mercury that were the paths of the rivers—

Then the rain again, erasing
footprints in the damp earth.
An implied path, like
a map without a crossroads.

8.

The implication was, it was necessary to abandon
childhood. The word "marry" was a signal.
You could also treat it as aesthetic advice;
the voice of the child was tiresome,
it had no lower register.
The word was a code, mysterious, like the Rosetta stone.
It was also a roadsign, a warning.
You could take a few things with you like a dowry.
You could take the part of you that thought.
"Marry" meant you should keep that part quiet.

9.

A night in summer. Outside,
sounds of a summer storm. Then the sky clearing.
In the window, constellations of summer.

I'm in a bed. This man and I,
we are suspended in the strange calm
sex often induces. Most sex induces.
Longing, what is that? Desire, what is that?

In the window, constellations of summer.
Once, I could name them.

10.

Abstracted
shapes, patterns.
The light of the mind. The cold, exacting
fires of disinterestedness, curiously

blocked by earth, coherent, glittering
in air and water,

the elaborate
signs that said *now plant, now harvest*—

I could name them, I had names for them:
two different things.

11.

Fabulous things, stars.

When I was a child, I suffered from insomnia.
Summer nights, my parents permitted me to sit by the lake;
I took the dog for company.

Did I say "suffered"? That was my parents' way of explaining
tastes that seemed to them
inexplicable: better "suffered" than "preferred to live with the dog."

Darkness. Silence that annulled mortality.
The tethered boats rising and falling.
When the moon was full, I could sometimes read the girls' names
painted to the sides of the boats:
Ruth Ann, Sweet Izzy, Peggy My Darling—

They were going nowhere, those girls.
There was nothing to be learned from them.

I spread my jacket in the damp sand,
the dog curled up beside me.
My parents couldn't see the life in my head;
when I wrote it down, they fixed the spelling.

Sounds of the lake. The soothing, inhuman
sounds of water lapping the dock, the dog scuffling somewhere
in the weeds—

12.

The assignment was to fall in love.
The details were up to you.
The second part was
to include in the poem certain words,
words drawn from a specific text
on another subject altogether.

13.

Spring rain, then a night in summer.
A man's voice, then a woman's voice.

You grew up, you were struck by lightning.
When you opened your eyes, you were wired forever to your true love.

It only happened once. Then you were taken care of,
your story was finished.

It happened once. Being struck was like being vaccinated;
the rest of your life you were immune,
you were warm and dry.

Unless the shock wasn't deep enough.
Then you weren't vaccinated, you were addicted.

14.

The assignment was to fall in love.
The author was female.
The ego had to be called the soul.

The action took place in the body.
Stars represented everything else: dreams, the mind, etc.

The beloved was identified
with the self in a narcissistic projection.
The mind was a subplot. It went nattering on.

Time was experienced
less as narrative than ritual.
What was repeated had weight.

Certain endings were tragic, thus acceptable.
Everything else was failure.

15.

Deceit. Lies. Embellishments we call
hypotheses—

There were too many roads, too many versions.
There were too many roads, no one path—

And at the end?

16.

List the implications of "crossroads."

Answer: a story that will have a moral.

Give a counter-example:

17.

The self ended and the world began.
They were of equal size,
commensurate,
one mirrored the other.

18.

The riddle was: why couldn't we live in the mind.

The answer was: the barrier of the earth intervened.

19.

The room was quiet.
That is, the room was quiet, but the lovers were breathing.

In the same way, the night was dark.
It was dark, but the stars shone.

The man in bed was one of several men
to whom I gave my heart. The gift of the self,
that is without limit.
Without limit, though it recurs.

The room was quiet. It was an absolute,
like the black night.

20.

A night in summer. Sounds of a summer storm.
The great plates invisibly shifting and changing—

And in the dark room, the lovers sleeping in each other's arms.

We are, each of us, the one who wakens first,
who stirs first and sees, there in the first dawn,
the stranger.

CRATER LAKE

There was a war between good and evil.
We decided to call the body good.

That made death evil.
It turned the soul
against death completely.

Like a foot soldier wanting
to serve a great warrior, the soul
wanted to side with the body.

It turned against the dark,
against the forms of death
it recognized.

Where does the voice come from
that says suppose the war
is evil, that says

suppose the body did this to us,
made us afraid of love—

ECHOES

I.

Once I could imagine my soul
I could imagine my death.
When I imagined my death
my soul died. This
I remember clearly.

My body persisted.
Not thrived, but persisted.
Why I do not know.

2.

When I was still very young
my parents moved to a small valley
surrounded by mountains
in what was called the lake country.
From our kitchen garden
you could see the mountains,
snow covered, even in summer.

I remember peace of a kind
I never knew again.

Somewhat later, I took it upon myself
to become an artist,
to give voice to these impressions.

3.

The rest I have told you already.
A few years of fluency, and then
the long silence, like the silence in the valley
before the mountains send back
your own voice changed to the voice of nature.

This silence is my companion now.
I ask: *of what did my soul die?*
and the silence answers

*if your soul died, whose life
are you living and
when did you become that person?*

FUGUE

1.

I was the man because I was taller.
My sister decided
when we should eat.
From time to time, she'd have a baby.

2.

Then my soul appeared.
Who are you, I said.
And my soul said,
I am your soul, the winsome stranger.

3.

Our dead sister
waited, undiscovered in my mother's head.
Our dead sister was neither
a man nor a woman. She was like a soul.

4.

My soul was taken in:
it attached itself to a man.
Not a real man, the man
I pretended to be, playing with my sister.

5.

It is coming back to me—lying on the couch
has refreshed my memory.
My memory is like a basement filled with old papers:
nothing ever changes.

6.

I had a dream: my mother fell out of a tree.
After she fell, the tree died:
it had outlived its function.
My mother was unharmed—her arrows disappeared, her wings
turned into arms. Fire creature: Sagittarius. She finds herself in—

a suburban garden. It is coming back to me.

7.

I put the book aside. What is a soul?
A flag flown
too high on the pole, if you know what I mean.

The body
cowers in the dreamlike underbrush.

8.

Well, we are here to do something about that.

(In a German accent.)

9.

I had a dream: we are at war.
My mother leaves her crossbow in the high grass.

(Sagittarius, the archer.)

My childhood, closed to me forever,
turned gold like an autumn garden,
mulched with a thick layer of salt marsh hay.

10.

A golden bow: a useful gift in wartime.

How heavy it was—no child could pick it up.

Except me: I could pick it up.

11.

Then I was wounded. The bow
was now a harp, its string cutting
deep into my palm. In the dream

it both makes the wound and seals the wound.

12.

My childhood: closed to me. Or is it
under the mulch—fertile.

But very dark. Very hidden.

13.

In the dark, my soul said
I am your soul.

No one can see me; only you—
only you can see me.

14.

And it said, you must trust me.

Meaning: if you move the harp,
you will bleed to death.

15.

Why can't I cry out?

I should be writing *my hand is bleeding*,
feeling pain and terror—what
I felt in the dream, as a casualty of war.

16.

It is coming back to me.

Pear tree. Apple tree.

I used to sit there
pulling arrows out of my heart.

17.

Then my soul appeared. It said
just as no one can see me, no one
can see the blood.

Also: no one can see the harp.

Then it said
I can save you. Meaning
this is a test.

18.

Who is "you"? As in

"Are you tired of invisible pain?"

19.

Like a small bird sealed off from daylight:

that was my childhood.

20.

I was the man because I was taller.

But I wasn't tall—
didn't I ever look in a mirror?

21.

Silence in the nursery,
the consulting garden. Then:

What does the harp suggest?

22.

I know what you want—
you want Orpheus, you want death.

Orpheus who said "Help me find Eurydice."

Then the music began, the lament of the soul
watching the body vanish.

II

THE EVENING STAR

Tonight, for the first time in many years,
there appeared to me again
a vision of the earth's splendor:

in the evening sky
the first star seemed
to increase in brilliance
as the earth darkened

until at last it could grow no darker.
And the light, which was the light of death,
seemed to restore to earth

its power to console. There were
no other stars. Only the one
whose name I knew

as in my other life I did her
injury: Venus,
star of the early evening,

to you I dedicate
my vision, since on this blank surface

you have cast enough light
to make my thought
visible again.

LANDSCAPE

—*for Keith Monley*

1.

The sun is setting behind the mountains,
the earth is cooling.
A stranger has tied his horse to a bare chestnut tree.
The horse is quiet—he turns his head suddenly,
hearing, in the distance, the sound of the sea.

I make my bed for the night here,
spreading my heaviest quilt over the damp earth.

The sound of the sea—
when the horse turns its head, I can hear it.

On a path through the bare chestnut trees,
a little dog trails its master.

The little dog—didn't he used to rush ahead,
straining the leash, as though to show his master
what he sees there, there in the future—

the future, the path, call it what you will.

Behind the trees, at sunset, it is as though a great fire
is burning between two mountains
so that the snow on the highest precipice
seems, for a moment, to be burning also.

Listen: at the path's end the man is calling out.
His voice has become very strange now,
the voice of a person calling to what he can't see.

Over and over he calls out among the dark chestnut trees.

Until the animal responds
faintly, from a great distance,
as though this thing we fear
were not terrible.

Twilight: the stranger has untied his horse.

The sound of the sea—
just memory now.

2.

Time passed, turning everything to ice.
Under the ice, the future stirred.
If you fell into it, you died.

It was a time
of waiting, of suspended action.

I lived in the present, which was
that part of the future you could see.
The past floated above my head,
like the sun and moon, visible but never reachable.

It was a time
governed by contradictions, as in
I felt nothing and
I was afraid.

Winter emptied the trees, filled them again with snow.
Because I couldn't feel, snow fell, the lake froze over.
Because I was afraid, I didn't move;
my breath was white, a description of silence.

Time passed, and some of it became this.

And some of it simply evaporated;
you could see it float above the white trees
forming particles of ice.

All your life, you wait for the propitious time.
Then the propitious time
reveals itself as action taken.

I watched the past move, a line of clouds moving
from left to right or right to left,
depending on the wind. Some days

there was no wind. The clouds seemed
to stay where they were,
like a painting of the sea, more still than real.

Some days the lake was a sheet of glass.
Under the glass, the future made
demure, inviting sounds:
you had to tense yourself so as not to listen.

Time passed; you got to see a piece of it.
The years it took with it were years of winter;
they would not be missed. Some days

there were no clouds, as though
the sources of the past had vanished. The world

was bleached, like a negative; the light passed
directly through it. Then
the image faded.

Above the world
there was only blue, blue everywhere.

3.

In late autumn a young girl set fire to a field
of wheat. The autumn

had been very dry; the field
went up like tinder.

Afterward there was nothing left.
You walk through it, you see nothing.

There's nothing to pick up, to smell.
The horses don't understand it—

Where is the field, they seem to say.
The way you and I would say
where is home.

No one knows how to answer them.
There is nothing left;
you have to hope, for the farmer's sake,
the insurance will pay.

It is like losing a year of your life.
To what would you lose a year of your life?

Afterward, you go back to the old place—
all that remains is char: blackness and emptiness.

You think: how could I live here?

But it was different then,
even last summer. The earth behaved

as though nothing could go wrong with it.

One match was all it took.
But at the right time—it had to be the right time.

The field parched, dry—
the deadness in place already
so to speak.

4.

I fell asleep in a river, I woke in a river,
of my mysterious
failure to die I can tell you
nothing, neither
who saved me nor for what cause—

There was immense silence.
No wind. No human sound.
The bitter century

was ended,
the glorious gone, the abiding gone,

the cold sun
persisting as a kind of curiosity, a memento,
time streaming behind it—

The sky seemed very clear,
as it is in winter,
the soil dry, uncultivated,

the official light calmly
moving through a slot in air

dignified, complacent,
dissolving hope,
subordinating images of the future to signs of the future's passing—

I think I must have fallen.
When I tried to stand, I had to force myself,
being unused to physical pain—

I had forgotten
how harsh these conditions are:

the earth not obsolete
but still, the river cold, shallow—

Of my sleep, I remember
nothing. When I cried out,
my voice soothed me unexpectedly.

In the silence of consciousness I asked myself:
why did I reject my life? And I answer
Die Erde überwältigt mich:
the earth defeats me.

I have tried to be accurate in this description
in case someone else should follow me. I can verify
that when the sun sets in winter it is
incomparably beautiful and the memory of it
lasts a long time. I think this means

there was no night.
The night was in my head.

5.

After the sun set
we rode quickly, in the hope of finding
shelter before darkness.

I could see the stars already,
first in the eastern sky:

we rode, therefore,
away from the light
and toward the sea, since
I had heard of a village there.

After some time, the snow began.
Not thickly at first, then
steadily until the earth
was covered with a white film.

The way we traveled showed
clearly when I turned my head—
for a short while it made
a dark trajectory across the earth—

Then the snow was thick, the path vanished.
The horse was tired and hungry;
he could no longer find
sure footing anywhere. I told myself:

I have been lost before, I have been cold before.
The night has come to me
exactly this way, as a premonition—

And I thought: if I am asked
to return here, I would like to come back
as a human being, and my horse

to remain himself. Otherwise
I would not know how to begin again.

A MYTH OF INNOCENCE

One summer she goes into the field as usual
stopping for a bit at the pool where she often
looks at herself, to see
if she detects any changes. She sees
the same person, the horrible mantle
of daughterliness still clinging to her.

The sun seems, in the water, very close.
That's my uncle spying again, she thinks—
everything in nature is in some way her relative.
I am never alone, she thinks,
turning the thought into a prayer.
Then death appears, like the answer to a prayer.

No one understands anymore
how beautiful he was. But Persephone remembers.
Also that he embraced her, right there,
with her uncle watching. She remembers
sunlight flashing on his bare arms.

This is the last moment she remembers clearly.
Then the dark god bore her away.

She also remembers, less clearly,
the chilling insight that from this moment
she couldn't live without him again.

The girl who disappears from the pool
will never return. A woman will return,
looking for the girl she was.

She stands by the pool saying, from time to time,
I was abducted, but it sounds
wrong to her, nothing like what she felt.
Then she says, *I was not abducted*.

Then she says, *I offered myself, I wanted
to escape my body.* Even, sometimes,
I willed this. But ignorance

cannot will knowledge. Ignorance
wills something imagined, which it believes exists.

All the different nouns—
she says them in rotation.
Death, husband, god, stranger.
Everything sounds so simple, so conventional.
I must have been, she thinks, a simple girl.

She can't remember herself as that person
but she keeps thinking the pool will remember
and explain to her the meaning of her prayer
so she can understand
whether it was answered or not.

ARCHAIC FRAGMENT

—for Dana Levin

I was trying to love matter.
I taped a sign over the mirror:
You cannot hate matter and love form.

It was a beautiful day, though cold.
This was, for me, an extravagantly emotional gesture.

. . . . your poem:
tried, but could not.

I taped a sign over the first sign:
Cry, weep, thrash yourself, rend your garments—

List of things to love:
dirt, food, shells, human hair.

. . . . said
tasteless excess. Then I

rent the signs.

AIAIAIAI cried
the naked mirror.

BLUE ROTUNDA

I am tired of having hands
she said
I want wings—

But what will you do without your hands
to be human?

I am tired of human
she said
I want to live on the sun—

.

Pointing to herself:

Not here.
There is not enough
warmth in this place.
Blue sky, blue ice

the blue rotunda
lifted over
the flat street—

And then, after a silence:

.

I want
my heart back
I want to feel everything again—

That's what
the sun meant: it meant
scorched—

.

It is not finally
interesting to remember.
The damage

is not interesting.
No one who knew me then
is still alive.

My mother
was a beautiful woman—
they all said so.

•

I have to imagine
everything
she said

I have to act
as though there is actually
a map to that place:

when you were a child—

•

And then:

I'm here
because it wasn't true; I

distorted it—

•

I want she said
a theory that explains
everything

in the mother's eye
the invisible
splinter of foil

the blue ice
locked in the iris—

.

Then:

I want it
to be my fault
she said
so I can fix it—

.

Blue sky, blue ice,
street like a frozen river

you're talking
about my life
she said

.

except
she said
you have to fix it

in the right order
not touching the father
until you solve the mother

.

a black space
showing
where the word ends

like a crossword saying
you should take a breath now

the black space meaning
when you were a child—

                •

And then:

the ice
was there for your own protection

to teach you
not to feel—

the truth
she said

I thought it would be like
a target, you would see

the center—

                •

Cold light filling the room.

I know where we are
she said
that's the window
when I was a child

That's my first home, she said
that square box—
go ahead and laugh.

Like the inside of my head:
you can see out
but you can't go out—

 .

Just think
the sun was there, in that bare place

the winter sun
not close enough to reach
the children's hearts

the light saying
you can see out
but you can't go out

Here, it says,
here is where everything belongs

A MYTH OF DEVOTION

When Hades decided he loved this girl
he built for her a duplicate of earth,
everything the same, down to the meadow,
but with a bed added.

Everything the same, including sunlight,
because it would be hard on a young girl
to go so quickly from bright light to utter darkness.

Gradually, he thought, he'd introduce the night,
first as the shadows of fluttering leaves.
Then moon, then stars. Then no moon, no stars.
Let Persephone get used to it slowly.
In the end, he thought, she'd find it comforting.

A replica of earth
except there was love here.
Doesn't everyone want love?

He waited many years,
building a world, watching
Persephone in the meadow.
Persephone, a smeller, a taster.
If you have one appetite, he thought,
you have them all.

Doesn't everyone want to feel in the night
the beloved body, compass, polestar,
to hear the quiet breathing that says
I am alive, that means also
you are alive, because you hear me,
you are here with me. And when one turns,
the other turns—

That's what he felt, the lord of darkness,
looking at the world he had
constructed for Persephone. It never crossed his mind
that there'd be no more smelling here,
certainly no more eating.

Guilt? Terror? The fear of love?
These things he couldn't imagine;
no lover ever imagines them.

He dreams, he wonders what to call this place.
First he thinks: *The New Hell.* Then: *The Garden.*
In the end, he decides to name it
Persephone's Girlhood.

A soft light rising above the level meadow,
behind the bed. He takes her in his arms.
He wants to say *I love you, nothing can hurt you*

but he thinks
this is a lie, so he says in the end
you're dead, nothing can hurt you
which seems to him
a more promising beginning, more true.

AVERNO

I.

You die when your spirit dies.
Otherwise, you live.
You may not do a good job of it, but you go on—
something you have no choice about.

When I tell this to my children
they pay no attention.
The old people, they think—
this is what they always do:
talk about things no one can see
to cover up all the brain cells they're losing.
They wink at each other;
listen to the old one, talking about the spirit
because he can't remember anymore the word for chair.

It is terrible to be alone.
I don't mean to live alone—
to *be* alone, where no one hears you.

I remember the word for chair.
I want to say—I'm just not interested anymore.

I wake up thinking
you have to prepare.
Soon the spirit will give up—
all the chairs in the world won't help you.

I know what they say when I'm out of the room.
Should I be seeing someone, should I be taking
one of the new drugs for depression.
I can hear them, in whispers, planning how to divide the cost.

And I want to scream out
you're all of you living in a dream.

Bad enough, they think, to watch me falling apart.
Bad enough without this lecturing they get these days
as though I had any right to this new information.

Well, they have the same right.

They're living in a dream, and I'm preparing
to be a ghost. I want to shout out

the mist has cleared—
It's like some new life:
you have no stake in the outcome;
you know the outcome.

Think of it: sixty years sitting in chairs. And now the mortal spirit
seeking so openly, so fearlessly—

To raise the veil.
To see what you're saying goodbye to.

2.

I didn't go back for a long time.
When I saw the field again, autumn was finished.
Here, it finishes almost before it starts—
the old people don't even own summer clothing.

The field was covered with snow, immaculate.
There wasn't a sign of what happened here.
You didn't know whether the farmer
had replanted or not.
Maybe he gave up and moved away.

The police didn't catch the girl.
After awhile they said she moved to some other country,
one where they don't have fields.

A disaster like this
leaves no mark on the earth.
And people like that—they think it gives them
a fresh start.

I stood a long time, staring at nothing.
After a bit, I noticed how dark it was, how cold.

A long time—I have no idea how long.
Once the earth decides to have no memory
time seems in a way meaningless.

But not to my children. They're after me
to make a will; they're worried the government
will take everything.

They should come with me sometime
to look at this field under the cover of snow.
The whole thing is written out there.

Nothing: I have nothing to give them.

That's the first part.
The second is: I don't want to be burned.

3.

On one side, the soul wanders.
On the other, human beings living in fear.
In between, the pit of disappearance.

Some young girls ask me
if they'll be safe near Averno—
they're cold, they want to go south a little while.
And one says, like a joke, but not too far south—

I say, as safe as anywhere,
which makes them happy.
What it means is nothing is safe.

You get on a train, you disappear.
You write your name on the window, you disappear.

There are places like this everywhere,
places you enter as a young girl,
from which you never return.

Like the field, the one that burned.
Afterward, the girl was gone.
Maybe she didn't exist,
we have no proof either way.

All we know is:
the field burned.
But we *saw* that.

So we have to believe in the girl,
in what she did. Otherwise
it's just forces we don't understand
ruling the earth.

The girls are happy, thinking of their vacation.
Don't take a train, I say.

They write their names in mist on a train window.
I want to say, you're good girls,
trying to leave your names behind.

4.

We spent the whole day
sailing the archipelago,
the tiny islands that were
part of the peninsula

until they'd broken off
into the fragments you see now
floating in the northern sea water.

They seemed safe to me,
I think because no one can live there.

Later we sat in the kitchen
watching the evening start and then the snow.
First one, then the other.

We grew silent, hypnotized by the snow
as though a kind of turbulence
that had been hidden before
was becoming visible,

something within the night
exposed now—

In our silence, we were asking
those questions friends who trust each other
ask out of great fatigue,
each one hoping the other knows more

and when this isn't so, hoping
their shared impressions will amount to insight.

Is there any benefit in forcing upon oneself
the realization that one must die?
Is it possible to miss the opportunity of one's life?

Questions like that.

The snow heavy. The black night
transformed into busy white air.

Something we hadn't seen revealed.
Only the meaning wasn't revealed.

5.

After the first winter, the field began to grow again.
But there were no more orderly furrows.
The smell of the wheat persisted, a kind of random aroma
intermixed with various weeds, for which
no human use has been as yet devised.

It was puzzling—no one knew
where the farmer had gone.
Some people thought he died.
Someone said he had a daughter in New Zealand,
that he went there to raise
grandchildren instead of wheat.

Nature, it turns out, isn't like us;
it doesn't have a warehouse of memory.
The field doesn't become afraid of matches,

of young girls. It doesn't remember
furrows either. It gets killed off, it gets burned,
and a year later it's alive again
as though nothing unusual has occurred.

The farmer stares out the window.
Maybe in New Zealand, maybe somewhere else.
And he thinks: *my life is over.*
His life expressed itself in that field;
he doesn't believe anymore in making anything
out of earth. The earth, he thinks,
has overpowered me.

He remembers the day the field burned,
not, he thinks, by accident.
Something deep within him said: *I can live with this,
I can fight it after awhile.*

The terrible moment was the spring after his work was erased,
when he understood that the earth
didn't know how to mourn, that it would change instead.
And then go on existing without him.

OMENS

I rode to meet you: dreams
like living beings swarmed around me
and the moon on my right side
followed me, burning.

I rode back: everything changed.
My soul in love was sad
and the moon on my left side
trailed me without hope.

To such endless impressions
we poets give ourselves absolutely,
making, in silence, omen of mere event,
until the world reflects the deepest needs of the soul.

after Alexander Pushkin

TELESCOPE

There is a moment after you move your eye away
when you forget where you are
because you've been living, it seems,
somewhere else, in the silence of the night sky.

You've stopped being here in the world.
You're in a different place,
a place where human life has no meaning.

You're not a creature in a body.
You exist as the stars exist,
participating in their stillness, their immensity.

Then you're in the world again.
At night, on a cold hill,
taking the telescope apart.

You realize afterward
not that the image is false
but the relation is false.

You see again how far away
each thing is from every other thing.

THRUSH

—for Noah Max Horwitz and Susan Kimmelman, in memory

Snow began falling, over the surface of the whole earth.
That can't be true. And yet it felt true,
falling more and more thickly over everything I could see.
The pines turned brittle with ice.

This is the place I told you about,
where I used to come at night to see the red-winged blackbirds,
what we call *thrush* here—
red flicker of the life that disappears—

But for me—I think the guilt I feel must mean
I haven't lived very well.

Someone like me doesn't escape. I think you sleep awhile,
then you descend into the terror of the next life
except

the soul is in some different form,
more or less conscious than it was before,
more or less covetous.

After many lives, maybe something changes.
I think in the end what you want
you'll be able to see—

Then you don't need anymore
to die and come back again.

In the second version, Persephone
is dead. She dies, her mother grieves—
problems of sexuality need not
trouble us here.

Compulsively, in grief, Demeter
circles the earth. We don't expect to know
what Persephone is doing.
She is dead, the dead are mysteries.

We have here
a mother and a cipher: this is
accurate to the experience
of the mother as

she looks into the infant's face. She thinks:
I remember when you didn't exist. The infant
is puzzled; later, the child's opinion is
she has always existed, just as

her mother has always existed
in her present form. Her mother
is like a figure at a bus stop,
an audience for the bus's arrival. Before that,
she was the bus, a temporary
home or convenience. Persephone, protected,
stares out the window of the chariot.

What does she see? A morning
in early spring, in April. Now

her whole life is beginning—unfortunately,
it's going to be
a short life. She's going to know, really,

only two adults: death and her mother.
But two is
twice what her mother has:
her mother has

one child, a daughter.
As a god, she could have had
a thousand children.

We begin to see here
the deep violence of the earth

whose hostility suggests
she has no wish
to continue as a source of life.

And why is this hypothesis
never discussed? Because
it is not *in* the story; it only
creates the story.

In grief, after the daughter dies,
the mother wanders the earth.
She is preparing her case;
like a politician
she remembers everything and admits
nothing.

For example, her daughter's
birth was unbearable, her beauty
was unbearable: she remembers this.
She remembers Persephone's
innocence, her tenderness—

What is she planning, seeking her daughter?
She is issuing
a warning whose implicit message is:
what are you doing outside my body?

You ask yourself:
why is the mother's body safe?

The answer is
this is the wrong question, since

the daughter's body
doesn't exist, except
as a branch of the mother's body
that needs to be
reattached at any cost.

When a god grieves it means
destroying others (as in war)
while at the same time petitioning
to reverse agreements (as in war also):

if Zeus will get her back,
winter will end.

Winter will end, spring will return.
The small pestering breezes
that I so loved, the idiot yellow flowers—

Spring will return, a dream
based on a falsehood:
that the dead return.

Persephone
was used to death. Now over and over
her mother hauls her out again—

You must ask yourself:
are the flowers real? If

Persephone "returns" there will be
one of two reasons:

either she was not dead or
she is being used
to support a fiction—

I think I can remember
being dead. Many times, in winter,
I approached Zeus. Tell me, I would ask him,
how can I endure the earth?

And he would say,
in a short time you will be here again.
And in the time between

you will forget everything:
those fields of ice will be
the meadows of Elysium.

A VILLAGE LIFE

(2009)

TO JAMES LONGENBACH

TWILIGHT

All day he works at his cousin's mill,
so when he gets home at night, he always sits at this one window,
sees one time of day, twilight.
There should be more time like this, to sit and dream.
It's as his cousin says:
Living—living takes you away from sitting.

In the window, not the world but a squared-off landscape
representing the world. The seasons change,
each visible only a few hours a day.
Green things followed by golden things followed by whiteness—
abstractions from which come intense pleasures,
like the figs on the table.

At dusk, the sun goes down in a haze of red fire between two poplars.
It goes down late in summer—sometimes it's hard to stay awake.

Then everything falls away.
The world for a little longer
is something to see, then only something to hear,
crickets, cicadas.
Or to smell sometimes, aroma of lemon trees, of orange trees.
Then sleep takes this away also.

But it's easy to give things up like this, experimentally,
for a matter of hours.

I open my fingers—
I let everything go.

Visual world, language,
rustling of leaves in the night,
smell of high grass, of woodsmoke.

I let it go, then I light the candle.

PASTORAL

The sun rises over the mountain.
Sometimes there's mist
but the sun's behind it always
and the mist isn't equal to it.
The sun burns its way through,
like the mind defeating stupidity.
When the mist clears, you see the meadow.

No one really understands
the savagery of this place,
the way it kills people for no reason,
just to keep in practice.

So people flee—and for a while, away from here,
they're exuberant, surrounded by so many choices—

But no signal from earth
will ever reach the sun. Thrash
against that fact, you are lost.

When they come back, they're worse.
They think they failed in the city,
not that the city doesn't make good its promises.
They blame their upbringing: youth ended and they're back,
silent, like their fathers.
Sundays, in summer, they lean against the wall of the clinic,
smoking cigarettes. When they remember,
they pick flowers for their girlfriends—

It makes the girls happy.
They think it's pretty here, but they miss the city, the afternoons
filled with shopping and talking, what you do
when you have no money...

To my mind, you're better off if you stay;
that way, dreams don't damage you.
At dusk, you sit by the window. Wherever you live,
you can see the fields, the river, realities
on which you cannot impose yourself—

To me, it's safe. The sun rises; the mist
dissipates to reveal
the immense mountain. You can see the peak,
how white it is, even in summer. And the sky's so blue,
punctuated with small pines
like spears—

When you got tired of walking
you lay down in the grass.
When you got up again, you could see for a moment where you'd been,
the grass was slick there, flattened out
into the shape of a body. When you looked back later,
it was as though you'd never been there at all.

Midafternoon, midsummer. The fields go on forever,
peaceful, beautiful.
Like butterflies with their black markings,
the poppies open.

TRIBUTARIES

All the roads in the village unite at the fountain.
Avenue of Liberty, Avenue of the Acacia Trees—
The fountain rises at the center of the plaza;
on sunny days, rainbows in the piss of the cherub.

In summer, couples sit at the pool's edge.
There's room in the pool for many reflections—
the plaza's nearly empty, the acacia trees don't get this far.
And the Avenue of Liberty is barren and austere; its image
doesn't crowd the water.

Interspersed with the couples, mothers with their younger children.
Here's where they come to talk to one another, maybe
meet a young man, see if there's anything left of their beauty.
When they look down, it's a sad moment: the water isn't encouraging.

The husbands are off working, but by some miracle
all the amorous young men are always free—
they sit at the edge of the fountain, splashing their sweethearts
with fountain water.

Around the fountain, there are clusters of metal tables.
This is where you sit when you're old,
beyond the intensities of the fountain.
The fountain is for the young, who still want to look at themselves.
Or for the mothers, who need to keep their children diverted.

In good weather, a few old people linger at the tables.
Life is simple now: one day cognac, one day coffee and a cigarette.
To the couples, it's clear who's on the outskirts of life, who's at the center.

The children cry, they sometimes fight over toys.
But the water's there, to remind the mothers that they love these children;
that for them to drown would be terrible.

The mothers are tired constantly, the children are always fighting,
the husbands at work or angry. No young man comes.
The couples are like an image from some faraway time, an echo coming
very faint from the mountains.

They're alone at the fountain, in a dark well.
They've been exiled by the world of hope,
which is the world of action,
but the world of thought hasn't as yet opened to them.
When it does, everything will change.

Darkness is falling, the plaza empties.
The first leaves of autumn litter the fountain.
The roads don't gather here anymore;
the fountain sends them away, back into the hills they came from.

Avenue of Broken Faith, Avenue of Disappointment,
Avenue of the Acacia Trees, of Olive Trees,
the wind filling with silver leaves,

Avenue of Lost Time, Avenue of Liberty that ends in stone,
not at the field's edge but at the foot of the mountain.

They're not grown up—more like a boy and girl, really.
School's over. It's the best part of the summer, when it's still beginning—
the sun's shining, but the heat isn't intense yet.
And freedom hasn't gotten boring.

So you can spend the whole day, all of it, wandering in the meadow.
The meadow goes on indefinitely, and the village keeps getting more and
more faint—

It seems a strange position, being very young.
They have this thing everyone wants and they *don't* want—
but they want to keep it anyway; it's all they can trade on.

When they're by themselves like this, these are the things they talk about.
How time for them doesn't race.
It's like the reel breaking at the movie theater. They stay anyway—
mainly, they just don't want to leave. But till the reel is fixed,
the old one just gets popped back in,
and all of a sudden you're back to long ago in the movie—
the hero hasn't even met the heroine. He's still at the factory,
he hasn't begun to go bad. And she's wandering around the docks, already bad.
But she never meant it to happen. She was good, then it happened to her,
like a bag pulled over her head.

The sky's completely blue, so the grass is dry.
They'll be able to sit with no trouble.
They sit, they talk about everything—then they eat their picnic.
They put the food on the blanket, so it stays clean.
They've always done it this way; they take the grass themselves.

The rest—how two people can lie down on the blanket—
they know about it but they're not ready for it.
They know people who've done it, as a kind of game or trial—
then you say, no, wrong time, I think I'll just keep being a child.

But your body doesn't listen. It knows everything now,
it says you're not a child, you haven't been a child for a long time.

Their thinking is, stay away from change. It's an avalanche—
all the rocks sliding down the mountain, and the child standing underneath
just gets killed.

They sit in the best place, under the poplars.
And they talk—it must be hours now, the sun's in a different place.
About school, about people they both know,
about being adult, about how you knew what your dreams were.

They used to play games, but that's stopped now—too much touching.
They only touch each other when they fold the blanket.

They know this in each other.
That's why it isn't talked about.
Before they do anything like that, they'll need to know more—
in fact, everything that can happen. Until then, they'll just watch
and stay children.

Today she's folding the blanket alone, to be safe.
And he looks away—he pretends to be too lost in thought to help out.

They know that at some point you stop being children, and at that point
you become strangers. It seems unbearably lonely.

When they get home to the village, it's nearly twilight.
It's been a perfect day; they talk about this,
about when they'll have a chance to have a picnic again.

They walk through the summer dusk,
not holding hands but still telling each other everything.

BEFORE THE STORM

Rain tomorrow, but tonight the sky is clear, the stars shine.
Still, the rain's coming,
maybe enough to drown the seeds.
There's a wind from the sea pushing the clouds;
before you see them, you feel the wind.
Better look at the fields now,
see how they look before they're flooded.

A full moon. Yesterday, a sheep escaped into the woods,
and not just any sheep—the ram, the whole future.
If we see him again, we'll see his bones.

The grass shudders a little; maybe the wind passed through it.
And the new leaves of the olives shudder in the same way.
Mice in the fields. Where the fox hunts,
tomorrow there'll be blood in the grass.
But the storm—the storm will wash it away.

In one window, there's a boy sitting.
He's been sent to bed—too early,
in his opinion. So he sits at the window—

Everything is settled now.
Where you are now is where you'll sleep, where you'll wake up in the morning.
The mountain stands like a beacon, to remind the night that the earth exists,
that it mustn't be forgotten.

Above the sea, the clouds form as the wind rises,
dispersing them, giving them a sense of purpose.

Tomorrow the dawn won't come.
The sky won't go back to being the sky of day; it will go on as night,
except the stars will fade and vanish as the storm arrives,
lasting perhaps ten hours altogether.
But the world as it was cannot return.

One by one, the lights of the village houses dim
and the mountain shines in the darkness with reflected light.

No sound. Only cats scuffling in the doorways.
They smell the wind: time to make more cats.
Later, they prowl the streets, but the smell of the wind stalks them.
It's the same in the fields, confused by the smell of blood,
though for now only the wind rises; stars turn the field silver.

This far from the sea and still we know these signs.
The night is an open book.
But the world beyond the night remains a mystery.

SUNSET

At the same time as the sun's setting,
a farm worker's burning dead leaves.

It's nothing, this fire.
It's a small thing, controlled,
like a family run by a dictator.

Still, when it blazes up, the farm worker disappears;
from the road, he's invisible.

Compared to the sun, all the fires here
are short-lived, amateurish—
they end when the leaves are gone.
Then the farm worker reappears, raking the ashes.

But the death is real.
As though the sun's done what it came to do,
made the field grow, then
inspired the burning of earth.

So it can set now.

IN THE CAFÉ

It's natural to be tired of earth.
When you've been dead this long, you'll probably be tired of heaven.
You do what you can do in a place
but after a while you exhaust that place,
so you long for rescue.

My friend falls in love a little too easily.
Every year or so a new girl—
If they have children he doesn't mind;
he can fall in love with children also.

So the rest of us get sour and he stays the same,
full of adventure, always making new discoveries.
But he hates moving, so the women have to come from here, or near here.

Every month or so, we meet for coffee.
In summer, we'll walk around the meadow, sometimes as far as the
    mountain.
Even when he suffers, he's thriving, happy in his body.
It's partly the women, of course, but not that only.

He moves into their houses, learns to like the movies they like.
It's not an act—he really does learn,
the way someone goes to cooking school and learns to cook.

He sees everything with their eyes.
He becomes not what they are but what they could be
if they weren't trapped in their characters.
For him, this new self of his is liberating because it's invented—

he absorbs the fundamental needs in which their souls are rooted,
he experiences as his own the rituals and preferences these give rise to—
but as he lives with each woman, he inhabits each version of himself
fully, because it isn't compromised by the normal shame and anxiety.

When he leaves, the women are devastated.
Finally they met a man who answered all their needs—
there was nothing they couldn't tell him.
When they meet him now, he's a cipher—
the person they knew doesn't exist anymore.
He came into existence when they met,
he vanished when it ended, when he walked away.

After a few years, they get over him.
They tell their new boyfriends how amazing it was,
like living with another woman, but without the spite, the envy,
and with a man's strength, a man's clarity of mind.

And the men tolerate this, they even smile.
They stroke the women's hair—
they know this man doesn't exist; it's hard for them to feel competitive.

You couldn't ask, though, for a better friend,
a more subtle observer. When we talk, he's candid and open,
he's kept the intensity we all had when we were young.
He talks openly of fear, of the qualities he detests in himself.
And he's generous—he knows how I am just by looking.
If I'm frustrated or angry, he'll listen for hours,
not because he's forcing himself, because he's interested.

I guess that's how he is with the women.
But the friends he never leaves—
with them, he's trying to stand outside his life, to see it clearly—

Today he wants to sit; there's a lot to say,
too much for the meadow. He wants to be face to face,
talking to someone he's known forever.

He's on the verge of a new life.
His eyes glow, he isn't interested in the coffee.
Even though it's sunset, for him
the sun is rising again, and the fields are flushed with dawn light,
rose-colored and tentative.

He's himself in these moments, not pieces of the women
he's slept with. He enters their lives as you enter a dream,
without volition, and he lives there as you live in a dream,
however long it lasts. And in the morning, you remember
nothing of the dream at all, nothing at all.

For two weeks he's been watching the same girl,
someone he sees in the plaza. In her twenties maybe,
drinking coffee in the afternoon, the little dark head
bent over a magazine.
He watches from across the square, pretending
to be buying something, cigarettes, maybe a bouquet of flowers.

Because she doesn't know it exists,
her power is very great now, fused to the needs of his imagination.
He is her prisoner. She says the words he gives her
in a voice he imagines, low-pitched and soft,
a voice from the south as the dark hair must be from the south.

Soon she will recognize him, then begin to expect him.
And perhaps then every day her hair will be freshly washed,
she will gaze outward across the plaza before looking down.
And after that they will become lovers.

But he hopes this will not happen immediately
since whatever power she exerts now over his body, over his emotions,
she will have no power once she commits herself—

she will withdraw into that private world of feeling
women enter when they love. And living there, she will become
like a person who casts no shadow, who is not present in the world;
in that sense, so little use to him
it hardly matters whether she lives or dies.

DAWN

1.

Child waking up in a dark room
screaming I want my duck back, I want my duck back

in a language nobody understands in the least—

There is no duck.

But the dog, all upholstered in white plush—
the dog is right there in the crib next to him.

Years and years—that's how much time passes.
All in a dream. But the duck—
no one knows what happened to that.

2.

They've just met, now
they're sleeping near an open window.

Partly to wake them, to assure them
that what they remember of the night is correct,
now light needs to enter the room,

also to show them the context in which this occurred:
socks half hidden under a dirty mat,
quilt decorated with green leaves—

the sunlight specifying
these but not other objects,
setting boundaries, sure of itself, not arbitrary,

then lingering, describing
each thing in detail,
fastidious, like a composition in English,
even a little blood on the sheets—

3.

Afterward, they separate for the day.
Even later, at a desk, in the market,
the manager not satisfied with the figures he's given,
the berries moldy under the topmost layer—

so that one withdraws from the world
even as one continues to take action in it—

You get home, that's when you notice the mold.
Too late, in other words.

As though the sun blinded you for a moment.

FIRST SNOW

Like a child, the earth's going to sleep,
or so the story goes.

But I'm not tired, it says.
And the mother says, You may not be tired but I'm tired—

You can see it in her face, everyone can.
So the snow has to fall, sleep has to come.
Because the mother's sick to death of her life
and needs silence.

EARTHWORM

Mortal standing on top of the earth, refusing
to enter the earth: you tell yourself
you are able to see deeply
the conflicts of which you are made but, facing death,
you will not dig deeply—if you sense
that pity engulfs you, you are not
delusional: not all pity
descends from higher to lesser, some
arises out of the earth itself, persistent
yet devoid of coercion. We can be split in two, but you are
mutilated at the core, your mind
detached from your feelings—
repression does not deceive
organisms like ourselves:
once you enter the earth, you will not fear the earth;
once you inhabit your terror,
death will come to seem a web of channels or tunnels like
a sponge's or honeycomb's, which, as part of us,
you will be free to explore. Perhaps
you will find in these travels
a wholeness that eluded you—as men and women
you were never free
to register in your body whatever left
a mark on your spirit.

AT THE RIVER

One night that summer my mother decided it was time to tell me about
what she referred to as *pleasure*, though you could see she felt
some sort of unease about this ceremony, which she tried to cover up
by first taking my hand, as though somebody in the family had just died—
she went on holding my hand as she made her speech,
which was more like a speech about mechanical engineering
than a conversation about pleasure. In her other hand,
she had a book from which, apparently, she'd taken the main facts.
She did the same thing with the others, my two brothers and sister,
and the book was always the same book, dark blue,
though we each got our own copy.

There was a line drawing on the cover
showing a man and woman holding hands
but standing fairly far apart, like people on two sides of a dirt road.

Obviously, she and my father did not have a language for what they did
which, from what I could judge, wasn't pleasure.
At the same time, whatever holds human beings together
could hardly resemble those cool black-and-white diagrams, which
    suggested,
among other things, that you could only achieve pleasure
with a person of the opposite sex,
so you didn't get two sockets, say, and no plug.

School wasn't in session.
I went back to my room and shut the door
and my mother went into the kitchen
where my father was pouring glasses of wine for himself and his invisible
    guest
who—surprise—doesn't appear.
No, it's just my father and his friend the Holy Ghost
partying the night away until the bottle runs out,
after which my father continues sitting at the table
with an open book in front of him.

Tactfully, so as not to embarrass the Spirit,
my father handled all the glasses,
first his own, then the other, back and forth like every other night.

By then, I was out of the house.
It was summer; my friends used to meet at the river.
The whole thing seemed a grave embarrassment
although the truth was that, except for the boys, maybe we didn't
    understand mechanics.
The boys had the key right in front of them, in their hands if they wanted,
and many of them said they'd already used it,
though once one boy said this, the others said it too,
and of course people had older brothers and sisters.

We sat at the edge of the river discussing parents in general
and sex in particular. And a lot of information got shared,
and of course the subject was unfailingly interesting.
I showed people my book, *Ideal Marriage*—we all had a good laugh over it.
One night a boy brought a bottle of wine and we passed it around for a while.

More and more that summer we understood
that something was going to happen to us
that would change us.
And the group, all of us who used to meet this way,
the group would shatter, like a shell that falls away
so the bird can emerge.
Only of course it would be two birds emerging, pairs of birds.

We sat in the reeds at the edge of the river
throwing small stones. When the stones hit,
you could see the stars multiply for a second, little explosions of light
flashing and going out. There was a boy I was beginning to like,
not to speak to but to watch.
I liked to sit behind him to study the back of his neck.

And after a while we'd all get up together and walk back through the dark
to the village. Above the field, the sky was clear,
stars everywhere, like in the river, though these were the real stars,
even the dead ones were real.

But the ones in the river—
they were like having some idea that explodes suddenly into a thousand
    ideas,
not real, maybe, but somehow more lifelike.

When I got home, my mother was asleep, my father was still at the table,
reading his book. And I said, Did your friend go away?
And he looked at me intently for a while,
then he said, Your mother and I used to drink a glass of wine together
after dinner.

A CORRIDOR

There's an open door through which you can see the kitchen—
always some wonderful smell coming from there,
but what paralyzes him is the warmth of that place,
the stove in the center giving out heat—

Some lives are like that.
Heat's at the center, so constant no one gives it a thought.
But the key he's holding unlocks a different door,
and on the other side, warmth isn't waiting for him.
He makes it himself—him and the wine.

The first glass is himself coming home.
He can smell the daube, a smell of red wine and orange peel mixed in with
    the veal.
His wife is singing in the bedroom, putting the children to sleep.
He drinks slowly, letting his wife open the door, her finger to her lips,
and then letting her eagerly rush toward him to embrace him.
And afterward there will be the daube.

But the glasses that follow cause her to disappear.
She takes the children with her; the apartment shrinks back to what it was.
He has found someone else—not another person exactly,
but a self who despises intimacy, as though the privacy of marriage
is a door that two people shut together
and no one can get out alone, not the wife, not the husband,
so the heat gets trapped there until they suffocate,
as though they were living in a phone booth—

Then the wine is gone. He washes his face, wanders around the apartment.
It's summer—life rots in the heat.
Some nights, he still hears a woman singing to her children;
other nights, behind the bedroom door, her naked body doesn't exist.

FATIGUE

All winter he sleeps.
Then he gets up, he shaves—
it takes a long time to become a man again,
his face in the mirror bristles with dark hair.

The earth now is like a woman, waiting for him.
A great hopefulness—that's what binds them together,
himself and this woman.

Now he has to work all day to prove he deserves what he has.
Midday: he's tired, he's thirsty.
But if he quits now he'll have nothing.

The sweat covering his back and arms
is like his life pouring out of him
with nothing replacing it.

He works like an animal, then
like a machine, with no feeling.
But the bond will never break
though the earth fights back now, wild in the summer heat—

He squats down, letting the dirt run through his fingers.

The sun goes down, the dark comes.
Now that summer's over, the earth is hard, cold;
by the road, a few isolated fires burn.

Nothing remains of love,
only estrangement and hatred.

BURNING LEAVES

Not far from the house and barn,
the farm worker's burning dead leaves.

They don't disappear voluntarily;
you have to prod them along
as the farm worker prods the leaf pile every year
until it releases a smell of smoke into the air.

And then, for an hour or so, it's really animated,
blazing away like something alive.

When the smoke clears, the house is safe.
A woman's standing in the back,
folding dry clothes into a willow basket.

So it's finished for another year,
death making room for life,
as much as possible,
but burning the house would be too much room.

Sunset. Across the road,
the farm worker's sweeping the cold ashes.
Sometimes a few escape, harmlessly drifting around in the wind.

Then the air is still.
Where the fire was, there's only bare dirt in a circle of rocks.
Nothing between the earth and the dark.

WALKING AT NIGHT

Now that she is old,
the young men don't approach her
so the nights are free,
the streets at dusk that were so dangerous
have become as safe as the meadow.

By midnight, the town's quiet.
Moonlight reflects off the stone walls;
on the pavement, you can hear the nervous sounds
of the men rushing home to their wives and mothers; this late,
the doors are locked, the windows darkened.

When they pass, they don't notice her.
She's like a dry blade of grass in a field of grasses.
So her eyes that used never to leave the ground
are free now to go where they like.

When she's tired of the streets, in good weather she walks
in the fields where the town ends.
Sometimes, in summer, she goes as far as the river.

The young people used to gather not far from here
but now the river's grown shallow from lack of rain, so
the bank's deserted—

There were picnics then.
The boys and girls eventually paired off;
after a while, they made their way into the woods
where it's always twilight—

The woods would be empty now—
the naked bodies have found other places to hide.

In the river, there's just enough water for the night sky
to make patterns against the gray stones. The moon's bright,
one stone among many others. And the wind rises;
it blows the small trees that grow at the river's edge.

When you look at a body you see a history.
Once that body isn't seen anymore,
the story it tried to tell gets lost—

On nights like this, she'll walk as far as the bridge
before she turns back.
Everything still smells of summer.
And her body begins to seem again the body she had as a young woman,
glistening under the light summer clothing.

VIA DELLE OMBRE

On most days, the sun wakes me.
Even on dark days, there's a lot of light in the mornings—
thin lines where the blinds don't come together.
It's morning—I open my eyes.
And every morning I see again how dirty this place is, how grim.
So I'm never late for work—this isn't a place to spend time in,
watching the dirt pile up as the sun brightens.

During the day at work, I forget about it.
I think about work: getting colored beads into plastic vials.
When I get home at dusk, the room is shadowy—
the shadow of the bureau covers the bare floor.
It's telling me whoever lives here is doomed.

When I'm in moods like that,
I go to a bar, watch sports on television.

Sometimes I talk to the owner.
He says moods don't mean anything—
the shadows mean night is coming, not that daylight will never return.
He tells me to move the bureau; I'll get different shadows, maybe
a different diagnosis.

If we're alone, he turns down the volume of the television.
The players keep crashing into each other
but all we hear are our own voices.

If there's no game, he'll pick a film.
It's the same thing—the sound stays off, so there's only images.
When the film's over, we compare notes, to see if we both saw the same story.
Sometimes we spend hours watching this junk.

When I walk home it's night. You can't see for once how shabby the houses are.
The film is in my head: I tell myself I'm following the path of the hero.

The hero ventures out—that's dawn.
When he's gone, the camera collects pictures of other things.
When he gets back, it already knows everything there is to know,
just from watching the room.

There's no shadows now.
Inside the room, it's dark; the night air is cool.
In summer, you can smell the orange blossoms.
If there's wind, one tree will do it—you don't need the whole orchard.

I do what the hero does.
He opens the window. He has his reunion with earth.

HUNTERS

A dark night—the streets belong to the cats.
The cats and whatever small thing they find to kill—
The cats are fast like their ancestors in the hills
and hungry like their ancestors.

Hardly any moon. So the night's cool—
no moon to heat it up. Summer's on the way out
but for now there's still plenty to hunt
though the mice are quiet, watchful like the cats.

Smell the air—a still night, a night for love.
And every once in a while a scream
rising from the street below
where the cat's digging his teeth into the rat's leg.

Once the rat screams, it's dead. That scream is like a map:
it tells the cat where to find the throat. After that,
the scream's coming from a corpse.

You're lucky to be in love on nights like this,
still warm enough to lie naked on top of the sheets,
sweating, because it's hard work, this love, no matter what anyone says.

The dead rats lie in the street, where the cat drops them.
Be glad you're not on the street now,
before the street cleaners come to sweep them away. When the sun rises,
it won't be disappointed with the world it finds,
the streets will be clean for the new day and the night that follows.

Just be glad you were in bed,
where the cries of love drown out the screams of the corpses.

A SLIP OF PAPER

Today I went to the doctor—
the doctor said I was dying,
not in those words, but when I said it
she didn't deny it—

What have you done to your body, her silence says.
We gave it to you and look what you did to it,
how you abused it.
I'm not talking only of cigarettes, she says,
but also of poor diet, of drink.

She's a young woman; the stiff white coat disguises her body.
Her hair's pulled back, the little female wisps
suppressed by a dark band. She's not at ease here,

behind her desk, with her diploma over her head,
reading a list of numbers in columns,
some flagged for her attention.
Her spine's straight also, showing no feeling.

No one taught me how to care for my body.
You grow up watched by your mother or grandmother.
Once you're free of them, your wife takes over, but she's nervous,
she doesn't go too far. So this body I have,
that the doctor blames me for—it's always been supervised by women,
and let me tell you, they left a lot out.

The doctor looks at me—
between us, a stack of books and folders.
Except for us, the clinic's empty.

There's a trap-door here, and through that door,
the country of the dead. And the living push you through,
they want you there first, ahead of them.

The doctor knows this. She has her books,
I have my cigarettes. Finally
she writes something on a slip of paper.
This will help your blood pressure, she says.

And I pocket it, a sign to go.
And once I'm outside, I tear it up, like a ticket to the other world.

She was crazy to come here,
a place where she knows no one.
She's alone; she has no wedding ring.
She goes home alone, to her place outside the village.
And she has her one glass of wine a day,
her dinner that isn't a dinner.

And she takes off that white coat:
between that coat and her body,
there's just a thin layer of cotton.
And at some point, that comes off too.

To get born, your body makes a pact with death,
and from that moment, all it tries to do is cheat—

You get into bed alone. Maybe you sleep, maybe you never wake up.
But for a long time you hear every sound.
It's a night like any summer night; the dark never comes.

BATS

There are two kinds of vision:
the seeing of things, which belongs
to the science of optics, versus
the seeing beyond things, which
results from deprivation. Man mocking the dark, rejecting
worlds you do not know: though the dark
is full of obstacles, it is possible to have
intense awareness when the field is narrow
and the signals few. Night has bred in us
thought more focused than yours, if rudimentary:
man the ego, man imprisoned in the eye,
there is a path you cannot see, beyond the eye's reach,
what the philosophers have called
the *via negativa*: to make a place for light
the mystic shuts his eyes—illumination
of the kind he seeks destroys
creatures who depend on things.

BURNING LEAVES

The fire burns up into the clear sky,
eager and furious, like an animal trying to get free,
to run wild as nature intended—

When it burns like this,
leaves aren't enough—it's
acquisitive, rapacious,

refusing to be contained, to accept limits—

There's a pile of stones around it.
Past the stones, the earth's raked clean, bare—

Finally the leaves are gone, the fuel's gone,
the last flames burn upwards and sidewards—

Concentric rings of stones and gray earth
circle a few sparks;
the farmer stomps on these with his boots.

It's impossible to believe this will work—
not with a fire like this, those last sparks
still resisting, unfinished,
believing they will get everything in the end

since it is obvious they are not defeated,
merely dormant or resting, though no one knows
whether they represent life or death.

MARCH

The light stays longer in the sky, but it's a cold light,
it brings no relief from winter.

My neighbor stares out the window,
talking to her dog. He's sniffing the garden,
trying to reach a decision about the dead flowers.

It's a little early for all this.
Everything's still very bare—
nevertheless, something's different today from yesterday.

We can see the mountain: the peak's glittering where the ice catches the light.
But on the sides the snow's melted, exposing bare rock.

My neighbor's calling the dog, making her unconvincing doglike sounds.
The dog's polite; he raises his head when she calls,
but he doesn't move. So she goes on calling,
her failed bark slowly deteriorating into a human voice.

All her life she dreamed of living by the sea
but fate didn't put her there.
It laughed at her dreams;
it locked her up in the hills, where no one escapes.

The sun beats down on the earth, the earth flourishes.
And every winter, it's as though the rock underneath the earth rises
higher and higher and the earth becomes rock, cold and rejecting.

She says hope killed her parents, it killed her grandparents.
It rose up each spring with the wheat
and died between the heat of summer and the raw cold.
In the end, they told her to live near the sea,
as though that would make a difference.

By late spring she'll be garrulous, but now she's down to two words,
never and *only*, to express this sense that life's cheated her.

Never the cries of the gulls, only, in summer, the crickets, cicadas.
Only the smell of the field, when all she wanted
was the smell of the sea, of disappearance.

The sky above the fields has turned a sort of grayish pink
as the sun sinks. The clouds are silk yarn, magenta and crimson.

And everywhere the earth is rustling, not lying still.
And the dog senses this stirring; his ears twitch.

He walks back and forth, vaguely remembering
from other years this elation. The season of discoveries
is beginning. Always the same discoveries, but to the dog,
intoxicating and new, not duplicitous.

I tell my neighbor we'll be like this
when we lose our memories. I ask her if she's ever seen the sea
and she says, once, in a movie.
It was a sad story, nothing worked out at all.

The lovers part. The sea hammers the shore, the mark each wave leaves
wiped out by the wave that follows.
Never accumulation, never one wave trying to build on another,
never the promise of shelter—

The sea doesn't change as the earth changes;
it doesn't lie.
You ask the sea, what can you promise me
and it speaks the truth; it says *erasure*.

Finally the dog goes in.
We watch the crescent moon,
very faint at first, then clearer and clearer
as the night grows dark.
Soon it will be the sky of early spring, stretching above the stubborn ferns
and violets.

Nothing can be forced to live.
The earth is like a drug now, like a voice from far away,
a lover or master. In the end, you do what the voice tells you.
It says forget, you forget.
It says begin again, you begin again.

A NIGHT IN SPRING

They told her she came out of a hole in her mother
but really it's impossible to believe
something so delicate could come out of something
so fat—her mother naked
looks like a pig. She wants to think
the children telling her were making fun of her ignorance;
they think they can tell her anything
because she doesn't come from the country, where people know these things.

She wants the subject to be finished, dead. It troubles her
to picture this space in her mother's body,
releasing human beings now and again,
first hiding them, then dropping them into the world,

and all along drugging them, inspiring the same feelings
she attaches to her bed, this sense of solitude, this calm,
this sense of being unique—

Maybe her mother still has these feelings.
This could explain why she never sees
the great differences between the two of them

because at one point they *were* the same person—

She sees her face in the mirror, the small nose
sunk in fat, and at the same time she hears
the children's laughter as they tell her
it doesn't start in the face, stupid,
it starts in the body—

At night in bed, she pulls the quilt as high as possible,
up to her neck—

She has found this thing, a self,
and come to cherish it,
and now it will be packed away in flesh and lost—

And she feels her mother did this to her, meant this to happen.
Because whatever she may try to do with her mind,
her body will disobey,
that its complacency, its finality, will make her mind invisible,
no one will see—

Very gently, she moves the sheet aside.
And under it, there is her body, still beautiful and new
with no marks anywhere. And it seems to her still
identical to her mind, so consistent with it as to seem
transparent, almost,

and once again
she falls in love with it and vows to protect it.

HARVEST

It's autumn in the market—
not wise anymore to buy tomatoes.
They're beautiful still on the outside,
some perfectly round and red, the rare varieties
misshapen, individual, like human brains covered in red oilcloth—

Inside, they're gone. Black, moldy—
you can't take a bite without anxiety.
Here and there, among the tainted ones, a fruit
still perfect, picked before decay set in.

Instead of tomatoes, crops nobody really wants.
Pumpkins, a lot of pumpkins.
Gourds, ropes of dried chilies, braids of garlic.
The artisans weave dead flowers into wreaths;
they tie bits of colored yarn around dried lavender.
And people go on for a while buying these things
as though they thought the farmers would see to it
that things went back to normal:
the vines would go back to bearing new peas;
the first small lettuces, so fragile, so delicate, would begin
to poke out of the dirt.

Instead, it gets dark early.
And the rains get heavier; they carry
the weight of dead leaves.

At dusk, now, an atmosphere of threat, of foreboding.
And people feel this themselves; they give a name to the season,
harvest, to put a better face on these things.

The gourds are rotting on the ground, the sweet blue grapes are finished.
A few roots, maybe, but the ground's so hard the farmers think
it isn't worth the effort to dig them out. For what?
To stand in the marketplace under a thin umbrella, in the rain, in the cold,
no customers anymore?

And then the frost comes; there's no more question of harvest.
The snow begins; the pretense of life ends.
The earth is white now; the fields shine when the moon rises.

I sit at the bedroom window, watching the snow fall.
The earth is like a mirror:
calm meeting calm, detachment meeting detachment.

What lives, lives underground.
What dies, dies without struggle.

CONFESSION

He steals sometimes, because they don't have their own tree
and he loves fruit. Not steals exactly—
he pretends he's an animal; he eats off the ground,
as the animals would eat. This is what he tells the priest,
that he doesn't think it should be a sin to take what would just lie there
    and rot,
this year like every other year.

As a man, as a human being, the priest agrees with the boy,
but as a priest he chastises him, though the penance is light,
so as to not kill off imagination: what he'd give
to a much younger boy who took something that wasn't his.

But the boy objects. He's willing to do the penance
because he likes the priest, but he refuses to believe that Jesus
gave this fig tree to this woman; he wants to know
what Jesus does with all the money he gets from real estate,
not just in this village but in the whole country.

Partly he's joking but partly he's serious
and the priest gets irritated—he's out of his depth with this boy,
he can't explain that though Christ doesn't deal in property,
still the fig tree belongs to the woman, even if she never picks the figs.
Perhaps one day, with the boy's encouragement,
the woman will become a saint and share her fig tree and her big house
    with strangers,
but for the moment she's a human being whose ancestors built this house.

The priest is pleased to have moved the conversation away from money,
which makes him nervous, and back to words like *family* or *tradition*,
where he feels more secure. The boy stares at him—

he knows perfectly well the ways in which he's taken advantage of a senile
    old lady,
the ways he's tried to charm the priest, to impress him. But he despises
speeches like the one beginning now;
he wants to taunt the priest with his own flight: if he loves family so much,
why didn't the priest marry as his parents married, continue the line from
    which he came.

But he's silent. The words that mean there will be
no questioning, no trying to reason—those words have been uttered.
"Thank you, Father," he says.

MARRIAGE

All week they've been by the sea again
and the sound of the sea colors everything.
Blue sky fills the window.
But the only sound is the sound of the waves pounding the shore—
angry. Angry at something. Whatever it is
must be why he's turned away. Angry, though he'd never hit her,
never say a word, probably.

So it's up to her to get the answer some other way,
from the sea, maybe, or the gray clouds suddenly
rising above it. The smell of the sea is in the sheets,
the smell of sun and wind, the hotel smell, fresh and sweet
because they're changed every day.

He never uses words. Words, for him, are for making arrangements,
for doing business. Never for anger, never for tenderness.

She strokes his back. She puts her face up against it,
even though it's like putting your face against a wall.

And the silence between them is ancient: it says
these are the boundaries.

He isn't sleeping, not even pretending to sleep.
His breathing's not regular: he breathes in with reluctance;
he doesn't want to commit himself to being alive.
And he breathes out fast, like a king banishing a servant.

Beneath the silence, the sound of the sea,
the sea's violence spreading everywhere, not finished, not finished,
his breath driving the waves—

But she knows who she is and she knows what she wants.
As long as that's true, something so natural can't hurt her.

Spring comes quickly: overnight
the plum tree blossoms,
the warm air fills with bird calls.

In the plowed dirt, someone has drawn a picture of the sun
with rays coming out all around
but because the background is dirt, the sun is black.
There is no signature.

Alas, very soon everything will disappear:
the bird calls, the delicate blossoms. In the end,
even the earth itself will follow the artist's name into oblivion.

Nevertheless, the artist intends
a mood of celebration.

How beautiful the blossoms are—emblems of the resilience of life.
The birds approach eagerly.

FIGS

My mother made figs in wine—
poached with cloves, sometimes a few peppercorns,
Black figs, from our tree.
And the wine was red, the pepper left a taste of smoke in the syrup.
I used to feel I was in another country.

Before that, there'd be chicken.
In autumn, sometimes filled with wild mushrooms.
There wasn't always time for that.
And the weather had to be right, just after the rain.
Sometimes it was just chicken, with a lemon inside.

She'd open the wine. Nothing special—
something she got from the neighbors.
I miss that wine—what I buy now doesn't taste as good.

I make these things for my husband,
but he doesn't like them.
He wants his mother's dishes, but I don't make them well.
When I try, I get angry—

He's trying to turn me into a person I never was.
He thinks it's a simple thing—
you cut up a chicken, throw a few tomatoes into the pan.
Garlic, if there's garlic.
An hour later, you're in paradise.

He thinks it's my job to learn, not his job
to teach me. What my mother cooked, I don't need to learn.
My hands already knew, just from smelling the cloves
while I did my homework.
When it was my turn, I was right. I did know.
The first time I tasted them, my childhood came back.

When we were young, it was different.
My husband and I—we were in love. All we ever wanted
was to touch each other.

He comes home, he's tired.
Everything is hard—making money is hard, watching your body change
is hard. You can take these problems when you're young—
something's difficult for a while, but you're confident.
If it doesn't work out, you'll do something else.

He minds summer most—the sun gets to him.
Here it's merciless, you can feel the world aging.
The grass turns dry, the gardens get full of weeds and slugs.

It was the best time for us once.
The hours of light when he came home from work—
we'd turn them into hours of darkness.
Everything was a big secret—
even the things we said every night.

And slowly the sun would go down;
we'd see the lights of the city come on.
The nights were glossy with stars—stars
glittered above the high buildings.

Sometimes we'd light a candle.
But most nights, no. Most nights we'd lie there in the darkness,
with our arms around each other.

But there was a sense you could control the light—
it was a wonderful feeling; you could make the whole room
bright again, or you could lie in the night air,
listening to the cars.

We'd get quiet after a while. The night would get quiet.
But we didn't sleep, we didn't want to give up consciousness.
We had given the night permission to carry us along;
we lay there, not interfering. Hour after hour, each one
listening to the other's breath, watching the light change
in the window at the end of the bed—

whatever happened in that window,
we were in harmony with it.

AT THE DANCE

Twice a year we hung the Christmas lights—
at Christmas for our Lord's birth, and at the end of August,
as a blessing on the harvest—
near the end but before the end,
and everyone would come to see,
even the oldest people who could hardly walk—

They had to see the colored lights,
and in summer there was always music, too—
music and dancing.

For the young, it was everything.
Your life was made here—what was finished under the stars
started in the lights of the plaza.
Haze of cigarettes, the women gathered under the colored awnings
singing along with whatever songs were popular that year,
cheeks brown from the sun and red from the wine.

I remember all of it—my friends and I, how we were changed by the music,
and the women, I remember how bold they were, the timid ones
along with the others—

A spell was on us, but it was a sickness too,
the men and women choosing each other almost by accident, randomly,
and the lights glittering, misleading,
because whatever you did then you did forever—

And it seemed at the time
such a game, really—lighthearted, casual,
dissipating like smoke, like perfume between a woman's breasts,
intense because your eyes are closed.

How were these things decided?
By smell, by feel—a man would approach a woman,
ask her to dance, but what it meant was
will you let me touch you, and the woman could say
many things, ask me later, she could say, ask me again.
Or she could say no, and turn away,
as though if nothing but you happened that night
you still weren't enough, or she could say yes, I'd love to dance
which meant yes, I want to be touched.

SOLITUDE

It's very dark today; through the rain,
the mountain isn't visible. The only sound
is rain, driving life underground.
And with the rain, cold comes.
There will be no moon tonight, no stars.

The wind rose at night;
all morning it lashed against the wheat—
at noon it ended. But the storm went on,
soaking the dry fields, then flooding them—

The earth has vanished.
There's nothing to see, only the rain
gleaming against the dark windows.
This is the resting place, where nothing moves—

Now we return to what we were,
animals living in darkness
without language or vision—

Nothing proves I'm alive.
There is only the rain, the rain is endless.

EARTHWORM

It is not sad not to be human
nor is living entirely within the earth
demeaning or empty: it is the nature of the mind
to defend its eminence, as it is the nature of those
who walk on the surface to fear the depths—one's
position determines one's feelings. And yet
to walk on top of a thing is not to prevail over it—
it is more the opposite, a disguised dependency,
by which the slave completes the master. Likewise
the mind disdains what it can't control,
which will in turn destroy it. It is not painful to return
without language or vision: if, like the Buddhists,
one declines to leave
inventories of the self, one emerges in a space
the mind cannot conceive, being wholly physical, not
metaphoric. What is your word? *Infinity*, meaning
that which cannot be measured.

OLIVE TREES

The building's brick, so the walls get warm in summer.
When the summer goes, they're still warm,
especially on the south side—you feel the sun there, in the brick,
as though it meant to leave its stamp on the wall, not just sail over it
on its way to the hills. I take my breaks here, leaning against the wall,
smoking cigarettes.

The bosses don't mind—they joke that if the business fails,
they'll just rent wall space. Big joke—everyone laughs very loud.
But you can't eat—they don't want rats here, looking for scraps.

Some of the others don't care about being warm, feeling the sun on their
    backs
from the warm brick. They want to know where the views are.
To me, it isn't important what I see. I grew up in those hills;
I'll be buried there. In between, I don't need to keep sneaking looks.

My wife says when I say things like this my mouth goes bitter.
She loves the village—every day she misses her mother.
She misses her youth—how we met there and fell in love.
How our children were born there. She knows she'll never go back
but she keeps hoping—

At night in bed, her eyes film over. She talks about the olive trees,
the long silver leaves shimmering in the sunlight.
And the bark, the trees themselves, so supple, pale gray like the rocks
    behind them.

She remembers picking the olives, who made the best brine.
I remember her hands then, smelling of vinegar.
And the bitter taste of the olives, before you knew not to eat them
fresh off the tree.

And I remind her how useless they were without people to cure them.
Brine them, set them out in the sun—
And I tell her all nature is like that to me, useless and bitter.
It's like a trap—and you fall into it because of the olive leaves,
because they're beautiful.

You grow up looking at the hills, how the sun sets behind them.
And the olive trees, waving and shimmering. And you realize that if you
    don't get out fast
you'll die, as though this beauty were gagging you so you couldn't
    breathe—

And I tell her I know we're trapped here. But better to be trapped
by decent men, who even re-do the lunchroom,
than by the sun and the hills. When I complain here,
my voice is heard—somebody's voice is heard. There's dispute, there's anger.
But human beings are talking to each other, the way my wife and I talk.
Talking even when they don't agree, when one of them is only pretending.

In the other life, your despair just turns into silence.
The sun disappears behind the western hills—
when it comes back, there's no reference at all to your suffering.
So your voice dies away. You stop trying, not just with the sun,
but with human beings. And the small things that made you happy
can't get through to you anymore.

I know things are hard here. And the owners—I know they lie sometimes.
But there are truths that ruin a life; the same way, some lies
are generous, warm and cozy like the sun on the brick wall.

So when you think of the wall, you don't think *prison*.
More the opposite—you think of everything you escaped, being here.

And then my wife gives up for the night, she turns her back.
Some nights she cries a little.
Her only weapon was the truth—it is true, the hills are beautiful.
And the olive trees really are like silver.

But a person who accepts a lie, who accepts support from it
because it's warm, it's pleasant for a little while—
that person she'll never understand, no matter how much she loves him.

SUNRISE

This time of year, the window boxes smell of the hills,
the thyme and rosemary that grew there,
crammed into the narrow spaces between the rocks
and, lower down, where there was real dirt,
competing with other things, blueberries and currants,
the small shrubby trees the bees love—
Whatever we ate smelled of the hills,
even when there was almost nothing.
Or maybe that's what nothing tastes like, thyme and rosemary.

Maybe, too, that's what it looks like—
beautiful, like the hills, the rocks above the tree line
webbed with sweet-smelling herbs,
the small plants glittering with dew—

It was a big event to climb up there and wait for dawn,
seeing what the sun sees as it slides out from behind the rocks,
and what you couldn't see, you imagined;

your eyes would go as far as they could, to the river, say,
and your mind would do the rest—

And if you missed a day, there was always the next,
and if you missed a year, it didn't matter,
the hills weren't going anywhere,
the thyme and rosemary kept coming back,
the sun kept rising, the bushes kept bearing fruit—

The streetlight's off: that's dawn here.
It's on: that's twilight.
Either way, no one looks up. Everyone just pushes ahead,
and the smell of the past is everywhere,
the thyme and rosemary rubbing against your clothes,
the smell of too many illusions—

I went back but I didn't stay.
Everyone I cared about was gone,
some dead, some disappeared into one of those places that don't exist,
the ones we dreamed about because we saw them from the top of the
    hills—
I had to see if the fields were still shining,
the sun telling the same lies about how beautiful the world is
when all you need to know of a place is, do people live there.
If they do, you know everything.

Between them, the hills and sky took up all the room.
Whatever was left, that was ours for a while.
But sooner or later the hills will take it back, give it to the animals.
And maybe the moon will send the seas there
and where we once lived will be a stream or river coiling around the base of
    the hills,
paying the sky the compliment of reflection—

Blue in summer. White when the snow falls.

A WARM DAY

Today the sun was shining
so my neighbor washed her nightdresses in the river—
she comes home with everything folded in a basket,
beaming, as though her life had just been
lengthened a decade. Cleanliness makes her happy—
it says you can begin again,
the old mistakes needn't hold you back.

A good neighbor—we leave each other
to our privacies. Just now,
she's singing to herself, pinning the damp wash to the line.

Little by little, days like this
will seem normal. But winter was hard:
the nights coming early, the dawns dark
with a gray, persistent rain—months of that,
and then the snow, like silence coming from the sky,
obliterating the trees and gardens.

Today, all that's past us.
The birds are back, chattering over seeds.
All the snow's melted; the fruit trees are covered with downy new growth.
A few couples even walk in the meadow, promising whatever they promise.

We stand in the sun and the sun heals us.
It doesn't rush away. It hangs above us, unmoving,
like an actor pleased with his welcome.

My neighbor's quiet a moment,
staring at the mountain, listening to the birds.

So many garments, where did they come from?
And my neighbor's still out there,
fixing them to the line, as though the basket would never be empty—

It's still full, nothing is finished,
though the sun's beginning to move lower in the sky;
remember, it isn't summer yet, only the beginning of spring;
warmth hasn't taken hold yet, and the cold's returning—

She feels it, as though the last bit of linen had frozen in her hands.
She looks at her hands—how old they are. It's not the beginning, it's the
    end.
And the adults, they're all dead now.
Only the children are left, alone, growing old.

BURNING LEAVES

The dead leaves catch fire quickly.
And they burn quickly; in no time at all,
they change from something to nothing.

Midday. The sky is cold, blue;
under the fire, there's gray earth.

How fast it all goes, how fast the smoke clears.
And where the pile of leaves was,
an emptiness that suddenly seems vast.

Across the road, a boy's watching.
He stays a long time, watching the leaves burn.
Maybe this is how you'll know when the earth is dead—
it will ignite.

CROSSROADS

My body, now that we will not be traveling together much longer
I begin to feel a new tenderness toward you, very raw and unfamiliar,
like what I remember of love when I was young—

love that was so often foolish in its objectives
but never in its choices, its intensities.
Too much demanded in advance, too much that could not be promised—

My soul has been so fearful, so violent:
forgive its brutality.
As though it were that soul, my hand moves over you cautiously,

not wishing to give offense
but eager, finally, to achieve expression as substance:

it is not the earth I will miss,
it is you I will miss.

BATS

—for Ellen Pinsky

Concerning death, one might observe
that those with authority to speak remain silent:
others force their way to the pulpit or
center stage—experience
being always preferable to theory, they are rarely
true clairvoyants, nor is conviction
the common aspect of insight. Look up into the night:
if distraction through the senses is the essence of life
what you see now appears to be a simulation of death, bats
whirling in darkness— But man knows
nothing of death. If how we behave is how you feel,
this is not what death is like, this is what life is like.
You too are blind. You too flail in darkness.
A terrible solitude surrounds all beings who
confront mortality. As Margulies says: death
terrifies us all into silence.

ABUNDANCE

A cool wind blows on summer evenings, stirring the wheat.
The wheat bends, the leaves of the peach trees
rustle in the night ahead.

In the dark, a boy's crossing the field:
for the first time, he's touched a girl
so he walks home a man, with a man's hungers.

Slowly the fruit ripens—
baskets and baskets from a single tree
so some rots every year
and for a few weeks there's too much:
before and after, nothing.

Between the rows of wheat
you can see the mice, flashing and scurrying
across the earth, though the wheat towers above them,
churning as the summer wind blows.

The moon is full. A strange sound
comes from the field—maybe the wind.

But for the mice it's a night like any summer night.
Fruit and grain: a time of abundance.
Nobody dies, nobody goes hungry.

No sound except the roar of the wheat.

MIDSUMMER

On nights like this we used to swim in the quarry,
the boys making up games requiring them to tear off the girls' clothes
and the girls cooperating, because they had new bodies since last summer
and they wanted to exhibit them, the brave ones
leaping off the high rocks—bodies crowding the water.

The nights were humid, still. The stone was cool and wet,
marble for graveyards, for buildings that we never saw,
buildings in cities far away.

On cloudy nights, you were blind. Those nights the rocks were dangerous,
but in another way it was all dangerous, that was what we were after.
The summer started. Then the boys and girls began to pair off
but always there were a few left at the end—sometimes they'd keep watch,
sometimes they'd pretend to go off with each other like the rest,
but what could they do there, in the woods? No one wanted to be them.
But they'd show up anyway, as though some night their luck would change,
fate would be a different fate.

At the beginning and at the end, though, we were all together.
After the evening chores, after the smaller children were in bed,
then we were free. Nobody said anything, but we knew the nights we'd meet
and the nights we wouldn't. Once or twice, at the end of summer,
we could see a baby was going to come out of all that kissing.

And for those two, it was terrible, as terrible as being alone.
The game was over. We'd sit on the rocks smoking cigarettes,
worrying about the ones who weren't there.

And then finally walk home through the fields,
because there was always work the next day.
And the next day, we were kids again, sitting on the front steps in the morning,
eating a peach. Just that, but it seemed an honor to have a mouth.
And then going to work, which meant helping out in the fields.

One boy worked for an old lady, building shelves.
The house was very old, maybe built when the mountain was built.

And then the day faded. We were dreaming, waiting for night.
Standing at the front door at twilight, watching the shadows lengthen.
And a voice in the kitchen was always complaining about the heat,
wanting the heat to break.

Then the heat broke, the night was clear.
And you thought of the boy or girl you'd be meeting later.
And you thought of walking into the woods and lying down,
practicing all those things you were learning in the water.
And though sometimes you couldn't see the person you were with,
there was no substitute for that person.

The summer night glowed; in the field, fireflies were glinting.
And for those who understood such things, the stars were sending
    messages:
You will leave the village where you were born
and in another country you'll become very rich, very powerful,
but always you will mourn something you left behind, even though you
    can't say what it was,
and eventually you will return to seek it.

THRESHING

The sky's light behind the mountain
though the sun is gone—this light
is like the sun's shadow, passing over the earth.

Before, when the sun was high,
you couldn't look at the sky or you'd go blind.
That time of day, the men don't work.
They lie in the shade, waiting, resting;
their undershirts are stained with sweat.

But under the trees it's cool,
like the flask of water that gets passed around.
A green awning's over their heads, blocking the sun.
No talk, just the leaves rustling in the heat,
the sound of the water moving from hand to hand.

This hour or two is the best time of day.
Not asleep, not awake, not drunk,
and the women far away
so that the day becomes suddenly calm, quiet and expansive,
without the women's turbulence.

The men lie under their canopy, apart from the heat,
as though the work were done.
Beyond the fields, the river's soundless, motionless—
scum mottles the surface.

To a man, they know when the hour's gone.
The flask gets put away, the bread, if there's bread.
The leaves darken a little, the shadows change.
The sun's moving again, taking the men along,
regardless of their preferences.

Above the fields, the heat's fierce still, even in decline.
The machines stand where they were left,
patient, waiting for the men's return.

The sky's bright, but twilight is coming.
The wheat has to be threshed; many hours remain
before the work is finished.
And afterward, walking home through the fields,
dealing with the evening.

So much time best forgotten.
Tense, unable to sleep, the woman's soft body
always shifting closer—
That time in the woods: that was reality.
This is the dream.

A VILLAGE LIFE

The death and uncertainty that await me
as they await all men, the shadows evaluating me
because it can take time to destroy a human being,
the element of suspense
needs to be preserved—

On Sundays I walk my neighbor's dog
so she can go to church to pray for her sick mother.

The dog waits for me in the doorway. Summer and winter
we walk the same road, early morning, at the base of the escarpment.
Sometimes the dog gets away from me—for a moment or two,
I can't see him behind some trees. He's very proud of this,
this trick he brings out occasionally, and gives up again
as a favor to me—

Afterward, I go back to my house to gather firewood.

I keep in my mind images from each walk:
monarda growing by the roadside;
in early spring, the dog chasing the little gray mice,

so for a while it seems possible
not to think of the hold of the body weakening, the ratio
of the body to the void shifting,

and the prayers becoming prayers for the dead.

Midday, the church bells finished. Light in excess:
still, fog blankets the meadow, so you can't see
the mountain in the distance, covered with snow and ice.

When it appears again, my neighbor thinks
her prayers are answered. So much light she can't control her happiness—
it has to burst out in language. *Hello*, she yells, as though
that is her best translation.

She believes in the Virgin the way I believe in the mountain,
though in one case the fog never lifts.
But each person stores his hope in a different place.

I make my soup, I pour my glass of wine.
I'm tense, like a child approaching adolescence.
Soon it will be decided for certain what you are,
one thing, a boy or girl. Not both any longer.
And the child thinks: I want to have a say in what happens.
But the child has no say whatsoever.

When I was a child, I did not foresee this.

Later, the sun sets, the shadows gather,
rustling the low bushes like animals just awake for the night.
Inside, there's only firelight. It fades slowly;
now only the heaviest wood's still
flickering across the shelves of instruments.
I hear music coming from them sometimes,
even locked in their cases.

When I was a bird, I believed I would be a man.
That's the flute. And the horn answers,
when I was a man, I cried out to be a bird.
Then the music vanishes. And the secret it confides in me
vanishes also.

In the window, the moon is hanging over the earth,
meaningless but full of messages.

It's dead, it's always been dead,
but it pretends to be something else,
burning like a star, and convincingly, so that you feel sometimes
it could actually make something grow on earth.

If there's an image of the soul, I think that's what it is.

I move through the dark as though it were natural to me,
as though I were already a factor in it.
Tranquil and still, the day dawns.
On market day, I go to the market with my lettuces.

FAITHFUL AND VIRTUOUS NIGHT

(2014)

PARABLE

First divesting ourselves of worldly goods, as St. Francis teaches,
in order that our souls not be distracted
by gain and loss, and in order also
that our bodies be free to move
easily at the mountain passes, we had then to discuss
whither or where we might travel, with the second question being
should we have a purpose, against which
many of us argued fiercely that such purpose
corresponded to worldly goods, meaning a limitation or constriction,
whereas others said it was by this word we were consecrated
pilgrims rather than wanderers: in our minds, the word translated as
a dream, a something-sought, so that by concentrating we might see it
glimmering among the stones, and not
pass blindly by; each
further issue we debated equally fully, the arguments going back and forth,
so that we grew, some said, less flexible and more resigned,
like soldiers in a useless war. And snow fell upon us, and wind blew,
which in time abated—where the snow had been, many flowers appeared,
and where the stars had shone, the sun rose over the tree line
so that we had shadows again; many times this happened.
Also rain, also flooding sometimes, also avalanches, in which
some of us were lost, and periodically we would seem
to have achieved an agreement, our canteens
hoisted upon our shoulders; but always that moment passed, so
(after many years) we were still at that first stage, still
preparing to begin a journey, but we were changed nevertheless;
we could see this in one another; we had changed although
we never moved, and one said, ah, behold how we have aged, traveling
from day to night only, neither forward nor sideward, and this seemed
in a strange way miraculous. And those who believed we should have a
    purpose
believed this was the purpose, and those who felt we must remain free
in order to encounter truth felt it had been revealed.

AN ADVENTURE

1.

It came to me one night as I was falling asleep
that I had finished with those amorous adventures
to which I had long been a slave. Finished with love?
my heart murmured. To which I responded that many profound
     discoveries
awaited us, hoping, at the same time, I would not be asked
to name them. For I could not name them. But the belief that they
     existed—
surely this counted for something?

2.

The next night brought the same thought,
this time concerning poetry, and in the nights that followed
various other passions and sensations were, in the same way,
set aside forever, and each night my heart
protested its future, like a small child being deprived of a favorite toy.
But these farewells, I said, are the way of things.
And once more I alluded to the vast territory
opening to us with each valediction. And with that phrase I became
a glorious knight riding into the setting sun, and my heart
became the steed underneath me.

3.

I was, you will understand, entering the kingdom of death,
though why this landscape was so conventional
I could not say. Here, too, the days were very long
while the years were very short. The sun sank over the far mountain.
The stars shone, the moon waxed and waned. Soon
faces from the past appeared to me:
my mother and father, my infant sister; they had not, it seemed,
finished what they had to say, though now
I could hear them because my heart was still.

4.

At this point, I attained the precipice
but the trail did not, I saw, descend on the other side;
rather, having flattened out, it continued at this altitude
as far as the eye could see, though gradually
the mountain that supported it completely dissolved
so that I found myself riding steadily through the air—
All around, the dead were cheering me on, the joy of finding them
obliterated by the task of responding to them—

5.

As we had all been flesh together,
now we were mist.
As we had been before objects with shadows,
now we were substance without form, like evaporated chemicals.
Neigh, neigh, said my heart,
or perhaps nay, nay—it was hard to know.

6.

Here the vision ended. I was in my bed, the morning sun
contentedly rising, the feather comforter
mounded in white drifts over my lower body.
You had been with me—
there was a dent in the second pillowcase.
We had escaped from death—
or was this the view from the precipice?

Small light in the sky appearing
suddenly between
two pine boughs, their fine needles

now etched onto the radiant surface
and above this
high, feathery heaven—

Smell the air. That is the smell of the white pine,
most intense when the wind blows through it
and the sound it makes equally strange,
like the sound of the wind in a movie—

Shadows moving. The ropes
making the sound they make. What you hear now
will be the sound of the nightingale, *chordata*,
the male bird courting the female—

The ropes shift. The hammock
sways in the wind, tied
firmly between two pine trees.

Smell the air. That is the smell of the white pine.

It is my mother's voice you hear
or is it only the sound the trees make
when the air passes through them

because what sound would it make,
passing through nothing?

FAITHFUL AND VIRTUOUS NIGHT

My story begins very simply: I could speak and I was happy.
Or: I could speak, thus I was happy.
Or: I was happy, thus speaking.
I was like a bright light passing through a dark room.

If it is so difficult to begin, imagine what it will be to end—
On my bed, sheets printed with colored sailboats
conveying, simultaneously, visions of adventure (in the form of
    exploration)
and sensations of gentle rocking, as of a cradle.

Spring, and the curtains flutter.
Breezes enter the room, bringing the first insects.
A sound of buzzing like the sound of prayers.

Constituent
memories of a large memory.
Points of clarity in a mist, intermittently visible,
like a lighthouse whose one task
is to emit a signal.

But what really is the point of the lighthouse?
This is north, it says.
Not: I am your safe harbor.

Much to his annoyance, I shared this room with my older brother.
To punish me for existing, he kept me awake, reading
adventure stories by the yellow nightlight.

The habits of long ago: my brother on his side of the bed,
subdued but voluntarily so,
his bright head bent over his hands, his face obscured—

At the time of which I'm speaking,
my brother was reading a book he called
the faithful and virtuous night.
Was this the night in which he read, in which I lay awake?
No—it was a night long ago, a lake of darkness in which
a stone appeared, and on the stone
a sword growing.

Impressions came and went in my head,
a faint buzz, like the insects.
When not observing my brother, I lay in the small bed we shared
staring at the ceiling—never
my favorite part of the room. It reminded me
of what I couldn't see, the sky obviously, but more painfully
my parents sitting on the white clouds in their white travel outfits.

And yet I too was traveling,
in this case imperceptibly
from that night to the next morning,
and I too had a special outfit:
striped pyjamas.

Picture if you will a day in spring.
A harmless day: my birthday.
Downstairs, three gifts on the breakfast table.

In one box, pressed handkerchiefs with a monogram.
In the second box, colored pencils arranged
in three rows, like a school photograph.
In the last box, a book called *My First Reader*.

My aunt folded the printed wrapping paper;
the ribbons were rolled into neat balls.
My brother handed me a bar of chocolate
wrapped in silver paper.

Then, suddenly, I was alone.

Perhaps the occupation of a very young child
is to observe and listen:

In that sense, everyone was occupied—
I listened to the various sounds of the birds we fed,
the tribes of insects hatching, the small ones
creeping along the windowsill, and overhead
my aunt's sewing machine drilling
holes in a pile of dresses—

Restless, are you restless?
Are you waiting for day to end, for your brother to return to his book?
For night to return, faithful, virtuous,
repairing, briefly, the schism between
you and your parents?

This did not, of course, happen immediately.
Meanwhile, there was my birthday;
somehow the luminous outset became
the interminable middle.

Mild for late April. Puffy
clouds overhead, floating among the apple trees.
I picked up *My First Reader*, which appeared to be
a story about two children—I could not read the words.

On page three, a dog appeared.
On page five, there was a ball—one of the children
threw it higher than seemed possible, whereupon
the dog floated into the sky to join the ball.
That seemed to be the story.

I turned the pages. When I was finished
I resumed turning, so the story took on a circular shape,
like the zodiac. It made me dizzy. The yellow ball

seemed promiscuous, equally
at home in the child's hand and the dog's mouth—

Hands underneath me, lifting me.
They could have been anyone's hands,
a man's, a woman's.
Tears falling on my exposed skin. Whose tears?
Or were we out in the rain, waiting for the car to come?

The day had become unstable.
Fissures appeared in the broad blue, or,
more precisely, sudden black clouds
imposed themselves on the azure background.

Somewhere, in the far backward reaches of time,
my mother and father
were embarking on their last journey,
my mother fondly kissing the new baby, my father
throwing my brother into the air.

I sat by the window, alternating
my first lesson in reading with
watching time pass, my introduction to
philosophy and religion.

Perhaps I slept. When I woke
the sky had changed. A light rain was falling,
making everything very fresh and new—

I continued staring
at the dog's frantic reunions
with the yellow ball, an object
soon to be replaced
by another object, perhaps a soft toy—

And then suddenly evening had come.
I heard my brother's voice
calling to say he was home.

How old he seemed, older than this morning.
He set his books beside the umbrella stand
and went to wash his face.
The cuffs of his school uniform
dangled below his knees.

You have no idea how shocking it is
to a small child when
something continuous stops.

The sounds, in this case, of the sewing room,
like a drill, but very far away—

Vanished. Silence was everywhere.
And then, in the silence, footsteps.
And then we were all together, my aunt and my brother.

Then tea was set out.
At my place, a slice of ginger cake
and at the center of the slice,
one candle, to be lit later.
How quiet you are, my aunt said.

It was true—
sounds weren't coming out of my mouth. And yet
they were in my head, expressed, possibly,
as something less exact, thought perhaps,
though at the time they still seemed like sounds to me.

Something was there where there had been nothing.
Or should I say, nothing was there
but it had been defiled by questions—

Questions circled my head; they had a quality
of being organized in some way, like planets—

Outside, night was falling. Was this
that lost night, star-covered, moonlight-spattered,
like some chemical preserving
everything immersed in it?

My aunt had lit the candle.

Darkness overswept the land
and on the sea the night floated
strapped to a slab of wood—

If I could speak, what would I have said?
I think I would have said
goodbye, because in some sense
it *was* goodbye—

Well, what could I do? I wasn't
a baby anymore.

I found the darkness comforting.
I could see, dimly, the blue and yellow
sailboats on the pillowcase.

I was alone with my brother;
we lay in the dark, breathing together,
the deepest intimacy.

It had occurred to me that all human beings are divided
into those who wish to move forward
and those who wish to go back.
Or you could say, those who wish to keep moving
and those who want to be stopped in their tracks
by the blazing sword.

My brother took my hand.
Soon it too would be floating away
though perhaps, in my brother's mind,
it would survive by becoming imaginary—

Having finally begun, how does one stop?
I suppose I can simply wait to be interrupted
as in my parents' case by a large tree—
the barge, so to speak, will have passed
for the last time between the mountains.
Something, they say, like falling asleep,
which I proceeded to do.

The next day, I could speak again.
My aunt was overjoyed—
it seemed my happiness had been
passed on to her, but then
she needed it more, she had two children to raise.

I was content with my brooding.
I spent my days with the colored pencils
(I soon used up the darker colors)
though what I saw, as I told my aunt,
was less a factual account of the world

than a vision of its transformation
subsequent to passage through the void of myself.

Something, I said, like the world in spring.

When not preoccupied with the world
I drew pictures of my mother
for which my aunt posed,
holding, at my request,
a twig from a sycamore.

As to the mystery of my silence:
I remained puzzled
less by my soul's retreat than
by its return, since it returned empty-handed—

How deep it goes, this soul,
like a child in a department store,
seeking its mother—

Perhaps it is like a diver
with only enough air in his tank
to explore the depths for a few minutes or so—
then the lungs send him back.

But something, I was sure, opposed the lungs,
possibly a death wish—
(I use the word *soul* as a compromise).

Of course, in a certain sense I was not empty-handed:
I had my colored pencils.
In another sense, that is my point:
I had accepted substitutes.

It was challenging to use the bright colors,
the ones left, though my aunt preferred them of course—
she thought all children should be lighthearted.

And so time passed: I became
a boy like my brother, later
a man.

I think here I will leave you. It has come to seem
there is no perfect ending.
Indeed, there are infinite endings.
Or perhaps, once one begins,
there are only endings.

Long, long ago, before I was a tormented artist, afflicted with longing yet incapable of forming durable attachments, long before this, I was a glorious ruler uniting all of a divided country—so I was told by the fortune-teller who examined my palm. Great things, she said, are ahead of you, or perhaps behind you; it is difficult to be sure. And yet, she added, what is the difference? Right now you are a child holding hands with a fortune-teller. All the rest is hypothesis and dream.

Let me tell you something, said the old woman.
We were sitting, facing each other,
in the park at ____, a city famous for its wooden toys.

At the time, I had run away from a sad love affair,
and as a kind of penance or self-punishment, I was working
at a factory, carving by hand the tiny hands and feet.

The park was my consolation, particularly in the quiet hours
after sunset, when it was often abandoned.
But on this evening, when I entered what was called the Contessa's
    Garden,
I saw that someone had preceded me. It strikes me now
I could have gone ahead, but I had been
set on this destination; all day I had been thinking of the cherry trees
with which the glade was planted, whose time of blossoming had nearly
    ended.

We sat in silence. Dusk was falling,
and with it came a feeling of enclosure
as in a train cabin.

When I was young, she said, I liked walking the garden path at twilight
and if the path was long enough I would see the moon rise.
That was for me the great pleasure: not sex, not food, not worldly
    amusement.
I preferred the moon's rising, and sometimes I would hear,
at the same moment, the sublime notes of the final ensemble
of *The Marriage of Figaro*. Where did the music come from?
I never knew.
Because it is the nature of garden paths
to be circular, each night, after my wanderings,
I would find myself at my front door, staring at it,
barely able to make out, in darkness, the glittering knob.

It was, she said, a great discovery, albeit my real life.

But certain nights, she said, the moon was barely visible through the clouds
and the music never started. A night of pure discouragement.
And still the next night I would begin again, and often all would be well.

I could think of nothing to say. This story, so pointless as I write it out,
was in fact interrupted at every stage with trance-like pauses
and prolonged intermissions, so that by this time night had started.

Ah the capacious night, the night
so eager to accommodate strange perceptions. I felt that some important
    secret
was about to be entrusted to me, as a torch is passed
from one hand to another in a relay.

My sincere apologies, she said.
I had mistaken you for one of my friends.
And she gestured toward the statues we sat among,
heroic men, self-sacrificing saintly women
holding granite babies to their breasts.
Not changeable, she said, like human beings.

I gave up on them, she said.
But I never lost my taste for circular voyages.
Correct me if I'm wrong.

Above our heads, the cherry blossoms had begun
to loosen in the night sky, or maybe the stars were drifting,
drifting and falling apart, and where they landed
new worlds would form.

Soon afterward I returned to my native city
and was reunited with my former lover.
And yet increasingly my mind returned to this incident,

studying it from all perspectives, each year more intensely convinced,
despite the absence of evidence, that it contained some secret.
I concluded finally that whatever message there might have been
was not contained in speech—so, I realized, my mother used to speak
    to me,
her sharply worded silences cautioning me and chastising me—

and it seemed to me I had not only returned to my lover
but was now returning to the Contessa's Garden
in which the cherry trees were still blooming
like a pilgrim seeking expiation and forgiveness,

so I assumed there would be, at some point,
a door with a glittering knob,
but when this would happen and where I had no idea.

VISITORS FROM ABROAD

1.

Sometime after I had entered
that time of life
people prefer to allude to in others
but not in themselves, in the middle of the night
the phone rang. It rang and rang
as though the world needed me,
though really it was the reverse.

I lay in bed, trying to analyze
the ring. It had
my mother's persistence and my father's
pained embarrassment.

When I picked it up, the line was dead.
Or was the phone working and the caller dead?
Or was it not the phone, but the door perhaps?

2.

My mother and father stood in the cold
on the front steps. My mother stared at me,
a daughter, a fellow female.
You never think of us, she said.

We read your books when they reach heaven.
Hardly a mention of us anymore, hardly a mention of your sister.
And they pointed to my dead sister, a complete stranger,
tightly wrapped in my mother's arms.

But for us, she said, you wouldn't exist.
And your sister—you have your sister's soul.
After which they vanished, like Mormon missionaries.

3.

The street was white again,
all the bushes covered with heavy snow
and the trees glittering, encased with ice.

I lay in the dark, waiting for the night to end.
It seemed the longest night I had ever known,
longer than the night I was born.

I write about you all the time, I said aloud.
Every time I say "I," it refers to you.

4.

Outside the street was silent.
The receiver lay on its side among the tangled sheets;
its peevish throbbing had ceased some hours before.

I left it as it was,
its long cord drifting under the furniture.

I watched the snow falling,
not so much obscuring things
as making them seem larger than they were.

Who would call in the middle of the night?
Trouble calls, despair calls.
Joy is sleeping like a baby.

ABORIGINAL LANDSCAPE

You're stepping on your father, my mother said,
and indeed I was standing exactly in the center
of a bed of grass, mown so neatly it could have been
my father's grave, although there was no stone saying so.

You're stepping on your father, she repeated,
louder this time, which began to be strange to me,
since she was dead herself; even the doctor had admitted it.

I moved slightly to the side, to where
my father ended and my mother began.

The cemetery was silent. Wind blew through the trees;
I could hear, very faintly, sounds of weeping several rows away,
and beyond that, a dog wailing.

At length these sounds abated. It crossed my mind
I had no memory of being driven here,
to what now seemed a cemetery, though it could have been
a cemetery in my mind only; perhaps it was a park, or if not a park,
a garden or bower, perfumed, I now realized, with the scent of roses—
douceur de vivre filling the air, the sweetness of living,
as the saying goes. At some point,

it occurred to me I was alone.
Where had the others gone,
my cousins and sister, Caitlin and Abigail?

By now the light was fading. Where was the car
waiting to take us home?

I then began seeking for some alternative. I felt
an impatience growing in me, approaching, I would say, anxiety.
Finally, in the distance, I made out a small train,

stopped, it seemed, behind some foliage, the conductor
lingering against a doorframe, smoking a cigarette.

Do not forget me, I cried, running now
over many plots, many mothers and fathers—

Do not forget me, I cried, when at last I reached him.
Madam, he said, pointing to the tracks,
surely you realize this is the end, the tracks do not go farther.
His words were harsh, and yet his eyes were kind;
this encouraged me to press my case harder.
But they go back, I said, and I remarked
their sturdiness, as though they had many such returns ahead of them.

You know, he said, our work is difficult: we confront
much sorrow and disappointment.
He gazed at me with increasing frankness.
I was like you once, he added, in love with turbulence.

Now I spoke as to an old friend:
What of you, I said, since he was free to leave,
have you no wish to go home,
to see the city again?

This is my home, he said.
The city—the city is where I disappear.

UTOPIA

When the train stops, the woman said, you must get on it. But how will I know, the child asked, it is the right train? It will be the right train, said the woman, because it is the right time. A train approached the station; clouds of grayish smoke streamed from the chimney. How terrified I am, the child thinks, clutching the yellow tulips she will give to her grandmother. Her hair has been tightly braided to withstand the journey. Then, without a word, she gets on the train, from which a strange sound comes, not in a language like the one she speaks, something more like a moan or a cry.

CORNWALL

A word drops into the mist
like a child's ball into high grass
where it remains seductively
flashing and glinting until
the gold bursts are revealed to be
simply field buttercups.

Word/mist, word/mist: thus it was with me.
And yet, my silence was never total—

Like a curtain rising on a vista,
sometimes the mist cleared: alas, the game was over.
The game was over and the word had been
somewhat flattened by the elements
so it was now both recovered and useless.

I was renting, at the time, a house in the country.
Fields and mountains had replaced tall buildings.
Fields, cows, sunsets over the damp meadow.
Night and day distinguished by rotating birdcalls,
the busy murmurs and rustlings merging into
something akin to silence.

I sat, I walked about. When night came,
I went indoors. I cooked modest dinners for myself
by the light of candles.
Evenings, when I could, I wrote in my journal.

Far, far away I heard cowbells
crossing the meadow.
The night grew quiet in its way.
I sensed the vanished words
lying with their companions,
like fragments of an unclaimed biography.

It was all, of course, a great mistake.
I was, I believed, facing the end:
like a fissure in a dirt road,
the end appeared before me—

as though the tree that confronted my parents
had become an abyss shaped like a tree, a black hole
expanding in the dirt, where by day
a simple shadow would have done.

It was, finally, a relief to go home.

When I arrived, the studio was filled with boxes.
Cartons of tubes, boxes of the various
objects that were my still lives,
the vases and mirrors, the blue bowl
I filled with wooden eggs.

As to the journal:
I tried. I persisted.
I moved my chair onto the balcony—

The streetlights were coming on,
lining the sides of the river.
The offices were going dark.
At the river's edge,
fog encircled the lights;
one could not, after a while, see the lights
but a strange radiance suffused the fog,
its source a mystery.

The night progressed. Fog
swirled over the lit bulbs.
I suppose that is where it was visible;

elsewhere, it was simply the way things were,
blurred where they had been sharp.

I shut my book.
It was all behind me, all in the past.

Ahead, as I have said, was silence.

I spoke to no one.
Sometimes the phone rang.

Day alternated with night, the earth and sky
taking turns being illuminated.

Reading what I have just written, I now believe
I stopped precipitously, so that my story seems to have been
slightly distorted, ending, as it did, not abruptly
but in a kind of artificial mist of the sort
sprayed onto stages to allow for difficult set changes.

Why did I stop? Did some instinct
discern a shape, the artist in me
intervening to stop traffic, as it were?

A shape. Or fate, as the poets say,
intuited in those few long-ago hours—

I must have thought so once.
And yet I dislike the term
which seems to me a crutch, a phase,
the adolescence of the mind, perhaps—

Still, it was a term I used myself,
frequently to explain my failures.
Fate, destiny, whose designs and warnings
now seem to me simply
local symmetries, metonymic
baubles within immense confusion—

Chaos was what I saw.
My brush froze—I could not paint it.

Darkness, silence: that was the feeling.

What did we call it then?
A "crisis of vision" corresponding, I believed,
to the tree that confronted my parents,

but whereas they were forced
forward into the obstacle,
I retreated or fled—

Mist covered the stage (my life).
Characters came and went, costumes were changed,
my brush hand moved side to side
far from the canvas,
side to side, like a windshield wiper.

Surely this was the desert, the dark night.
(In reality, a crowded street in London,
the tourists waving their colored maps.)

One speaks a word: *I*.
Out of this stream
the great forms—

I took a deep breath. And it came to me
the person who drew that breath
was not the person in my story, his childish hand
confidently wielding the crayon—

Had I been that person? A child but also
an explorer to whom the path is suddenly clear, for whom
the vegetation parts—

And beyond, no longer screened from view, that exalted
solitude Kant perhaps experienced
on his way to the bridges—
(We share a birthday.)

Outside, the festive streets
were strung, in late January, with exhausted Christmas lights.

A woman leaned against her lover's shoulder
singing Jacques Brel in her thin soprano—

Bravo! the door is shut.
Now nothing escapes, nothing enters—

I hadn't moved. I felt the desert
stretching ahead, stretching (it now seems)
on all sides, shifting as I speak,

so that I was constantly
face-to-face with blankness, that
stepchild of the sublime,

which, it turns out,
has been both my subject and my medium.

What would my twin have said, had my thoughts
reached him?

Perhaps he would have said
in my case there was no obstacle (for the sake of argument)
after which I would have been
referred to religion, the cemetery where
questions of faith are answered.

The mist had cleared. The empty canvases
were turned inward against the wall.

The little cat is dead (so the song went).

Shall I be raised from death, the spirit asks.
And the sun says yes.
And the desert answers
your voice is sand scattered in wind.

MIDNIGHT

At last the night surrounded me;
I floated on it, perhaps in it,
or it carried me as a river carries
a boat, and at the same time
it swirled above me,
star-studded but dark nevertheless.

These were the moments I lived for.
I was, I felt, mysteriously lifted above the world
so that action was at last impossible
which made thought not only possible but limitless.

It had no end. I did not, I felt,
need to do anything. Everything
would be done for me, or done to me,
and if it was not done, it was not
essential.

I was on my balcony.
In my right hand I held a glass of Scotch
in which two ice cubes were melting.

Silence had entered me.
It was like the night, and my memories—they were like stars
in that they were fixed, though of course
if one could see as do the astronomers
one would see they are unending fires, like the fires of hell.
I set my glass on the iron railing.

Below, the river sparkled. As I said,
everything glittered—the stars, the bridge lights, the important
illumined buildings that seemed to stop at the river
then resume again, man's work
interrupted by nature. From time to time I saw

the evening pleasure boats; because the night was warm,
they were still full.

This was the great excursion of my childhood.
The short train ride culminating in a gala tea by the river,
then what my aunt called our promenade,
then the boat itself that cruised back and forth over the dark water—

The coins in my aunt's hand passed into the hand of the captain.
I was handed my ticket, each time a fresh number.
Then the boat entered the current.

I held my brother's hand.
We watched the monuments succeeding one another
always in the same order
so that we moved into the future
while experiencing perpetual recurrences.

The boat traveled up the river and then back again.
It moved through time and then
through a reversal of time, though our direction
was forward always, the prow continuously
breaking a path in the water.

It was like a religious ceremony
in which the congregation stood
awaiting, beholding,
and that was the entire point, the beholding.

The city drifted by,
half on the right side, half on the left.

See how beautiful the city is,
my aunt would say to us. Because

it was lit up, I expect. Or perhaps because
someone had said so in the printed booklet.

Afterward we took the last train.
I often slept, even my brother slept.
We were country children, unused to these intensities.
You boys are spent, my aunt said,
as though our whole childhood had about it
an exhausted quality.
Outside the train, the owl was calling.

How tired we were when we reached home.
I went to bed with my socks on.

The night was very dark.
The moon rose.
I saw my aunt's hand gripping the railing.

In great excitement, clapping and cheering,
the others climbed onto the upper deck
to watch the land disappear into the ocean—

THE SWORD IN THE STONE

My analyst looked up briefly.
Naturally I couldn't see him
but I had learned, in our years together,
to intuit these movements. As usual,
he refused to acknowledge
whether or not I was right. My ingenuity versus
his evasiveness: our little game.

At such moments, I felt the analysis
was flourishing: it seemed to bring out in me
a sly vivaciousness I was
inclined to repress. My analyst's
indifference to my performances
was now immensely soothing. An intimacy

had grown up between us
like a forest around a castle.

The blinds were closed. Vacillating
bars of light advanced across the carpeting.
Through a small strip above the windowsill,
I saw the outside world.

All this time I had the giddy sensation
of floating above my life. Far away
that life occurred. But was it
still occurring: that was the question.

Late summer: the light was fading.
Escaped shreds flickered over the potted plants.

The analysis was in its seventh year.
I had begun to draw again—
modest little sketches, occasional

three-dimensional constructs
modeled on functional objects—

And yet, the analysis required
much of my time. From what
was this time deducted: that
was also the question.

I lay, watching the window,
long intervals of silence alternating
with somewhat listless ruminations
and rhetorical questions—

My analyst, I felt, was watching me.
So, in my imagination, a mother stares at her sleeping child,
forgiveness preceding understanding.

Or, more likely, so my brother must have gazed at me—
perhaps the silence between us prefigured
this silence, in which everything that remained unspoken
was somehow shared. It seemed a mystery.

Then the hour was over.

I descended as I had ascended;
the doorman opened the door.

The mild weather of the day had held.
Above the shops, striped awnings had unfurled
protecting the fruit.

Restaurants, shops, kiosks
with late newspapers and cigarettes.
The insides grew brighter
as the outside grew darker.

Perhaps the drugs were working?
At some point, the streetlights came on.

I felt, suddenly, a sense of cameras beginning to turn;
I was aware of movement around me, my fellow beings
driven by a mindless fetish for action—

How deeply I resisted this!
It seemed to me shallow and false, or perhaps
partial and false—
Whereas truth—well, truth as I saw it
was expressed as stillness.

I walked awhile, staring into the windows of the galleries—
my friends had become famous.

I could hear the river in the background,
from which came the smell of oblivion
interlaced with potted herbs from the restaurants—

I had arranged to join an old acquaintance for dinner.
There he was at our accustomed table;
the wine was poured; he was engaged with the waiter,
discussing the lamb.

As usual, a small argument erupted over dinner, ostensibly
concerning aesthetics. It was allowed to pass.

Outside, the bridge glittered.
Cars rushed back and forth, the river
glittered back, imitating the bridge. Nature
reflecting art: something to that effect.
My friend found the image potent.

He was a writer. His many novels, at the time,
were much praised. One was much like another.
And yet his complacency disguised suffering
as perhaps my suffering disguised complacency.
We had known each other many years.

Once again, I had accused him of laziness.
Once again, he flung the word back—

He raised his glass and turned it upside-down.
This is your purity, he said,
this is your perfectionism—
The glass was empty; it left no mark on the tablecloth.

The wine had gone to my head.
I walked home slowly, brooding, a little drunk.
The wine had gone to my head, or was it
the night itself, the sweetness at the end of summer?

It is the critics, he said,
the critics have the ideas. We artists
(he included me)—we artists
are just children at our games.

After the orchestra had been playing for some time, and had passed the andante, the scherzo, the poco adagio, and the first flautist had put his head on the stand because he would not be needed until tomorrow, there came a passage that was called the forbidden music because it could not, the composer specified, be played. And still it must exist and be passed over, an interval at the discretion of the conductor. But tonight, the conductor decides, it must be played—he has a hunger to make his name. The flautist wakes with a start. Something has happened to his ears, something he has never felt before. His sleep is over. Where am I now, he thinks. And then he repeated it, like an old man lying on the floor instead of in his bed. Where am I now?

THE OPEN WINDOW

An elderly writer had formed the habit of writing the words THE END on a piece of paper before he began his stories, after which he would gather a stack of pages, typically thin in winter when the daylight was brief, and comparatively dense in summer when his thought became again loose and associative, expansive like the thought of a young man. Regardless of their number, he would place these blank pages over the last, thus obscuring it. Only then would the story come to him, chaste and refined in winter, more free in summer. By these means he had become an acknowledged master.

He worked by preference in a room without clocks, trusting the light to tell him when the day was finished. In summer, he liked the window open. How then, in summer, did the winter wind enter the room? You are right, he cried out to the wind, this is what I have lacked, this decisiveness and abruptness, this surprise—O, if I could do this I would be a god! And he lay on the cold floor of the study watching the wind stirring the pages, mixing the written and unwritten, the end among them.

THE MELANCHOLY ASSISTANT

I had an assistant, but he was melancholy,
so melancholy it interfered with his duties.
He was to open my letters, which were few,
and answer those that required answers,
leaving a space at the bottom for my signature.
And under my signature, his own initials,
in which formality, at the outset, he took great pride.
When the phone rang, he was to say
his employer was at the moment occupied,
and offer to convey a message.

After several months, he came to me.
Master, he said (which was his name for me),
I have become useless to you; you must turn me out.
And I saw that he had packed his bags
and was prepared to go, though it was night
and the snow was falling. My heart went out to him.
Well, I said, if you cannot perform these few duties,
what can you do? And he pointed to his eyes,
which were full of tears. I can weep, he said.
Then you must weep for me, I told him,
as Christ wept for mankind.

Still he was hesitant.
Your life is enviable, he said;
what must I think of when I cry?
And I told him of the emptiness of my days,
and of time, which was running out,
and of the meaninglessness of my achievement,
and as I spoke I had the odd sensation
of once more feeling something
for another human being—

He stood completely still.
I had lit a small fire in the fireplace;
I remember hearing the contented murmurs of the dying logs—

Master, he said, you have given
meaning to my suffering.

It was a strange moment.
The whole exchange seemed both deeply fraudulent
and profoundly true, as though such words as emptiness and
    meaninglessness
had stimulated some remembered emotion
which now attached itself to this occasion and person.

His face was radiant. His tears glinted
red and gold in the firelight.
Then he was gone.

Outside the snow was falling,
the landscape changing into a series
of bland generalizations
marked here and there with enigmatic
shapes where the snow had drifted.
The street was white, the various trees were white—
Changes of the surface, but is that not really
all we ever see?

I found the stairs somewhat more difficult than I had expected and so I sat down, so to speak, in the middle of the journey. Because there was a large window opposite the railing, I was able to entertain myself with the little dramas and comedies of the street outside, though no one I knew passed by, no one, certainly, who could have assisted me. Nor were the stairs themselves in use, as far as I could see. You must get up, my lad, I told myself. Since this seemed suddenly impossible, I did the next best thing: I prepared to sleep, my head and arms on the stair above, my body crouched below. Sometime after this, a little girl appeared at the top of the staircase, holding the hand of an elderly woman. Grandmother, cried the little girl, there is a dead man on the staircase! We must let him sleep, said the grandmother. We must walk quietly by. He is at that point in life at which neither returning to the beginning nor advancing to the end seems bearable; therefore, he has decided to stop, here, in the midst of things, though this makes him an obstacle to others, such as ourselves. But we must not give up hope; in my own life, she continued, there was such a time, though that was long ago. And here, she let her granddaughter walk in front of her so they could pass me without disturbing me.

I would have liked to hear the whole of her story, since she seemed, as she passed by, a vigorous woman, ready to take pleasure in life, and at the same time forthright, without illusions. But soon their voices faded into whispers, or they were far away. Will we see him when we return, the child murmured. He will be long gone by then, said her grandmother, he will have finished climbing up or down, as the case may be. Then I will say goodbye now, said the little girl. And she knelt below me, chanting a prayer I recognized as the Hebrew prayer for the dead. Sir, she whispered, my grandmother tells me you are not dead, but I thought perhaps this would soothe you in your terrors, and I will not be here to sing it at the right time.

When you hear this again, she said, perhaps the words will be less intimidating, if you remember how you first heard them, in the voice of a little girl.

APPROACH OF THE HORIZON

One morning I awoke unable to move my right arm.
I had, periodically, suffered from considerable
pain on that side, in my painting arm,
but in this instance there was no pain.
Indeed, there was no feeling.

My doctor arrived within the hour.
There was immediately the question of other doctors,
various tests, procedures—
I sent the doctor away
and instead hired the secretary who transcribes these notes,
whose skills, I am assured, are adequate to my needs.
He sits beside the bed with his head down,
possibly to avoid being described.

So we begin. There is a sense
of gaiety in the air,
as though birds were singing.
Through the open window come gusts of sweet scented air.

My birthday (I remember) is fast approaching.
Perhaps the two great moments will collide
and I will see my selves meet, coming and going—
Of course, much of my original self
is already dead, so a ghost would be forced
to embrace a mutilation.

The sky, alas, is still far away,
not really visible from the bed.
It exists now as a remote hypothesis,
a place of freedom utterly unconstrained by reality.
I find myself imagining the triumphs of old age,
immaculate, visionary drawings
made with my left hand—
"left," also, as "remaining."

The window is closed. Silence again, multiplied.
And in my right arm, all feeling departed.
As when the stewardess announces the conclusion
of the audio portion of one's in-flight service.

Feeling has departed—it occurs to me
this would make a fine headstone.

But I was wrong to suggest
this has occurred before.
In fact, I have been hounded by feeling;
it is the gift of expression
that has so often failed me.
Failed me, tormented me, virtually all my life.

The secretary lifts his head,
filled with the abstract deference
the approach of death inspires.
It cannot help, really, but be thrilling,
this emerging of shape from chaos.

A machine, I see, has been installed by my bed
to inform my visitors
of my progress toward the horizon.

My own gaze keeps drifting toward it,
the unstable line gently
ascending, descending,
like a human voice in a lullaby.

And then the voice grows still.
At which point my soul will have merged
with the infinite, which is represented
by a straight line,
like a minus sign.

I have no heirs
in the sense that I have nothing of substance
to leave behind.
Possibly time will revise this disappointment.
Those who know me well will find no news here;
I sympathize. Those to whom
I am bound by affection
will forgive, I hope, the distortions
compelled by the occasion.

I will be brief. This concludes,
as the stewardess says,
our short flight.

And all the persons one will never know
crowd into the aisle, and all are funnelled
into the terminal.

One day continuously followed another.
Winter passed. The Christmas lights came down
together with the shabby stars
strung across the various shopping streets.
Flower carts appeared on the wet pavements,
the metal pails filled with quince and anemones.

The end came and went.
Or should I say, at intervals the end approached;
I passed through it like a plane passing through a cloud.
On the other side, the vacant sign still glowed above the lavatory.

My aunt died. My brother moved to America.

On my wrist, the watch face glistened in the false darkness
(the movie was being shown).
This was its special feature, a kind of bluish throbbing
which made the numbers easy to read, even in the absence of light.
Princely, I always thought.

And yet the serene transit of the hour hand
no longer represented my perception of time
which had become a sense of immobility
expressed as movement across vast distances.

The hand moved;
the twelve, as I watched, became the one again.

Whereas time was now this environment in which
I was contained with my fellow passengers,
as the infant is contained in his sturdy crib
or, to stretch the point, as the unborn child
wallows in his mother's womb.

Outside the womb, the earth had fallen away;
I could see flares of lightning striking the wing.

When my funds were gone,
I went to live for a while
in a small house on my brother's land
in the state of Montana.

I arrived in darkness;
at the airport, my bags were lost.

It seemed to me I had moved
not horizontally but rather from a very low place
to something very high,
perhaps still in the air.

Indeed, Montana was like the moon—
My brother drove confidently over the icy road,
from time to time stopping to point out
some rare formation.

We were, in the main, silent.
It came to me we had resumed
the arrangements of childhood,
our legs touching, the steering wheel
now substituting for the book.

And yet, in the deepest sense, they were interchangeable:
had not my brother always been steering,
both himself and me, out of our bleak bedroom
into a night of rocks and lakes
punctuated with swords sticking up here and there—

The sky was black. The earth was white and cold.

I watched the night fading. Above the white snow
the sun rose, turning the snow a strange pinkish color.

Then we arrived.
We stood awhile in the cold hall, waiting for the heat to start.
My brother wrote down my list of groceries.
Across my brother's face,
waves of sadness alternated with waves of joy.

I thought, of course, of the house in Cornwall.
The cows, the monotonous summery music of the bells—

I felt, as you will guess, an instant of stark terror.

And then I was alone.
The next day, my bags arrived.

I unpacked my few belongings.
The photograph of my parents on their wedding day
to which was now added
a photograph of my aunt in her aborted youth, a souvenir
she had cherished and passed on to me.

Beyond these, only toiletries and medications,
together with my small collection of winter clothes.

My brother brought me books and journals.
He taught me various new world skills
for which I would soon have no use.

And yet this was to me the new world:
there was nothing, and nothing was supposed to happen.

The snow fell. Certain afternoons,
I gave drawing lessons to my brother's wife.

At some point, I began to paint again.

It was impossible to form
any judgment of the work's value.
Suffice to say the paintings were
immense and entirely white. The paint had been
applied thickly, in great irregular strokes—

Fields of white and glimpses, flashes
of blue, the blue of the western sky,
or what I called to myself
watch-face blue. It spoke to me of another world.

I have led my people, it said,
into the wilderness
where they will be purified.

My brother's wife would stand mesmerized.
Sometimes my nephew came
(he would soon become my life companion).
I see, she would say, the face of a child.

She meant, I think, that feelings emanated from the surface,
feelings of helplessness or desolation—

Outside, the snow was falling.
I had been, I felt, accepted into its stillness.
And at the same time, each stroke was a decision,
not a conscious decision, but a decision nevertheless,
as when, for example, the murderer pulls the trigger.

This, he is saying. This is what I mean to do.
Or perhaps, what I need to do.
Or, this is all I can do.
Here, I believe, the analogy ends
in a welter of moral judgments.

Afterward, I expect, he remembers nothing.
In the same way, I cannot say exactly
how these paintings came into being, though in the end
there were many of them, difficult to ship home.

When I returned, Harry was with me.
He is, I believe, a gentle boy
with a taste for domesticity.
In fact, he has taught himself to cook
despite the pressures of his academic schedule.

We suit each other. Often he sings as he goes about his work.
So my mother sang (or, more likely, so my aunt reported).
I request, often, some particular song to which I am attached,
and he goes about learning it. He is, as I say,
an obliging boy. The hills are alive, he sings,
over and over. And sometimes, in my darker moods,
the Jacques Brel which has haunted me.

The little cat is dead, meaning, I suppose,
one's last hope.

The cat is dead, Harry sings,
he will be pointless without his body.
In Harry's voice, it is deeply soothing.

Sometimes his voice shakes, as with great emotion,
and then for a while the hills are alive overwhelms
the cat is dead.

But we do not, in the main, need to choose between them.

Still, the darker songs inspire him; each verse acquires variations.

The cat is dead: who will press, now,
his heart over my heart to warm me?

The end of hope, I think it means,
and yet in Harry's voice it seems a great door is swinging open—

The snow-covered cat disappears in the high branches;
O what will I see when I follow?

THE HORSE AND RIDER

Once there was a horse, and on the horse there was a rider. How handsome they looked in the autumn sunlight, approaching a strange city! People thronged the streets or called from the high windows. Old women sat among flowerpots. But when you looked about for another horse or another rider, you looked in vain. My friend, said the animal, why not abandon me? Alone, you can find your way here. But to abandon you, said the other, would be to leave a part of myself behind, and how can I do that when I do not know which part you are?

A WORK OF FICTION

As I turned over the last page, after many nights, a wave of sorrow enveloped me. Where had they all gone, these people who had seemed so real? To distract myself, I walked out into the night; instinctively, I lit a cigarette. In the dark, the cigarette glowed, like a fire lit by a survivor. But who would see this light, this small dot among the infinite stars? I stood awhile in the dark, the cigarette glowing and growing small, each breath patiently destroying me. How small it was, how brief. Brief, brief, but inside me now, which the stars could never be.

THE STORY OF A DAY

I.

I was awakened this morning as usual
by the narrow bars of light coming through the blinds
so that my first thought was that the nature of light
was incompleteness—

I pictured the light as it existed before the blinds stopped it—
how thwarted it must be, like a mind
dulled by too many drugs.

2.

I soon found myself
at my narrow table; to my right,
the remains of a small meal.

Language was filling my head, wild exhilaration
alternated with profound despair—

But if the essence of time is change,
how can anything become nothing?
This was the question I asked myself.

3.

Long into the night I sat brooding at my table
until my head was so heavy and empty
I was compelled to lie down.
But I did not lie down. Instead, I rested my head on my arms
which I had crossed in front of me on the bare wood.
Like a fledgling in a nest, my head
lay on my arms.

It was the dry season.
I heard the clock tolling, three, then four—

I began at this point to pace the room
and shortly afterward the streets outside
whose turns and windings were familiar to me
from nights like this. Around and around I walked,
instinctively imitating the hands of the clock.
My shoes, when I looked down, were covered with dust.

By now the moon and stars had faded.
But the clock was still glowing in the church tower—

4.

Thus I returned home.
I stood a long time
on the stoop where the stairs ended,
refusing to unlock the door.

The sun was rising.
The air had become heavy,
not because it had greater substance
but because there was nothing left to breathe.

I closed my eyes.
I was torn between a structure of oppositions
and a narrative structure—

5.

The room was as I left it.
There was the bed in the corner.
There was the table under the window.

There was the light battering itself against the window
until I raised the blinds
at which point it was redistributed
as flickering among the shade trees.

A SUMMER GARDEN

1.

Several weeks ago I discovered a photograph of my mother
sitting in the sun, her face flushed as with achievement or triumph.
The sun was shining. The dogs
were sleeping at her feet where time was also sleeping,
calm and unmoving as in all photographs.

I wiped the dust from my mother's face.
Indeed, dust covered everything; it seemed to me the persistent
haze of nostalgia that protects all relics of childhood.
In the background, an assortment of park furniture, trees, and shrubbery.

The sun moved lower in the sky, the shadows lengthened and darkened.
The more dust I removed, the more these shadows grew.
Summer arrived. The children
leaned over the rose border, their shadows
merging with the shadows of the roses.

A word came into my head, referring
to this shifting and changing, these erasures
that were now obvious—

it appeared, and as quickly vanished.
Was it blindness or darkness, peril, confusion?

Summer arrived, then autumn. The leaves turning,
the children bright spots in a mash of bronze and sienna.

2.

When I had recovered somewhat from these events,
I replaced the photograph as I had found it
between the pages of an ancient paperback,
many parts of which had been

annotated in the margins, sometimes in words but more often
in spirited questions and exclamations
meaning "I agree" or "I'm unsure, puzzled"—

The ink was faded. Here and there I couldn't tell
what thoughts occurred to the reader
but through the blotches I could sense
urgency, as though tears had fallen.

I held the book awhile.
It was *Death in Venice* (in translation);
I had noted the page in case, as Freud believed,
nothing is an accident.

Thus the little photograph
was buried again, as the past is buried in the future.
In the margin there were two words,
linked by an arrow: "sterility" and, down the page, "oblivion"—

"And it seemed to him the pale and lovely
Summoner out there smiled at him and beckoned . . ."

3.

How quiet the garden is;
no breeze ruffles the Cornelian cherry.
Summer has come.

How quiet it is
now that life has triumphed. The rough

pillars of the sycamores
support the immobile
shelves of the foliage,

the lawn beneath
lush, iridescent—

And in the middle of the sky,
the immodest god.

Things are, he says. They are, they do not change;
response does not change.

How hushed it is, the stage
as well as the audience; it seems
breathing is an intrusion.

He must be very close,
the grass is shadowless.

How quiet it is, how silent,
like an afternoon in Pompeii.

4.

Mother died last night,
Mother who never dies.

Winter was in the air,
many months away
but in the air nevertheless.

It was the tenth of May.
Hyacinth and apple blossom
bloomed in the back garden.

We could hear
Maria singing songs from Czechoslovakia—

How alone I am—
songs of that kind.

How alone I am,
no mother, no father—
my brain seems so empty without them.

Aromas drifted out of the earth;
the dishes were in the sink,
rinsed but not stacked.

Under the full moon
Maria was folding the washing;
the stiff sheets became
dry white rectangles of moonlight.

How alone I am, but in music
my desolation is my rejoicing.

It was the tenth of May
as it had been the ninth, the eighth.

Mother slept in her bed,
her arms outstretched, her head
balanced between them.

5.

Beatrice took the children to the park in Cedarhurst.
The sun was shining. Airplanes
passed back and forth overhead, peaceful because the war was over.

It was the world of her imagination:
true and false were of no importance.

Freshly polished and glittering—
that was the world. Dust
had not yet erupted on the surface of things.

The planes passed back and forth, bound
for Rome and Paris—you couldn't get there
unless you flew over the park. Everything
must pass through, nothing can stop—

The children held hands, leaning
to smell the roses.
They were five and seven.

Infinite, infinite—that
was her perception of time.

She sat on a bench, somewhat hidden by oak trees.
Far away, fear approached and departed;
from the train station came the sound it made.

The sky was pink and orange, older because the day was over.

There was no wind. The summer day
cast oak-shaped shadows on the green grass.

THE COUPLE IN THE PARK

A man walks alone in the park and beside him a woman walks, also alone.
How does one know? It is as though a line exists between them, like a line
on a playing field. And yet, in a photograph they might appear a married
couple, weary of each other and of the many winters they have endured
together. At another time, they might be strangers about to meet by acci-
dent. She drops her book; stooping to pick it up, she touches, by accident,
his hand and her heart springs open like a child's music box. And out of
the box comes a little ballerina made of wood. I have created this, the man
thinks; though she can only whirl in place, still she is a dancer of some kind,
not simply a block of wood. This must explain the puzzling music coming
from the trees.

INDEX OF TITLES